Science and Sensibility

Science and Sensibility

From the Heavens Above to the Earth Below

David Howe

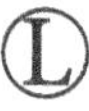

The Lutterworth Press

The Lutterworth Press

P.O. Box 60
Cambridge
CB1 2NT
United Kingdom

www.lutterworth.com.
publishing@lutterworth.com

Paperback ISBN: 978 0 7188 9809 0
PDF ISBN: 978 0 7188 9810 6
ePub ISBN: 978 0 7188 9811 3

British Library Cataloguing-in-Publication Data
A record is available from the British Library

First published by The Lutterworth Press, 2025

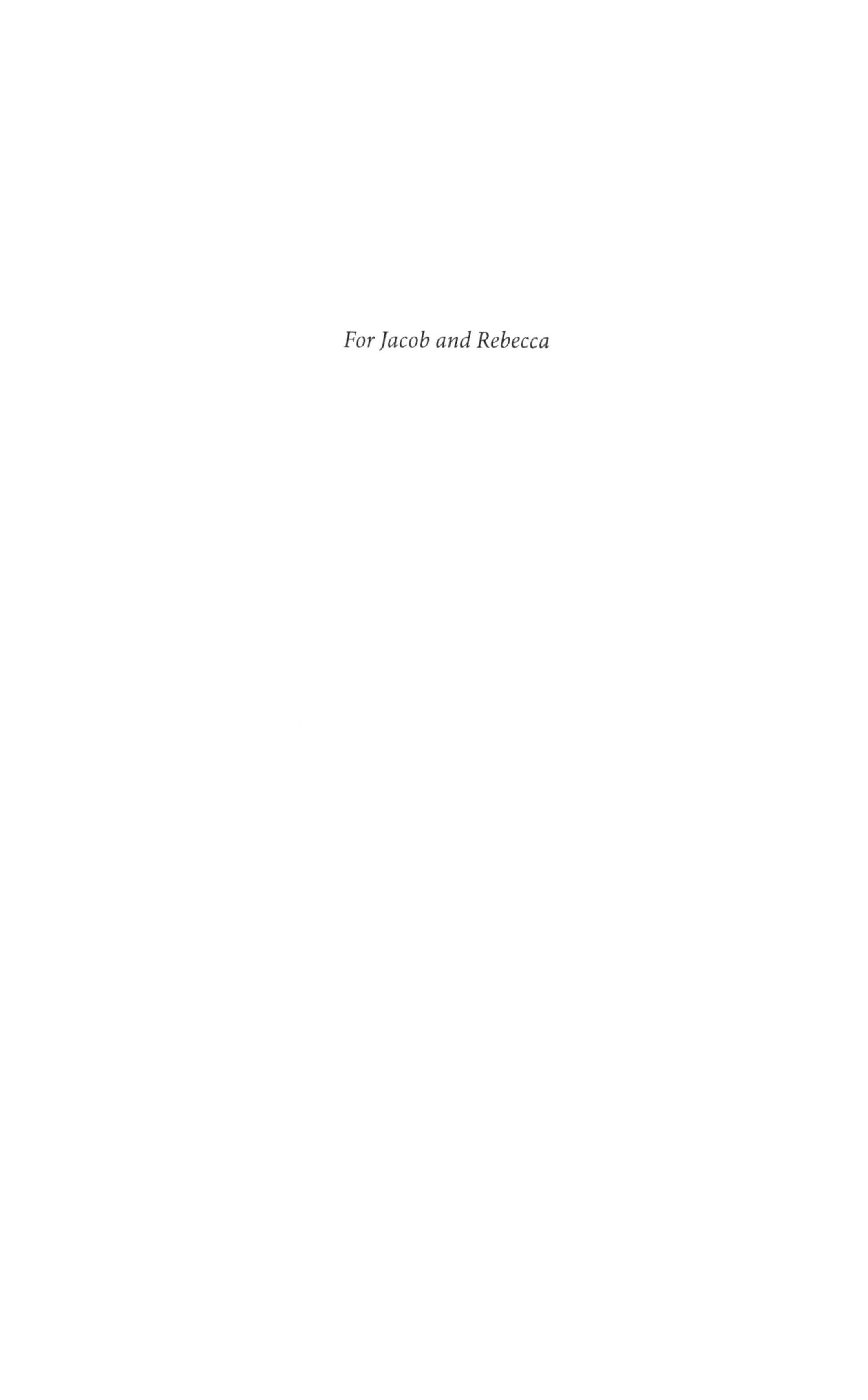

For Jacob and Rebecca

Contents

Part V: Life

Part VI: Elements

Part VII: One World

Acknowledgements

Many thanks to the team at Lutterworth Press for supporting the book through all its stages. Thanks, too, to Dorothy Luckhurst for her eagle-eyed copyediting. And a huge thanks, in particular, to my editors, Georgina Melia and Sarah Algar-Hughes, for their invaluable advice and suggestions, enthusiasm and encouragement, Georgina also designed the book's lovely cover. Any errors that remain are my own.

Part I

Order and Romance

1

Wondering High and Low

It had been one of those summer days when the air is still and thick with heat. The walk up the fell had been ambitious, foolish even, given the forecast of record high temperatures. But I was now down from the tops, sitting with my feet dangling in the deliciously cold waters of the beck. A kaleidoscope of pebbles, smooth and sensuously shiny in their lizard greens and browns, pale yellows and reds, glistening beneath the ripples and rills.

I lay back on the grass. The sky was a soft, milky blue. In the distance, clouds were beginning to rise and tower. A buzzard, too, was catching the last of the day's thermals as it leisurely circled high above. It was late afternoon and the sun was sinking behind Bow Fell. Shadows stretched down the dale, and although struggling to be seen, a faint half-moon was rising low in the east, circling the Earth as the Earth circles the Sun.

Socks back on, boots laced and a slow walk back to the car. Great Langdale, a valley in the English Lake District, is an ancient landscape. Its rocky roots stretch back nearly half a billion years. Like all mountains, the fells inspire both poetry and prose. They evoke feelings of the sublime. In her book, *Vesper Flights*, the writer and naturalist Helen Macdonald talks of times when, immersed in nature, the world 'stutters, turns and fills with unexpected meaning. When rapturousness claims a moment and transfigures it. … Love, beauty, mystery. Epiphanies, I suppose. Occasions of grace.'[1]

Samuel Taylor Coleridge felt that untamed landscapes, and raw nature in particular, have the power to excite and cause us to wonder.

In 1802, finding himself alone on the summit of Scafell, he noticed storm clouds approaching. In his eagerness to get down, he took what proved to be a precipitous and hazardous route that left him in a thrilling state of tremble and terror: 'the sight of the Crags above me on each side, and the impetuous clouds just over them, posting so luridly and so rapidly northward, overawed me. I lay in a state of almost prophetic Trance and Delight.'[2]

High on the summit of Ben Hope, the writer Robert Macfarlane also felt, and feared, the majestic indifference of nature. 'All travellers to wild places', he wrote, 'will have felt some version of this, a brief blazing perception of the world's disinterest. In small measures it exhilarates. But in full form it annihilates.'[3]

I reached the car park. There was a distant rumble of thunder, another reminder of nature's power to frighten and excite.

Sensually then, there was a lot going on. I was pleasantly tired. The heat only added to a drowsy contentment. I had drunk most of my water. The hotel bar by the car park was doing a brisk trade. I bought a pint of ice-cold shandy and sat down in the shade of a table umbrella.

Another distant thundery growl. The clouds boiled higher, darker as the fast-rising, humid air cooled and condensed. Two hundred years earlier, two Lakeland characters had taken a particular interest in the weather, in general, and clouds and water vapour, in particular. A threatening storm would certainly have excited their interest.

John Dalton was born on 6 September 1766, one of six children. His father was a weaver. The family lived in Eaglesfield, a small village a couple of miles south-west of Cockermouth below the Lake District's western Fells. Elihu Robinson, a fellow Quaker and a leading figure in Eaglesfield, took an interest in the young boy, who was clearly bright and keen to learn. He taught Dalton to think scientifically and encouraged him to observe and record the weather using a variety of measuring instruments. From the age of twenty-two until his death fifty-seven years later, Dalton kept a daily record of the weather. However, his lasting fame is not as a meteorologist, although he did important work in that field, but rather as the father of the atomic theory of chemistry and how the elements combine to form compounds.[4]

Jonathan Otley was born in Nook House near Loughrigg Tarn on 19 January 1766, the same year as John Dalton. The house, also known less prettily as Scroggs House, was tucked beneath the western slopes of Loughrigg Fell, only a few miles down the dale from where I was finishing my shandy. Otley became a watchmaker and instrument repairer based in Keswick.[5]

Dalton and Otley first met by accident on 6 July 1812. They were both on their way up Skiddaw when they bumped into each other. Otley noticed that Dalton was carrying a barometer to measure air pressure and estimate height. Naturally this piqued Otley's professional interest. The two men got talking and learned that they shared a deep fascination with the weather, including their taking daily readings of the wind and rain, humidity and temperature, pressure and height. This was the beginnings of a sustained friendship forged by a mutual interest, obsession even, with all things wet and windy.

Although Dalton lived most of his adult life in Manchester, he would holiday in the Lakes were he continued his practice of taking daily weather readings. His favourite mountain was Helvellyn. Over the course of his life, he reckoned he'd climbed the fell over forty times, always taking note of the wind and the rain, temperature and humidity, always taking a scientific interest in whatever was happening around him.

However, Dalton was not the only famous scientist to enjoy climbing Helvellyn. As a young man, the chemist Humphry Davy had become friends with the poets Robert Southey and Samuel Taylor Coleridge when all three were living in Bristol. In 1795 Coleridge married Sarah Fricker. A couple of months later Southey married Sarah's sister Edith. In 1800 the Coleridges moved into Greta Hall in Keswick, Lakeland. This allowed the family to remain in neighbourly proximity with their friends, William, Mary, his wife, and Dorothy Wordsworth, his sister, who were then living in Dove Cottage, Grasmere. In the late summer of 1803, Southey and Edith travelled up to Keswick to holiday with the Coleridges. The plan was to stay a couple of months but, in the event, the Southeys spent the rest of their lives living in the town.

Coleridge had been growing increasingly unhappy with his marriage to Sarah. In December 1803, restless and depressed, he walked out on his wife and children. Southey decided to do the decent thing. He and Edith stayed on at Greta Hall to help support and look after Sarah – Coleridge's abandoned wife – and her three living children.[6]

Humphry Davy would make periodic visits to the Lake District, on these occasions staying at Greta Hall with the Southeys, Coleridges' wife Sarah and their children. It was during one of these visits that Davy finally met the Wordsworths. On one famous occasion in 1805, Davy joined Southey, Wordsworth and the novelist Walter Scott on a walk to the top of Helvellyn. Although Davy was destined to become a world-famous scientist, he never gave up his love of poetry, not just reading verse but also writing poems himself.[7]

Lakes, hills and weather have a habit of inspiring, not just poets but scientists too. The scientists wanted to explain and make sense of what they saw, both above and below. Why do clouds form as humid air rises over mountains? What are rocks made of? How old are they? By the late eighteenth century, mountains, in particular, were beginning to attract increasing scientific interest. Botanists, meteorologists, geologists, mineralogists, physicists, astronomers and mapmakers all began climbing the hills, collecting flowers, examining rocks, measuring the pressure of the air, testing humidity and looking up at the stars.

These pioneering naturalists were also keen, as Simon Bainbridge points out in his book, *Mountaineering and British Romanticism*, to describe their ascents 'among the rocks and precipices'.[8] They experienced the craggy tops as sublime, dangerous and perilous. They viewed their exploits as brave and heroic, but all done in the name of science. The grandeur and beauty seemed to fire their scientific imagination every bit as much as the poet's sensibilities. From these great heights, the world was being seen anew. Nature's mysteries lay all around, her secrets ready to be unveiled.

In contrast, the poets sought to understand and communicate what they *felt* and *experienced* as they wandered over the fells and amongst the flowers. They wanted to explore the human condition. What is our relationship with nature? What is our place in a world seemingly indifferent to our existence? In his poem, *The Prelude*, Wordsworth described himself as a 'Child of the mountains'. Like many Romantic poets, he felt that his relationship with mountains was visceral. Although no fell walker himself, William Blake said that: 'Great things are done when men and mountains meet.'[9]

Sitting by a tumbling stream, with all our senses alert, the world is experienced without division. Sight, sound, the brush of the breeze, the smell of grass immerse us in a seamless reality. Dissolved in nature, we enjoy the continuous flow of sensation. Indeed, the most fundamental aspect of being human is having a body. Experience is only possible because we have a body with senses. We know the world through our senses. For poets, climbing rugged terrains brought all the senses into play, the inner self could be experienced in all its registers, and the imagination could soar.

However, there were others who thought there was a tension between the poetic gaze and the scientific quest. The historian Theodore Roszak saw a conflict between the objective consciousness of the scientist and the vision and imagination of seers, mystics and artists, who felt themselves to be in touch with a different kind of reality.[10] William Blake feared that scientists were squeezing the mystery out of the universe, while poets, he famously wrote in the opening lines of his poem, *Auguries of Innocence*, were able:

To see a World in a Grain of Sand
And a Heaven in a Wild Flower,
Hold Infinity in the palm of your hand
And Eternity in an hour.

However, the argument in this book is that in both cases, to be at their creative best, scientists and poets alike first need to feel an overwhelming sense of wonder. In the minds of the curious, nature in all its glorious confusion, profusion and complexity invites the question, 'what's it all about?'[11]

The ancient Greeks were amongst the first to appreciate that wonder has the power to stretch the imagination. Feelings of wonder lead us to philosophise. Our thoughts are stimulated by nature's mysteries and secrets. We are curious whenever we meet the puzzling and peculiar. Our feelings, too, are heightened when we experience the sublime and beautiful. It is our capacity to wonder that gives rise to both the arts and sciences.

When we turn our gaze outwards and examine the world objectively, we want to explain. We ask, what is going on here? Why do things do what they do? Why are things like they are? Most dizzying of all, why is there something rather than nothing? These are the questions posed by natural philosophers and the men and women of science.

It is also the case, however, that, when we look out across a boundless sea or stare into a starry sky, our senses tremble. We feel ecstatic. In such moments, romance outshines reason. We reflect on our inner selves and our subjective experiences of being in the world. We even think about the very meaning of life and our presence in the universe. This is how poets, painters and musicians respond to nature.

Moreover, it's not just the grand and cosmic that can evoke such feelings. The exquisitely small can also enrapture us. Julian of Norwich, born in 1343, was an anchoress. In her little cell attached to St Julian's church, she meditated on life and its wonders. In her book, *Revelations of Divine Love* – the first book believed to have been written in English by a woman – she reflects:

> And in this he showed me a little thing, the quantity of a hazel nut, lying in the palm of my hand, as it seemed. And it was as round as any ball. I looked upon it with the eye of my understanding, and thought, 'What may this be?' And it was answered generally thus, 'It is all that is made.' I marvelled how it might last, for I thought it might suddenly have fallen to nothing for littleness.[12]

* * *

The biographer, Richard Holmes, describes the late eighteenth and early nineteenth centuries as *The Age of Wonder.*[13] It was a time of Romantic science as well as Romantic poetry. Davy and Dalton were celebrating the power of human reason to fathom nature's deepest secrets. Science was revealing nature to be more fluid, dynamic and energetic than previously thought. Constant change lay beneath the fabric of reality.

Coleridge and Wordsworth preferred to experience nature directly through the senses, unmediated by thought or theory. Amongst the flowers, by the streams, in the mountains, they sought to 're-enchant' nature. 'My opinion', wrote Coleridge, 'is that deep Thinking is only attainable by a man of deep Feeling, and that all truth is a species of Revelation.'[14] It was on their shared walk up the slopes of Helvellyn that both scientists and poets had cause to wonder as they climbed over ancient rocks, rambled by tumbling becks and wandered beneath vast skies.

* * *

The gift of wonder is often at its most intense when we meet the strange and surprising. But we can also find ourselves wondering whenever we see and think about the everyday and familiar in a new light. Some people have a talent for this kind of thinking. Einstein's remarkable thought experiments allowed him to develop his revolutionary ideas about space and time. In his mind he wondered what things would look like if you could ride on a wave of light, at the speed of light. This talent to see the world from a different or unusual point of view can promote an original turn of mind.

Aronson and his colleagues give the example of Richard Feynman, the Nobel prize-winning physicist.[15] When he was a boy, Feynman's father would challenge the child's intellect by, for example, asking him to pretend that he was a tiny creature living in the carpet. What would the world look like if you were very, very small? Would the carpet's fibres rise like giant, branchless trees into a distant magnolia coloured sky? Such 'games' encourage children to see things from an unusual point of view. Feynman was famous for his brilliant ability to understand and explain the complexity and weirdness of the world at the sub-atomic, quantum level using images and ideas that could be grasped even by those who struggle with the abstract world of mathematics.

It is when we wonder that we also wish to understand. We become curious and begin to ask questions. Wonder and curiosity are the twin drivers that fire our imaginations and fuel our creativity. The beginnings of these creative urges are further aided by two other human characteristics; and it is these two proclivities that spin and spill their way throughout this book. On the one hand, there is the urge to discover *order* and see *patterns* in the world: science; and, on the other, there is our need to tell *stories* and *find meaning*: art.

2

Order and Meaning

We are pattern-seekers. We look for order and logic in what otherwise might appear random, meaningless and, indeed, chaotic. In her memoir, the novelist Penelope Lively explains her need for order.[1] She likes to name things, specifically. She has to know whether a fossil ammonite is some kind of asteroceras or promicroceras. The desire to label, organise and make sense of the natural world became particularly strong in the eighteenth century. Both scientists and artists thought that understanding the mysteries of life offered a sublime experience.[2] They classified clouds. They observed sequences in the rocks. They saw order in the living world, a world in which Charles Darwin saw 'endless forms most beautiful'.[3]

Reality bubbles and seethes. There is ceaseless activity and process, emergence and evolution, death and decay. The order we impose does not exist in nature itself. We can never really know things in themselves. Or, as the theoretical physicist, Richard Feynman put it: 'If our small minds, for some convenience, divide this universe into parts … – physics, biology, geology, astronomy, psychology, and so on – remember that the universe does not know it!'[4] But when trying to make sense of nature, men and women, via their minds and senses, do seek to connect up appearances. It is we who impose shape on the flux of experience.[5]

Any order seen in nature is therefore a human construct, but one that helps us make sense of the world around us. Our apprehensions of things are not actually constituent parts of the things apprehended.

The way we understand and apprehend the world is through our senses and they are tuned into only a limited range of reality. What objects may be in themselves remains unknown to us. The sensations we experience are not inherent in the things seen, heard, touched, tasted and smelled. However, for us these sensations are real and they can be joyous. Once we understand this, our imagination can excite our intellect. The world becomes a more enchanting place. And in such a world, we can experience our self and being more fully, more wonderfully.

The most creative artists, including poets and novelists, painters and musicians, have the imagination to experience the world more richly. There are scientists, too, gifted with the ability to hear the world's deeper notes. If someone responds to a work of art or scientific insight predominantly with their intellect, they have already misunderstood it. Thus, concludes the philosopher Bryan Magee, we *do* have a direct knowledge of one thing from the inside, that is our own inner experience. He describes both the arts and sciences as 'truth-seeking activities ... penetrating beneath the surface of appearances'.[6]

* * *

The order perceived often reflects what is of interest and importance for that person and his or her society at that time. Our intellects don't operate independently of time and place. Our minds are an organic part of the world and as such become active players in shaping and construing what we see and how we see it. Our time and place, culture and history determine *what* we see and *how* we see it. The same natural phenomenon might generate different orders and alternative classifications at different times and in other places.

In the sixteenth and seventeenth centuries, it was the fashion amongst the gentry to collect random objects of interest and place them in ornate wooden cases. They were known as 'cabinets of curiosities', in which might be placed fossils, stuffed birds, minerals, bits of Roman pottery, religious relics, indeed anything that interested the collector. The Germans called them *Wunderkammern*, 'cabinets of wonder'. There was no obvious logic or order to what was being collected and displayed other than the objects could provoke feelings of curiosity and a sense of wonder.

In one of Jorge Luis Borges' critical essays, *The Analytical Language of John Wilkins*, he cites 'a certain Chinese encyclopaedia'.

The encyclopaedia is a fiction of Borges' creative mind. Nevertheless, the paragraph has often been quoted by those who wish to ponder our obsession with ordering the world:

> These ambiguities, redundancies and deficiencies remind us of those which doctor Franz Kuhn attributes to a certain Chinese encyclopaedia entitled 'Celestial Empire of benevolent Knowledge'. In its remote pages it is written that the animals are divided into: (a) belonging to the emperor, (b) embalmed, (c) tame, (d) sucking pigs, (e) sirens, (f) fabulous, (g) stray dogs, (h) included in the present classification, (i) frenzied, (j) innumerable, (k) drawn with a very fine camelhair brush, (l) et cetera, (m) having just broken the water pitcher, (n) that from a long way off look like flies.[7]

Although this quote is both funny and mischievous, there is, nevertheless, merit in creating order. It would be difficult to survive in a world that seemed forever arbitrary and random. Finding rhythms and regularities makes life easier. We like predictability and, to some extent, the familiar and recognisable. Too much uncertainty makes us anxious. Seeing patterns and making some kind of sense is satisfying. It can also be very useful.

We know that summer follows spring, and winter follows autumn. Tides ebb and flow in phase with the moon and sun. From ancient times, knowing that the North Star, or Polaris, lies pretty much in a direct line with the Earth's rotational axis, men and women began to appreciate that from the ground it always appears as if it's 'above' the North Pole. Over the course of a clear night, the star therefore looks relatively motionless. All the other stars in the northern sky appear to rotate and spin around it. Long exposure photographs show this beautifully with the North Star at the still centre of a whirlpool of cosmic starlight. As you locate and look up at the North Star, whatever time of night it happens to be, you know you are looking due north. This is very useful if you are sailing far out at sea on the blackest of nights, or trying to find your way home on a dark, featureless moor.

One of the other skills of those who order and classify is to observe similarities and differences in whatever bits of the natural world that happen to interest them. For example, there are plants that flower and plants that do not. Amongst the flowering plants, there are some whose seeds contain only one embryonic leaf (the monocotyledons), including orchids, grasses and, if we are still in the Lake District, daffodils. There are others which contain two embryonic leaves (the dicotyledons), including magnolias, bay trees and avocados. Botanists and agriculturists find these distinctions interesting as well as useful.

Running alongside the classifiers and pattern-seekers are the explainers and theorists. They look at the natural world and see one thing following another. Theorists consider the order observed in nature and then look for the underlying processes generating these surface properties.[8] It is certainly interesting, they might say, to recognise that there are some clouds that hover around mountain tops and others that feather the sky with milky wisps far above but what are the causes and effects? What processes lie behind the formation of mountain mists, on the one hand, and high, thin clouds on the other? Why does the westerly wind that blows up and over Scafell often hide it in cloud? Why does it rain so much in the Lake District?

The classifiers, pattern-seekers, order-makers and taxonomists ask *what* questions. Theorists ask *why* questions? Nonetheless, both are trying to make sense of the world and both outlooks can bubble and fizz in the same head. These are the people who observe and *describe* and then go on to *explain*. Men and women who are curious, who wonder, first see order then puzzle over why such order might exist. Today we call them *scientists*, those who use thinking and logic to try to make sense of what they find and see.

The artistic stance is different but complementary. The psychologist, Jerome Bruner, contrasts the scientific way of understanding with that of storytelling.[9] Storytellers seek to endow experience with meaning. Storytelling gives us wisdom. In contrast, rational scientific analysis generates information. Science convinces us rationally. Art and literature move us emotionally. Science reveals what is there, though often hidden. Art looks at what's there and then creates something new, something that never existed before. Artists find form in apparent chaos. As Richard Holloway puts it, 'As well as reading stories *out of* what we perceive, we also read stories *into* what we perceive.'[10] The novelist, Iris Murdoch, believed that storytelling was an entirely natural thing that we humans do. One of the deep motives of literature or art of any sort, she says, 'is defeating the formlessness of the world', to impose order on disorder, to find sense and meaning.[11]

* * *

Bruner believes that good science and effective storytelling both need a strong imagination. We have already met Einstein riding on a sunbeam and Feynman shrinking to the size of an ant to help them understand the very big and the very small. When artists contemplate nature, they engage it with both their internal and external worlds. They seek to communicate the meaning of their experience using words, music and paint. Bruner calls the artistic way of making sense the *narrative* mode.[12] Stories and art give life shape and meaning.

The narrative bent in our psychological make-up crops up surprisingly often as we look and listen. Unless we are expert meteorologists, we rarely think of the fair-weather clouds that float along in the blue of a summer sky as nice examples of the cumulus variety. If anything, in our imagination we are more inclined to see one of them taking the shape of a dragon, only a few minutes later to morph into a crocodile. Plump, cottony cumulus clouds continuously shape-shift. A dolphin one moment and an eagle the next. In Shakespeare's Hamlet, Act 3, scene 2, Hamlet asks Polonius: 'Do you see yonder cloud that's almost in shape of a camel?' Coleridge, too, mused on the sky's power to inspire the imagination. He titled one of his later sonnets, 'Fancy in Nubibus, Or, The Poet in the Clouds'. It was first published in *The Courier* on 30 January 1818. Here are the first three lines:

> O, it is pleasant, with a heart at ease,
> Just after sunset, or by moonlight skies,
> To make the shifting clouds be what you please …

Whether it's clouds or seas, mountains or woods, poets have the imaginative skill to find meaning in nature's profusion. In their artistic explorations of the world around them, they also ponder the mysteries of human existence. The shifting, evolving impermanence of clouds and our brief appearance on life's stage resonates particularly well with the poetic vision.

But it's not only poets who see agency in the world around them. Finding meaning and looking for reason in what happens around us is a fundamental characteristic of being human. There is a curious, indeed, famous experiment reported in 1944 by two psychologists, Fritz Heider and Marianne Simmel.[13] In essence, what they found was that, when presented with a film of the random movements of several geometrical shapes, and then asked what was going on, most people saw a 'story' being played out. Many variations of this experiment have taken place over the years. It seems that, when we see objects, let's say red squares, green triangles and blue circles *randomly* moving around a screen, sometimes bumping into each other, sometimes wandering away, we see agency, intention and purpose. Feelings and motives might be invoked to account for the green triangle 'avoiding' the red square. 'Friendship' might be suggested when the triangle heads towards the circle. Stories are told to explain the random movements of the figures. As Bruner deduced, we are just as likely to engage with the world in the *narrative* mode as we are to adopt a scientific stance.

* * *

By the nineteenth century, natural philosophy had resolved itself into a number of distinct sciences. We recognise them today as biology, chemistry, physics, geology, meteorology and astronomy. The early pioneers in each of these disciplines, although particularly gifted with the ability to wonder and imagine, nevertheless came up with ideas that most of us could, and still can, grasp, at least in broad terms. The order and patterns they saw in nature are easily appreciated by the lay enthusiast.

In contrast, modern sciences are sub-divided into dozens and dozens of specialisms. Each specialism requires great expertise, arcane knowledge and often years of advanced study. Although non-specialists might have a crude sense of what the specialist scientists do and how they do it, the skills and understanding needed to follow their findings and investigations require rare talents and prolonged training. So, for example, within the broad field of biology there are zoologists, botanists, microbiologists, virologists, mathematical biologists, molecular geneticists, and many, many other sub-specialisms. In physics we have classical mechanics, thermodynamics, fluid dynamics, nuclear physics, optics, quantum mechanics, and so on.

However, in this book, I want to begin with the sense of wonder and the search for order that inspired people to shape the early ideas of the modern sciences. These early scientists were certainly astute observers. They saw pattern and order in the everyday and familiar. They classified the natural world and began to see reason and logic behind material reality. In their eyes, the formless took on form. Regularities began to appear in nature's rich and dense fabric. They collected and catalogued, observed and classified, then they theorised and explained. They asked *what* and *when*, then went on to wonder *how* and *why*. Their gaze fell on the stars above and the rocks below, the fish in the sea and the birds in the air, the flowers in the meadow and the trees of the forest. We shall follow their eyes as they looked up as well as down, and we shall try to capture some of the imaginative genius that helped lay the foundations of the basic sciences.

The late afternoon in Great Langdale is as good a place to start as any. If you recall, there is a thundery sky above, rocky ground beneath my feet, ferns on the fells, and sheep in the fields. Looking up then gradually turning our eyes earthwards will be the order in which we explore the life and work of the pioneering men and women of science; and, while these scientists were trying to make sense of the world out there, the poets and painters were helping us to understand what it means to be in that world, personally and emotionally, aesthetically and existentially.

We begin with galaxies and the *stars*, the planets and the moon. The diamond-studded night sky has been a source of wonder from the most ancient of days and *astronomy*, via astrology, one of the earliest sciences.

The weather, in general, and *clouds*, in particular, hold an equal fascination. Wind, rain and sun have been the concern of farmers and sailors, builders and travellers for countless generations. In around 350 BCE, Aristotle wrote a treatise on the weather and the interaction between the four classical elements. He titled his work, *Meteorology*, from the Greek meaning the 'discussion of high things', and it covered everything above the earth and beneath the moon, including meteors or shooting stars. However, it was not until the eighteenth century that *meteorology* as a science of the weather and atmosphere began to take its first tentative steps.

This then brings us down to earth, to the *rocks* themselves. *Geology* emerged as people began to take a closer look at landforms and landscapes. People studied the rocks that lay beneath the ground. They wanted to know the age of the Earth.

The land and sea beneath the sky also teem with *life*. There is such richness and variety in the living world that it took particularly keen minds to see order there, then, having found order, to hazard explanations. Once the *biological sciences* had built their taxonomic base, there was no looking back for the life sciences.

Finally, and most fundamental of all, are the *elements* out of which all matter, including life, rocks, clouds and the stars above are made.

This brings us full circle, from the heavens above to the earth below, high to low, up and down, and back again. All the naturally occurring elements that make up the world were born in the early universe and the fiery hearts of long dead stars. So, let us begin with the stars and the night sky.

Part II

Stars

3

Star Struck

Cities are not a good place to study the night sky. Urban nights are never pitch-black. There is always a light shining somewhere close by. Regimented rows of street lights, car headlights, lights from house windows, blinding security lights, the neon lights above shops and garages, LCD screens advertising this and that. Above the bright streets, low clouds reflect the city glow. Even when there are no clouds, city skies remain matt and featureless save for the occasional blinking lights of a high-flying passenger jet or, if you're very lucky, the international space station as it makes one of its silent loops 200 miles above the planet every 93 minutes.

So city folk rarely look up. There's not much to see; perhaps a handful of stars and, if it's there, the moon, of course. True, the Evening Star – the planet Venus – can defeat most light-polluted skies. Sirius, too, and Alpha Centauri can twinkle faintly in the luminescent black, if you know where to look. In the main, however, urban souls see few stars, even when they turn their eyes skywards.

People have always created light in attempts to banish the dark: fires to keep warm, ward off animals and flicker comfortingly in the middle of gathered family groups; burning torches to find your way on moonless nights along huddled streets or over open moors; candles and oil lamps to cast a dull yellow light across sitting rooms and corridors, upstairs and into bedrooms. Their light is weak and short-lived, however, and fires die out, and candles and oil lamps are snuffed as people make their way early to bed.

First gas, then electricity changed all that. By the early nineteenth century, London, Paris and Baltimore were amongst the first cities to install street gas lights. It was Thomas Edison, though, who revolutionised the world when he created incandescent light bulbs that were robust and practical and powered by electricity. A number of other inventors had also come up with similar designs for the incandescent light bulb, most notably Joseph Swan of Newcastle, but it was Edison's design that eventually won the day. By the end of the nineteenth century, electric light bulbs could be found inside homes, illuminating shops and offices, lighting up streets and blotting out the stars.

In our 24-hour world there are fewer and fewer places where we can see the wonders of a starry night. The majority of the world's population now lives in cities. Nevertheless, if you can get away from the endless urban sprawl and off the beaten track, with not a motorway in sight, then the night sky becomes a different place. In the pens of poets, the dark becomes 'bible black', 'velvet black', 'star-studded', where a sense of the infinite invites us 'to dance beneath the diamond sky'.[1]

In attempts to recover the beauty of night skies unpolluted by artificial light, many countries have designated some of their more remote places as 'dark sky' areas. In the UK, both the Northumberland National Park and the Snowdonia Dark Sky Reserve have been recognised as International Dark Sky Places. The United States has several internationally recognised areas including Canyonlands National Park, Utah and, the darkest place of all, with no hint of understatement, the Cosmic Campground, New Mexico.

However, for large optical telescopes, the best sites for the clearest skies tend to be on the tops of mountains (less air for the starlight to shine through) in areas where the air is dry (less water to absorb the light waves). They also need to be far away from populated places. The Atacama Desert in the Chilean Andes, La Palma in the Canary Islands, Maunakea in Hawaii and the Canadian Rockies host some of the world's biggest telescopes. Blackest of all, of course, is space itself which is where we find the Hubble, Gaia, James Webb and several other telescopes.

* * *

Before electricity and the banishment of infinite black, people would have been much more aware of stars and their profusion in the night sky. On the clearest of nights and with the sharpest of eyes, you can see roughly 4,500 stars if you live in the northern hemisphere and a similar number if you live in the southern hemisphere. The most spectacular sight on the darkest of moonless nights is the majestic arc of the Milky Way, our own galaxy. It contains billions of stars, but the merest fraction can be distinguished as individual points of light with the naked eye. Our galaxy appears as a hazy band of light arching across the black vault.

The breath-taking beauty of a star-strewn night sky has thrilled and fascinated people of all cultures from time immemorial. Gerard Manley Hopkins captures these feelings of excitement with the opening lines of his poem 'The Starlight Night':

> Look at the stars! look, look up at the skies!
> O look at all the fire-folk sitting in the air![2]

Similar exuberance is shown by Vincent van Gogh in his swirling interpretation, *The Starry Night.* He painted the picture in 1889 during his stay at the asylum of Saint-Paul-de-Mausole in Provence. Van Gogh painted other nocturnes that also have the power to trouble and thrill the viewer. These include the *Café Terrace at Night*, painted in Arles, and *Starry Night (Over the Rhône).* Equally magnificent are the photographs of Ansel Adams, particularly his spellbinding *Milky Way Shining Briefly Over Banner Peak and One-Thousand Island Lake.*

* * *

Ancient knowledge of the position and movement of the sun, moon and stars certainly helped farmers decide when to sow. It helped sailors to navigate the seas. Nearly 4,000 years ago Babylonian astrologers saw patterns in the night sky. Most early cultures believed that the planets and stars had religious significance. Priests became expert in recognising and interpreting what they observed as they looked up at the stellar-studded blackness of a desert night sky. For some the heavens were the realm of the gods. For others, the patterns of light made by the stars and the wandering of the planets had the power to foretell events down here on the Earth. This marked the beginnings of astrology, the belief that what was going on above influenced what was happening below. The idea that the date when you were born and the disposition of the stars and planets at that time determined your character gained credence.

However, by the seventeenth century and the emergence of a scientifically based astronomy, it soon became obvious that astrology was little more than a pseudo-science. Because of their vast distances from our planet, we don't see the stars move but they do, at enormous speeds, around the galactic centre. Their position in the night sky changes, imperceptibly slowly. Given our fleeting lives, we don't notice. However, the position and patterns of the stars are constantly shifting so that in 10,000 years, a million years, a billion years, the night sky will appear different, and then different again.

Nevertheless, the early efforts that went into studying the planets and stars, for whatever reasons, did act as a stimulus to the discipline of mathematics and helped in the development of calendars, the recognition of annual cycles, and an appreciation of the rhythms of the year. It was with the aid of maths that the Polish polymath, Nicolaus Copernicus, revolutionised the way we thought about the sun and the planets. He was born on 19 February 1473 in the Polish city of Toruń. He studied and travelled throughout Europe, developing a particular interest in the stars and planets.

Although the idea that the sun might be at the centre of the celestial world had been around, off and on, for centuries, the received Aristotelian and Ptolemaic wisdom up until Copernicus's time was that the planets, sun and stars revolved around the Earth. However, whereas the stars appeared fixed in their patterns of movement, the planets shifted their position from night to night. They were known as 'wandering stars'. The six known planets would appear to weave their way amongst the stars and across constellations with no obvious logic, mathematical or astronomical. This posed major problems if you were intent on trying to model the planets as bodies that revolved around the Earth.

Copernicus had been thinking about placing the sun at the centre of the planetary system for a while but he didn't go public with his ideas. His 'heliocentric' theory made sense of why the planets appeared to move so erratically across the night skies. By placing the sun at the centre, the planets' wanderings only appeared random from the Earth's viewpoint because the Earth, too, was orbiting the sun.

One of the problems of displacing the Earth from the centre of the universe was that it went against the teachings of the Church. It was at odds with what was written in the Bible. Putting the sun at the centre of the planetary system was therefore seen as blasphemous and, if voiced, could incur severe penalties, including the possibility of death. However, by 1543 when he was nearly seventy years of age, Copernicus decided to publish his mathematical description of the sun, moon and planets. *De revolutionibus orbium coelestium* (*On the Revolutions of the Heavenly Spheres*) described the planets, including the Earth, as a single system circling the sun.[3] In the book, he writes:

> [The sphere of the fixed stars] is followed by the first of the planets, Saturn, which completes its circuit in 30 years. After Saturn, Jupiter accomplishes its revolution in 12 years. Then Mars revolves in 2 years. The annual revolution takes the series' fourth place, which contains the Earth … together with the lunar sphere as an epicycle. In the fifth place Venus returns in 9 months. Lastly, the sixth place is held by Mercury, which revolves in a period of 80 days.

He went further and suggested that the universe is much larger than was previously thought. Astronomical distances, he said, were vast. In an instant, the universe and our tiny place in it, was transformed. No longer were men, women and the Earth at the centre, with the rest of the universe spinning around us in neat, ever-widening circles. We were displaced. This would not go down well with the religious authorities. Unfortunately, or perhaps fortunately, Copernicus died later that year on 15 May 1543 in his native Poland.

* * *

Not long after the death of Copernicus, the study of the stars was about to receive another huge boost. For a while, Dutch lens makers had been producing some of the best glass lenses in the world for fitting into spectacles. The microscope had been invented and the world of the very small was being revealed in marvellous detail.

'Spyglasses' or telescopes were also in development allowing the far away to appear near and close. The first person to apply for a patent for a telescope was a Dutch eyeglass-maker named Hans Lippershey in 1608, although there was fierce rivalry between Lippershey and some of his fellow countrymen, including Zacharias Jansen and Jacob Metius about who made the best, if not the first telescope.[4]

Born in Pisa in 1564, the same year as William Shakespeare, the young Galileo Galilei began to develop an interest in natural philosophy. Galileo soon established himself as an expert in physics, engineering and mathematics. His skills as a lens grinder allowed him to make improvements to the recently invented microscope.[5] When he heard about the Dutch 'perspective glasses', he set about making his own telescopes. By 1609 his improvements were allowing him to magnify distant objects 20 to 30 times, a significant increase in power over other telescopes around at the time. However, whereas most 'spyglass' enthusiasts were training their telescopes horizontally to look out for ships on the horizon on their way into port or to spy enemy soldiers lining up on distant hillsides, Galileo turned his telescope up, vertically, to look at the sky.[6]

His powerful telescopes were soon revealing 'stars in their myriads', ten times as many as had ever been seen by the naked eye. Suddenly, the universe was not only bigger than previously thought, but teeming with stars, far more than ever had been imagined.

Copernicus had based his ideas of a heliocentric solar system on getting the planetary mathematics to add up. In contrast, Galileo developed his understanding of the stars and planets by making observations using his increasingly powerful telescopes. His approach marked the birth of astronomy as an empirical science. In no time at all he was seeing craters on the moon, dark spots on the sun, phases of Venus, rings around Saturn, moons spinning about Jupiter and a band of light arcing across the clear black, night sky that we now know is an end-on view of our own galaxy, the Milky Way.

In 1592 he moved to the Venetian city of Padua where he took the chair in mathematics. However, it was as a practical scientist that it became clear to Galileo that Copernicus was right. The Earth could no longer be seen as the centre of the universe. Along with the other planets, it revolved around the sun. The Roman Catholic Church continued to view such ideas as heretical. Any challenge to its view of the world and its divinely ordained hierarchy was a challenge to its authority. Under threats from the Church, Galileo had to back-pedal. Although he was allowed to discuss the sun-centred view of the universe as a philosophical idea, he could not openly endorse it. For a while, he played safe and kept quiet. Gradually, however, it seemed as if the religious authorities might be growing more tolerant of debates about how the cosmos might be structured.

In 1632, Galileo thought he had gained papal approval to publish his book, *Dialogue Concerning the Two Chief World Systems*, in which he could mention helio-centrism but certainly not support it. However, he was up against powerful forces who would have no truck with the belief 'that the Earth is not at the centre of heaven'. In February 1633, Galileo was charged with heresy and brought before the pope's inquisitor, Vincenzo Maculani da Firenzuola. During his trial, Galileo insisted that he had kept his promise not to defend the Copernican view of the universe. However, under pressure, including the threat of torture, he conceded that perhaps anyone reading his book might get the impression that Copernicus could be right and that the sun, indeed, was at the centre of the solar system.

Galileo was found guilty of heresy and of holding views contrary to the teachings of the Bible. He was required to 'abjure, curse and detest' all ideas that suggested the Earth revolved around the sun. He was placed under house arrest. His book, *Dialogue*, was banned. During his years of confinement, Galileo devoted himself to writing another book, *Discorsi e dimostrazioni matematiche intorno a due nuove scienze* (*Discourses and Mathematical Demonstrations Relating to Two New Sciences*), published in 1638 in Protestant Holland, just to be on the safe side. The book summarised much of his life's work and earned him the title 'Father of Modern Physics' from none other than Albert Einstein.

Of course, in spite of his recantation of heliocentrism, Galileo, being an unrepentant empirical scientist, didn't really think the Earth was at the centre of the universe, but he was careful never to mention it, except possibly at the very end of his life when he was rumoured to have muttered, 'E pur si muove' – 'and yet it moves'.

Galileo's trial put the brakes on the scientific revolution in and around the Mediterranean states. As a result, the centre of scientific brilliance shifted to the Protestant north. Galileo died in 1642, the same year that saw the birth of Isaac Newton.

Over the next few centuries, astronomy's scientific credentials, having been given a solid footing by Galileo, went from strength to strength. Galileo's contemporary, the German astronomer, Johannes Kepler, had already worked out that the planets revolved around the sun in elliptical, rather than perfectly circular orbits. His calculations have given us Kepler's laws of planetary motion. He was one of the first to give astronomy a strong mathematical footing. He also realised that the moon governed the movement of the tides, something with which Galileo disagreed.

Isaac Newton's genius gave the world his three laws of motion, his laws of universal gravitation, the calculation that the planets did not move around the sun in perfect circles but ellipses, and the maths to make them all work. Appointed by Newton as a demonstrator for the Royal Society, and populariser of Newton's theories, John Theophilus Desaguliers[7] went so far as to write a poem about suns, kings, gravity and the six known planets of the time including the lines:

> Six Worlds sweep round his Throne in Mystick Dance.
> He turns their Motion from its Devious Course,
> And bends their Orbits by Attractive Force.

Improvements in the design and power of telescopes meant that not only were more and more stars being observed, but other cosmic phenomena, many not seen before, began to reveal their far away presence. In 1655, the Dutchman, Christiaan Huygens, refined Galileo's view of Saturn's rings. He also discovered that the planet had a moon which would later be named Titan. The British astronomer, Edmond Halley, calculated that a comet that had famously appeared in the year 1066 and features in the Bayeux tapestry, actually re-appears every 76 years (modern calculations work it out to be 75.32 years). He confidently predicted that it would re-appear in 1758 and, indeed, it did and so, in honour of his success, the comet was named Halley's Comet.

* * *

One of the greatest astronomers of the eighteenth century was William Herschel, who, along with his sister, Caroline, realised that the universe was big, very big, much bigger than even Copernicus had imagined. Herschel was born in the German city of Hanover on 15 November 1738. His younger sister, with whom he worked in close partnership, was born twelve years later on 16 March 1750.[8]

William's early career was as a musician. Under French army occupation, it was felt by the family that the eighteen-year old William would be safer abroad. In 1757, he was smuggled out of Hanover. He eventually fetched up in England, where he was soon to be joined by his older brother, Jacob. The pair were penniless. Music was their salvation. William could play the oboe, violin, harpsichord and, in time, the organ. The brothers performed in concerts and began to earn money.

After only a year or so, Jacob returned to Germany. William was on his own. For a number of years he supported himself as a freelance musician and teacher. He found work in various places including

Newcastle, Sunderland, Durham, Darlington and Leeds. However, in 1766, he landed the permanent position of organist at the Octagon Chapel in Bath.

It would not be until 1772 that young sister Caroline would join her brother, who was still living in Bath, still earning his living as a musician. In 1780, Herschel was appointed director of the Bath orchestra. Caroline, also musically talented, would often perform as a soloist, singing soprano.

William read a great deal and developed a particular interest in natural philosophy, including optics and astronomy. In William's mind, there were deep resonances between music, harmonics and mathematics, all of which leant themselves wonderfully to studying the stars, the planets and the 'music' of the spheres.

After taking lessons from local craftsmen, William learnt to grind mirrors and then build his own telescopes. Caroline and their brother, Alexander, also helped in the long and laborious task of carefully and accurately polishing mirrors to ensure that the stars would be magnified manyfold and seen clearly, without distortion. Over the years, William and his siblings built bigger and better telescopes culminating in the famous giant reflecting telescope which they built in the grounds of a house in Slough. It had a mirror that was 49½ inches in diameter with a focal length of 40 feet.

As the fame of Herschel and his telescopes spread, he began to receive strings of distinguished visitors. When Byron peered through the Slough telescope, he was particularly affected by the sight of so many stars. He sensed humanity's insignificance and the universe's indifference to our being. 'It was the comparative insignificance of ourselves, and *our world*, when placed in competition with the *mighty whole*, of which it is an atom, that first led me to imagine that our pretensions to eternity might be … *over-rated*', said Byron, cited by Richard Holmes.[9] In sensing the infinite, poets experienced the sublime. The Nobel Laureate, Louise Glück, offers similar sentiments in her 2005 poem, 'The Telescope'. As the stargazer journeys in the silence of the night sky she realises that in the vastness of the cosmos human life has no meaning.[10]

With their various telescopes and total dedication to observing the night skies, William and Caroline began to clock up success after success. William discovered a new planet that was eventually named Uranus, after the Greek god, 'father of the sky'. The existence of a new planet not only excited the scientists of the day, but poets too.

Some 35 years later, John Keats wrote a sonnet, 'On First Looking into Chapman's Homer', in which he celebrates the emotional power of art and scientific discovery, giving a clear nod to Herschel's cosmic findings:

> Much have I travell'd in the realms of gold,
> And many goodly states and kingdoms seen;
> Round many western islands have I been
> Which bards in fealty to Apollo hold.
> Oft of one wide expanse had I been told
> That deep-brow'd Homer ruled as his demesne;
> Yet did I never breathe its pure serene
> Till I heard Chapman speak out loud and bold:
> Then felt I like some watcher of the skies
> When a new planet swims into his ken;
> Or like stout Cortez when with eagle eyes
> He star'd at the Pacific – and with all his men
> Look'd at each other with a wild surmise –
> Silent, upon a peak in Darien.[11]

William Herschel went on to discover yet more moons around Saturn and Uranus. He saw asteroids between Mars and Jupiter. He found that stars emitted infrared, heat radiation as well as visible light. Caroline observed many comets never seen before. Under their sibling gaze, the sheer number of stars observed became unimaginably huge.

William also began to train his telescopes on the faint, diffuse smudges of light that were known as nebula, the Latin for 'cloud'. Quite what they were was not immediately apparent but he realised that some existed inside our own galaxy, the Milky Way, while others seemed to lie even further beyond in the far depths of space. Over the years he observed, catalogued and classified over 2,000 nebulae. His eight-fold classification ran as follows: (I) bright nebulae, (II) faint nebulae, (III) very faint nebulae, (IV) planetary nebulae, (V) very large nebulae, (VI) very compressed and rich clusters of stars, (VII) compressed clusters of small and large stars, and (VIII) coarsely scattered clusters of stars.

More eccentrically, Herschel believed the moon and the planets were populated. Bizarrely, he even speculated that people might be living inside the sun. Nevertheless, none of these wilder thoughts detract from the number and variety of astronomical insights and discoveries that William and Caroline made during their many years of dedicated study of the night skies. Brother and sister published over a hundred scientific papers for the Royal Society. Their observational brilliance, writes the biographer Richard Holmes, 'would change not only the public perception of the solar system, but of the whole Milky Way galaxy and the structure and meaning of the universe itself'.[12] In recognition of his astronomical genius, William was knighted in 1816.

William died in 1822, aged 83. His son, John was destined to follow in his father's footsteps as a scientist and astronomer. William's death left Caroline grief-stricken. She returned to Hanover where she died in 1848, aged 97. Brother and sister left the world with a universe that was far bigger, busier and more exotic than when they first turned their telescopes to look at the night skies of southern England.

Herschel's ideas represented a radical departure from the belief that the world was a stable, static, ordained place. His universe was dynamic, constantly on the move and ever-evolving. Stars were born, aged and died. Vast passages of time would see galaxies form, change shape and mature. Erasmus Darwin, Charles Darwin's grandfather, wrote a poem, 'The Botanic Garden' (1791), in which he celebrates Herschel's vision of an evolving universe, one far bigger and older than was previously imagined, writing that the stars too must yield to age before rushing 'Headlong, extinct, to one dark centre fall, / And Death and Night and Chaos mingle all!'[13]

It was towards the end of his life that Herschel himself said: 'I have looked further into space than ever human being did before me. I have observed stars of which the light, it can be proved, must take two millions of years to reach this globe.'[14] Moreover, in the spirit of this book, Herschel felt that there was beauty in all this variety and vastness, pattern and order. In his mind the search for structure in the beauty of the universe became a life-long passion: 'If one observes the whole Natural World as one, one finds everything in the most Beautiful Order; it is my favourite maxim: *Tout est dans l'ordre.*'[14]

4

Let Me Play among the Stars

The French polymath, Pierre-Simon Laplace, took Herschel's belief that stars and galaxies had a life in which they were born, grew old and died and applied it to the formation of solar systems including our own.[1] In his five-volume *Traité de mécanique céleste*, published between 1798 and 1825, he argued that stars, including our sun, formed as nebular dust and gases that had gradually condensed under the force of gravity. Any remaining stardust left spinning around the newly formed star would eventually gather and coalesce to form planets. Such thoughts were viewed by many as heretical, and even worse, atheistic. In Laplace's challenging view, the Earth formed without the need for divine intervention.

It was also becoming apparent that not all stars are like our sun. Some are old, some are young, some are big, others are small, a few are near, the majority are far, very far away. Most of space is empty. The distances between even close stars is enormous. Light travels at about 300,000 kilometres a second. In a calendar year there are 31,536,000 seconds. A light year therefore equals 300,000 × 31,536,000 kilometres, which is to say about 9.46 trillion kilometres (5.88 trillion miles).

The nearest star to our own sun is Proxima Centauri. It is 4.24 light years away, or 40,208,000,000,000 kilometres distance from our solar system. That's an awfully long way – and that's our nearest star. Our own galaxy, the Milky Way, contains roughly 200 billion stars that form a spiral disc well over 100,000 light years in diameter. If you could fly in a spaceship at a speed of one million miles per hour

(1.6 million kilometres per hour), it would take you about 65 million years to cross our galaxy and 1,600 million years to reach our nearest neighbouring galaxy, Andromeda.

A key breakthrough in the study of stars was made by the Bavarian physicist and lens grinder, Joseph Ritter von Fraunhofer, born on 6 March 1787.[2] With his optical know-how he invented the spectroscope, or spectrometer. This instrument uses either prisms or very fine gratings on a reflective surface to diffract light; and, just like Newton's famous experiments with prisms and light, the spectrometer spreads any white light that hits it into the colours of the rainbow.

During the early years of the nineteenth century, what Fraunhofer discovered was that along these spectra of starlight, many dark lines also appeared. It was eventually realised that these dark lines represented particular wavelengths which were being absorbed by individual elements that were present in the light source. This meant that these particular wavelengths were not being radiated within the propagated light spectrum. Somewhere along their path, they were being absorbed.

It was gradually appreciated that each element had a unique profile of these dark absorption and bright emission lines. It was deduced that you could 'read' the number and distribution of these lines, rather in the manner of a bar code, and determine what elements are present in the radiating object. All of which meant that you could project the light from any source into a spectrometer, including starlight, and work out the elemental composition of the light emitting body. If you trained your telescope on a particular star and then processed the light through a spectrometer, you could determine the composition of that star's gaseous make-up.

In recognition of his discovery, the dark lines in the spectrum are now known as Fraunhofer lines. During an eclipse of the sun in 1868, astronomers noticed emission lines that they hadn't spotted before. The British astronomer, Norman Lockyer, suggested that this indicated the presence of an element unknown on Earth. He called it *helium*, after the Greek word for the sun. It would be another thirty years before helium was found within certain minerals, rocks and natural gases here on Earth.

By the end of the nineteenth century, two key pieces of the cosmic jigsaw were now in place. The universe as described by Herschel was enormously big and probably very old. Up until Herschel's day, it was generally assumed that bright stars were big stars and faint ones small. Herschel proposed the radical idea that perhaps many faint stars were faint, not because they were small but because they were very far away. It was becoming apparent to all astronomers that the universe was populated with untold numbers of stars of varying size, age and brightness.

The second piece of the jigsaw was the findings revealed by the spectrographic analysis of starlight. The existence of Fraunhofer lines allowed astronomers to work out the composition of individual stars.

With these two bits of information it was now possible to think about classifying the stars, looking for sequences of development, working out their elemental composition, and finding a pattern in their evolution.

* * *

The American amateur astronomer, Henry Draper, was amongst the first to attempt a star classification. His work formed the basis of many subsequent schemes. Annie Jump Cannon was born in Delaware in 1863.[3] Her mother encouraged Annie's burgeoning interest in maths and science. She taught her daughter to recognise and name the constellations. As a young woman, Annie lost most of her hearing. Nevertheless, she attended the prestigious Wellesley College in Massachusetts from which she graduated with a degree in physics in 1884, achieving some of the highest grades of her year.

By 1896, Annie Jump Cannon had secured herself a job working with the team at the Harvard Observatory. Under the directorship of Edward C. Pickering, the team was tasked with developing and expanding Draper's classification. Cannon became extraordinarily skilled at reading and interpreting each star's spectral profile. She published her first star catalogue, based on spectral analysis, in 1901. Her pioneering work formed the basis of the Harvard Classification Scheme and, in recognition of her major contributions to astronomy, she received many honours, both nationally and internationally. In 1938, she was appointed the William C. Bond Astronomer at Harvard University. Annie died in 1941, aged 77.

The British-born, American astronomer, Cecilia Payne, using Cannon's understanding of spectral lines, made another breakthrough. In her 1925 doctoral thesis, she showed that all stars are composed mainly of hydrogen and helium.[4]

In 1806, the same decade William and Caroline Herschel realised that deep space equals deep time, the English poet, Jane Taylor wrote a short couplet for young children called 'The Star'. The words were later adapted and used in the familiar lullaby:

> Twinkle, twinkle little star,
> How I wonder what you are.

Over a century later, Norman Lockyer and Cecilia Payne could answer that the stars are essentially giant balls of gaseous hydrogen and helium which differ in size, colour and temperature.

Harking back to Herschel and other nineteenth-century astronomers, if stars are mainly made of hydrogen and helium, but nevertheless vary in their appearance, perhaps the most straightforward way to classify them was simply on their colour, size and brightness. These are the characteristics on which modern classifications are based. The most common system was introduced in 1943 by two American astronomers, William Wilson Morgan and Philip C. Keenan. It is therefore known as the Morgan-Keenan, or MK, system.[5]

Given the fact that there are trillions of stars in hundreds of billions of galaxies, there is a huge variety of stars differing in size, colour and temperature. Each star is categorised along a sequence from the hottest and most blue, to the coolest and most orange, and from the brightest to the dimmest.

There are blue-to-white stars six times hotter than our sun, burning away at the surface at 30,000 °C. There are cool, orange-to-red stars glowing at a mere 2,500 °C, half as hot as the sun. Some stars are hundreds of times bigger than the sun, but typically much less dense. These are the giants and super-giants. The most common stars are smaller than the sun, including the red dwarfs which have radii typically less than half that of our local star.

* * *

Let's follow the story of star types and their development in a little more detail, although even this simplified story hides a fiercely complex area of science.

First off in the classification are *protostars*. Many of these are the nebulae spotted by the Herschels towards the end of the eighteenth century. They are giant clouds of mainly hydrogen that are still in the process of collapsing under the force of gravity. They are almost, but not quite, at the point of becoming fully formed suns. As the gases condense and become energised under gravitational pull, they heat up, and the stars begin to emit a faint light.

It is not until the gases have collapsed into a sufficiently dense and hot state that they become fully-fledged stars. The extremely high pressures and temperatures of up to 15 million °C in their cores allows nuclear fusion to take place. Hydrogen is converted first into helium, then in later stages into even heavier elements. Fusion also releases enormous amounts of energy in the form of heat and light. At this point in their life story, stars are said to enter the *main sequence*.

Most stars in the universe are main sequence stars. Our sun and our near neighbours, Sirius and Alpha Centauri A, are main sequence stars. Our sun turns out to be rather ordinary. It is classified as a main sequence, yellow dwarf star with a surface temperature of 5,500 °C, a core temperature of about 15 million °C and a diameter of nearly a million miles. On our planet, we experience the energy released by the processes of nuclear fusion taking place at the centre of the sun as warm sunlight. It is the sun's heat and light that gives rise to and sustains life on Earth.

From the moment of their birth, just as William Herschel proposed, stars develop, mature, grow old and, at some distant point in the future, die. However, the key value that determines a star's life course, evolution and longevity is its size at birth; and, perhaps counter-intuitively, the bigger the star, the shorter its life.

The fate of small- to medium-sized stars like our sun is to end their days as *red giants*. As the processes of nuclear fusion gradually wind down and generate less energy, pressures fall, stars relax and they become more diffuse and less dense. As a result, they also become less hot, turn from yellow to red, and grow hugely in size, anything up to one hundred times larger than when they were in their prime.

Our sun formed about 4.6 billion years ago. It's now middle aged, half-way through its life. In about another five billion years, it will have exhausted its nuclear supplies. It will quietly ease into a flabby old age, expand enormously in size and become a red giant, engulfing the inner planets of Mercury and Venus and possibly the Earth in the process. The red giant phase lasts only a few hundred million years. When that stage ends and the sun has burned away a third of its mass, its helium core will suddenly ignite violently. This is known as a helium flash. A third of the remaining mass will turn into carbon in a matter of minutes. It will then shrink to a tenth of its current size, undergo another low density expansion before finally collapsing into a dense *white dwarf*, not much bigger than the Earth, although in this highly condensed, compact state, much more massive.

White dwarves do continue to shine because their remaining cores were once very hot. However, as white dwarfs cannot generate any new heat, very, very slowly, they cool down. Their internal heat and light radiate away. Only after a staggering few hundred billion years do they finally stop shining, cold cinders invisible in the black night of the cosmos. From yellow average star to red giant to white dwarf in around 10 billion years, that's our sun's life story in a nutshell.

The most common types of star in the universe are *red dwarfs*. These are also main sequence stars but they have much lower masses than our sun. Their upper limit is, at most, half the mass of the Sun, but often much less. Their less dense cores mean that the processes of nuclear fusion are more limited and not so energetic. Red dwarfs burn their hydrogen more slowly, although in the end they consume more of the gas than their larger, white and yellow-hot cousins. All of this means that red dwarfs carry on quietly glowing with their dull light for a very long time, for hundreds of billions, even trillions of years. In comparison, our sun's active life of ten billion years is relatively brief. But like the sun, red dwarfs, too, will eventually end their days as tiny white, slowly cooling, dwarf stars.

The fate of main sequence stars that are a little larger than our sun, say about four to ten times as massive, is a little more dramatic. They avoid a distended old age. They don't slacken into red giants. When nuclear fusion is no longer sustainable, after a mere ten million years or so, these big stars explode. They form *supernovae*, instantly emitting huge amounts of energy equivalent to a hundred billion suns. This energy, in the form of heat, light and hot gases, blasts out into the surrounding cosmos. For a brief while, supernovae can appear as the brightest objects in the night sky. As astronomers are fond of saying, in the case of very big stars, they live fast and die young.

However, after their spectacular, explosive finales, massive stars do leave behind their cores. These spent cores are still sufficiently massive to collapse under powerful gravitational forces. They end up as extremely small, dense stars known as *neutron stars*. Under intense gravity, the star's positively charged protons and negatively charged electrons become so crushed and compressed that they fuse to form an electrically neutral sub-atomic particle, the neutron.

Neutron stars are tiny, only a few miles across, not much bigger than a large city. However, because the neutrons out of which they are made are so incredibly densely packed, their mass can be several times that of the sun, all compressed into a ball, a few miles in diameter. This means that a teaspoonful of a neutron star could weigh a billion metric tonnes. Neutron stars also spin, very fast, anything between one and a hundred times a second. They often emit pulses of light which, because the stars spin, beam out across the blackness of space, rather like a souped-up lighthouse. In these cases, the neutron stars are also known as *pulsars*. Pulsars were first detected by the Irish astronomer, Jocelyn Bell Burnell, when she was a postgraduate student at the University of Cambridge.[6]

If the mass of the star's core after it has exploded as a supernova is particularly great, gravitational forces become so powerful and extreme that not even a neutron star is possible. The star's spent matter collapses to such a degree that it forms a *black hole*. In the centre of a black hole is a gravitational singularity. This is a one-dimensional point. It contains the entire mass of the collapsed core in an infinitely small space. This means that density and gravity also become infinite and space-time curves infinitely. Gravity is so strong that not even light can escape. The once giant star has become a black hole in space. It is the blackest of black. Other types of black hole also exist, but their origins are tied up with the very early stages of the universe's history. They are therefore known as *primordial black holes*, with many *supermassive* ones, thousands, millions, even billions times more massive than the sun, sitting at the centre of every galaxy.

Finally, stars that are ten, twenty, even thirty times the mass of the sun, live the fastest and die the youngest of all. They are the *supergiants*. After fewer than ten million years, a supergiant ends its days as a supernova, but one so cataclysmically violent that not even the core remains. The whole star disintegrates, its remains being blasted into the heavens to become stardust, the interstellar motes that one day might collapse to become part of a new generation of stars and planets, and you and me.

* * *

Up until the 1920s, many astronomers, though not William Herschel, still thought that all the stars were part of the Milky Way. However, the work of the American astronomer, Edwin Hubble, established that the Milky Way was just one of many galaxies in the universe.[7] The next few paragraphs introduce more numbers that are breathtakingly huge. As Douglas Adams says in *The Hitchhiker's Guide to the Galaxy*, 'Space is big. You just won't believe how vastly, hugely, mind-bogglingly big it is.' It really is that big.

Let's begin with the Milky Way, our own galaxy, in which our sun lies some two thirds from the centre on one of the spiral arms of the galactic catherine wheel. On average, our sun is 93 million miles away from planet Earth. It takes just over eight minutes for its heat and light to reach us.

As we've learned, the visible parts of the Milky Way are at least a 100,000 light years across. This is equivalent to a diameter of roughly 600,000 trillion miles. And that's just one galaxy, our own.

The next nearest galaxy is Andromeda. It is 2.3 million light years distant from the Milky Way. We won't convert this number of light years into miles because the numbers get even more outrageous, and totally unimaginable. As telescopes get more powerful, estimates for the number of galaxies in the observable universe increase each year. Current estimates suggest that there upwards of 200 billion galaxies. The furthest observed so far are over around 13.4 billion light years away, that is, it has taken the light from them 13.4 billion years to reach us today. We see them as they were 13.4 billion years ago, only a short while after the birth of the universe itself which exploded into existence about 13.8 billion years ago.

All of which means that the universe really is, as we've established, unimaginably, 'mind-bogglingly big'; and somewhere in this boundless universe, we find ourselves, living on an insignificant speck of rock, spinning around a very ordinary star sitting in the outer reaches of an average galaxy. You can appreciate the profound implications of this realisation, philosophically and existentially. In his 1882 novel, *Two on a Tower*, Thomas Hardy describes feelings of swirling vertigo experienced by his two star-crossed lovers as they looked into the deep night sky through a telescope:

> At night … there is nothing to moderate the blow which the infinitely great, the stellar universe, strikes down upon the infinitely little, the mind of the beholder; and this was the case now. Having got closer to immensity than their fellow creatures, they saw at once the beauty and its frightfulness. They more and more felt the contrast between their own tiny magnitude and those amongst which they

> had recklessly plunged, till they were oppressed with the presence of a vastness they could not cope with even as an idea ...[8]

Whether it's wild mountains, boundless oceans or the infinite black of a night sky, we feel a shivering thrill as we sense nature's majestic indifference to our small, short lives.

* * *

One of the next major milestones in our understanding of the night sky was to realise that the galaxies themselves, with the exception of our immediate neighbours in our local cluster, were all getting further and further away. In 1912, Vesto Slipher, an American astronomer, observed that the light from distant galaxies had shifted towards the red end of the spectrum. Red light has a longer wavelength than the orange, yellow, green and blue parts of the spectrum. As objects speed away from us, the wavelength of the light they emit becomes stretched and slightly elongated. Hence, light from receding objects is described as 'red-shifted.' We can therefore interpret any red-shift in the light analysed from a galaxy as indicating that it is speeding away from us, just as the pitch of a police car siren drops as it speeds past and away from us.

A few years later, other astronomers reached similar conclusions, including the Soviet physicist, Alexander Friedmann in 1922, and the Belgian priest and mathematician, Georges Lemaître in 1927. Lemaître might have been in Rose Tremain's mind when she has Nadia, a character in her novel, *The Swimming Pool Season*, say that a monk had a telescope on his roof, 'but I don't know what some monk is being an astronomer for. Maybe he's looking for heaven?'[9]

Two years after Lemaître's observations, the American astronomer, Edwin Hubble, also confirmed from his results that the further away a galaxy was, the faster it was receding.[10] Indeed, all galaxies outside their local clusters are speeding away from all other galaxies. The more distant the galaxy, the faster it recedes. This is now known as 'Hubble's Law'. Moreover, because it takes time for light to travel, the more distant the galaxy the further back in time we are looking. We don't see them as they are 'now' but as they were when their light left them and the time it took for that light to reach us here on Earth.

The conclusion was clear, if rather extraordinary. The universe is expanding, or more technically, space itself is expanding carrying the galaxies with it. However, if the universe is expanding, then this must also mean that, if you project backwards in time, all the galaxies must have been closer together. Push this thought to its logical conclusion and it means that the entire universe and everything in it, as well as time and space themselves must have expanded from a single point. Or, as Katie Mack clarifies, a singularity doesn't actually have to be a single point, it can 'just be an infinitely dense state of an infinitely large universe', in which points were therefore present before space and time began.[11] The stars and galaxies aren't actually expanding into anything. There's no beyond or outside to expand into. It is the universe and space itself that are expanding carrying the stars and galaxies ever-outwards like the dots on a balloon being blown ever bigger from an infinitesimally small point.

The distinguished British astronomer Fred Hoyle was not convinced that the universe began as a singularity. He thought the universe existed in a 'steady state'. In 1950, he argued against those who said that the universe began, as he facetiously put it, in a 'big bang'. In spite of Hoyle's dismissive intentions, the name stuck. Today, we all know the origins of the universe as the Big Bang Theory. Indeed, more recent observations suggest the universe is not only expanding but also that the rate of expansion is actually increasing. As the galaxies race away, their speed of retreat is increasing, perhaps all driven by the mysterious force of dark energy.

The ultimate fate of the universe, so current thinking tells us, is to expand and expand, and, under the inexorable laws of entropy, slowly, slowly run itself down. Order evaporates. Structure dwindles. Trillions of years into the future, way past the time when our sun has died, the night skies will darken as first galaxies disappear beyond the edge of the observable universe, then the stars stop shining, and finally even matter itself decays into nothing but an invisible radiation of electrons, protons and neutrinos, spread impossibly thin throughout a still expanding, structureless, utterly black universe.

* * *

This, then, is the story of the universe, our night sky, and what a story. It is a tale that has taken several centuries to tell. It has involved many extraordinary minds: Copernicus, Galileo, Newton, the Herschels, Lemaître, Einstein, Morgan, Cannon, Keenan, Hubble, Bell Burnell and countless others. It has involved patient science and remarkable imaginations.

'We are a species that delights in story', says the physicist Brian Greene. 'We look out on reality, we grasp patterns, and we join them into narratives that can captivate, inform, startle, amuse, and thrill.'[12] From nothing, the universe explodes, inflates, exponentially expands and, in less than a trillionth of a second, it roars into glorious existence. Stars form. Planets gather. Galaxies mass and cluster. The heavens evolve, mature, age and die.

Somewhere along this story line, on at least one tiny, insignificant planet around one average star that shines for a cosmically brief ten billion years, in a spiral arm of a regular galaxy, life appeared. Life that became conscious of its own existence. Life that asks questions about itself. Life that could wonder why there is something rather than nothing. Life that found itself self-conscious in an unconscious, indifferent universe and wondered what it all means. Life that could tell the story of how the universe came to be and how it might end.

Nonetheless, in spite of the universe's indifference to our fleeting presence, the philosophical genius of that self-conscious life, is also capable of giving our lives meaning. As Sarah Williams says in her 1868 poem, 'The Old Astronomer', there is nothing to be afraid of:

> Though my soul may set in darkness, it will rise in perfect
> light;
> I have loved the stars too truly to be fearful of the night.[13]

It is the living of life itself that becomes the source of its own meaning. In his poem, 'The More Loving One' (1957), W.H. Auden recognises the indifference of the stars to our brief lives: whether we are loved or not, whatever the relationship, 'let the more loving one be me.[14]

Part III

Clouds

5

Head in the Clouds

We see the stars by night. We see the clouds by day. Yet there are a number of beautiful exceptions to this simple divide. When the sun sets and the sun rises, its light is reflected by Venus as she makes her night entry as the brilliant Evening Star and bids farewell as the Morning Star. On nights when there is a full moon and thin, broken clouds slip silently across black skies, for brief moments we see their ghostly presence as they glide over the cold, clear lunar light.

Perhaps most ethereal of all are *noctilucent clouds*. Literally translated these are 'night shining' clouds. They are made of wisps of ice crystals that form 50 miles high. They might be seen during the summer months in the higher latitudes, between 50 degrees and 70 degrees both north and south of the Equator. When the sun has set below the horizon and we are in the shadow of evening, the very highest clouds remain in sunlight for a short while longer. If conditions are right, these *mesospheric clouds* reflect the light and appear in dusky north-western skies as luminescent streams of blue and white light.

In this chapter, we are still looking up at the sky, but it's now daylight and our sights are lower. We have come down to earth, almost. We have left the cold, star-studded black of expanding space and have fallen into Earth's outermost layer – the gaseous atmosphere.

* * *

The sky and clouds have always held a deep fascination for writers, poets and artists. In a short essay reproduced in Edward Cook's and

Alexander Wedderburn's edited book, *The Works of John Ruskin*, the art critic and polymath, Ruskin wrote that the atmosphere is 'Sometimes gentle, sometimes capricious, sometimes awful, never the same for two moments together; almost human in its passions, almost spiritual in its tenderness, almost divine in its infinity.'[1]

When Virginia Woolf was experiencing a nervous breakdown, she wrote an essay, 'On Being Ill', in which she valued the opportunities that being unwell gave her, including the chance to reflect on things both big and small. The essay was originally published in 1926. Here she is writing about looking up at the clouds and the sky:

> The first impression of that extraordinary spectacle is strangely overcoming ... this incessant making up of shapes and casting them down, this buffeting of clouds together, and drawing vast trains of ships and waggons from North to South. ... One should not let this gigantic cinema play perpetually to an empty house. But watch a little longer and another emotion drowns the stirrings of civic ardour. Divinely beautiful it is also divinely heartless.[2]

At first her reactions to clouds are similar to those of other poets and prose writers. She sees shapes in the ever-shifting cloudscape. However, she then goes on to ask more serious questions about the human condition and nature's indifference to our being. Although clouds in themselves can offer no consolation, they can inspire our imaginations. It is in the creative response to nature that we find meaning, freedom and contentment. In this, Woolf is following in the footsteps of William Wordsworth, Samuel Taylor Coleridge and Thomas de Quincy. It was Woolf's image of the sky as a giant cinema that inspired the poet Alice Oswald and her co-editor, Paul Keegan, to publish an anthology of weather-related prose and poems with the title, *Gigantic Cinema: A Weather Anthology*, in which the editors claim their ruling idea was to have no ideas: to dispense with writing 'about' weather, 'writing that knows what it's talking about', in favour of 'writing that is "like" weather', nebulous, shifting, surreal.[3]

It is the air that surrounds our planet that makes life possible. It is held there by Earth's gravity. Yet, relatively speaking, this life-giving layer is as thin as it is precious. Ninety per cent of the atmosphere lies below 52,000 feet, just ten miles above the ground. Above this height, the air gets thinner and thinner. When you reach around 300,000 feet, almost 60 miles up, the atmosphere ends and space begins.

It is just under 4,000 miles from the centre of the Earth to its surface. A further 60 miles and you have reached the very top of the atmosphere. This thin skin of gas is a mere 1.5 per cent of the radius of the Earth from its centre to the edge of space but it's vital for our existence and we need to look after it.

We learn at school that air is made up of 78 per cent nitrogen, 21 per cent oxygen and one per cent argon. A few other gases occur but in very small amounts. In 1900, levels of carbon dioxide in the atmosphere measured below 300 parts per million or 0.03 per cent by volume. Present-day levels have risen sharply, approaching 420 parts per million in 2023. As we burn more fossil fuels, we pump more carbon dioxide into the atmosphere and, because it is a 'greenhouse' gas, any increase also means an increase in atmospheric heat retention, a rise in global heating and ultimately climate change. If we don't care for the air, the air won't care for us.

The air also contains water molecules in the form of a gas known as water vapour, also a greenhouse gas. The amount of water vapour in the atmosphere varies depending on temperature and height. At sea level, on average, there is about one per cent of water vapour present. As temperatures rise, so the air can hold more water. For example, if the temperature of the air is 30 °C at sea level it can hold up to four per cent water vapour by volume. Conversely, on very cold days, below freezing, these levels can drop to well below one per cent.

Water vapour gets into the air through evaporation as the sun shines on rivers, lakes and oceans, and beams down on damp soil, melting snow and slushy ice. When animals respire and plants transpire, they breathe moisture into the atmosphere. These processes mark the beginning of the *water cycle*. Clouds form when water vapour (a gas) cools and condenses to form water droplets (a liquid). However, these droplets are so small they stay aloft. Before they can become rain, the water droplets must grow. As they gain more water, they become larger and heavier. They can no longer float around in the sky as clouds. They fall to Earth. It begins to rain and, to quote the poet Shelley, 'bring fresh showers for the thirsting flowers'. The water is returned to the rivers, lakes and oceans. The cycle is complete, ready to begin all over again. It was in his poem, 'The Cloud', published in 1820, that Percy Bysshe Shelley offered his own take on the water cycle:[4]

I am the daughter of Earth and Water,
And the nursling of the Sky;
I pass through the pores of the ocean and shores;
I change, but I cannot die.
For after the rain when with never a stain
The pavilion of Heaven is bare,
And the winds and sunbeams with their convex gleams
Build up the blue dome of air,
I silently laugh at my own cenotaph,
And out of the caverns of rain,
Like a child from the womb, like a ghost from the tomb,
I arise and unbuild it again.

Water vapour, then, is critical for the formation of clouds; and clouds, their types and behaviour are the main interest of this chapter.

* * *

We first met John Dalton in Chapter 1. He is remembered and celebrated first and foremost as the father of atomic chemistry and we shall meet him again in Chapter 15.[5] As well as chemistry, Dalton also made significant contributions to the new science of meteorology. For over 50 years he took daily readings of the weather, measuring the temperature, air pressure, rainfall, wind speed and direction. His very last reading was taken on 26 July 1844. He reported: '60, 71, 30.18, SW 1, Little Rain.' Translated, this tells us that on this day, there was an outside temperature of 60 °F, an inside temperature of 71 °F, an air pressure of 30.18 inches of mercury, a south-westerly wind and, of course, a 'little rain'. Dalton died the very next day, aged 77. His final weather report appeared posthumously in the *Manchester Guardian*. In honour of a remarkable life, Manchester Corporation organised a mile-long funeral procession which was attended by 40,000 mourners.[6,7]

Amongst his many meteorological observations, Dalton took a particular interest in water vapour and cloud formation. He appreciated that, as moist winds rose, they cooled and, as they cooled, any gaseous water vapour they held condensed to liquid water, and clouds formed. This was particularly evident over the mountains of the Lake District, his home country. He knew that the prevailing winds were westerlies and that they had travelled over the Atlantic Ocean and Irish Sea. They were therefore saturated with water vapour. As the winds rose over the fells, the air chilled. Mists formed and clouds thickened and, more often than not, rain would fall. It was no surprise to Dalton that the wettest parts of the British Isles were the mountains of the west.

Dalton was interested in the weather for its own sake but, more particularly, he was interested in the properties of gases, including air, and the presence of water vapour in the atmosphere. Indeed, it was probably his experiments with gases and water vapour that first gave him the idea of atoms and their relative weights in compounds and molecules. Moreover, although he confirmed and developed the idea of the water cycle, he didn't say much about clouds and their types. Dalton was certainly a child of his age, the Age of Reason. However, the late eighteenth century was still waiting for someone to look at clouds specifically, observe them carefully, collect good facts,and then see if any patterns or laws might emerge.

Up until the eighteenth century, clouds either did not interest scientists, or, if they did wonder about them, their fleeting, morphing appearance, high above and beyond reach, didn't seem to offer a promising subject for careful study. Clouds were described as 'ornaments of the sky' and to study them, to quote Luke Howard, might 'be deemed a useless pursuit of shadows, an attempt to define forms which, being the sport of winds, must be ever varying, and therefore not to be defined'[8]. In an essay, Rhodri Lewis notes that Shakespeare was also drawn to 'inconstant clouds' and their metaphorical potential. Lewis saw them as possessing 'a particular kind of mutability, one closely tied up with the transformative power of the poetic-artistic imagination'.[9]

Even the Latin word for cloud, *nebulosus*, has given us the English adjective 'nebulous', which describes things seen as vague, foggy, cloudy and not clearly defined. However, at the turn of the nineteenth century, ways of thinking about clouds were about to change, and with that change came the prospect of meteorology becoming a sharper and, ironically, less nebulous science.

* * *

Luke Howard was born in London in 1772. Like Dalton, he was a Quaker.[10] His interest in the weather developed when he was a child. In his mid-teens, he set up a weather station in the garden of the family home in Stamford Hill, London. After leaving school in Oxfordshire, he was apprenticed to a pharmacist in Stockport, Cheshire, before eventually establishing his own pharmacy in Fleet

Street, London in 1794. He was aged 21. His return to the capital also gave him the opportunity to attend public lectures on science. It was at these lectures that Howard got to know William Allen. He was a Quaker, pacifist and, like Howard, a supporter of the anti-slavery movement. Allen was also a successful pharmacist with premises in Plough Court, Lombard Street in London.

In 1796, Allen and Howard, along with other Quakers, founded the Askesian Society. This was a debating and self-improvement club to encourage research and education. Members met weekly and presented papers. In 1798, Allen and Howard went into partnership and opened a new pharmaceutical company based in Plaistow, East London.

It was not long after this joint venture was established that Howard had a minor accident. He had to take time off work. His active and enquiring mind, though, didn't rest. Being a pharmacist, he had an interest in botany and the medical properties of plants. Using his microscope he decided to take a look at plant pollen. In 1800 he presented a paper to the Linnean Society of London titled, 'Account of a Microscopical Investigation of Several Species of Pollen, with Remarks and Questions on the Structure and Use of that Part of Vegetables'. It was published in the society's transactions a couple of years later.

East London is flat and the skies, at least then, were big and without interruption. There was plenty of opportunity for Howard to indulge in his other scientific passion, meteorology. He was already familiar with John Dalton's book, *Meteorological Observations and Essays*, published in 1793. Howard's work on pollens and his paper presented to the Linnean Society also meant he knew all about the work of the Swedish botanist, Carl Linnaeus. We shall meet Linnaeus again in Chapter 10, but he is the person who developed the modern system, still used today, for classifying and naming plants and animals using Latin as the *lingua franca*. Linnaeus is known as the 'father of modern taxonomy'.

Howard's genius was to combine his interest in the weather, observations of what was going on in the sky, readings of Dalton's work on meteorology, and knowledge and appreciation of Linnaeus's methods of classifying plants and animals. He then applied his understanding to the studies he'd made of clouds. He brought order to their shape-shifting, transient presence. In 1802 he presented a paper to the Askesian Society on the classification of clouds titled as 'On the Modifications of Clouds, and on the Principles of their Production, Suspension and Destruction'. It was subsequently published as an essay in 1803.[11]

By 1807 Howard had branched out on his own as a pharmaceutical manufacturer. He moved his business a mile up the road from Plaistow to Stratford. The company was a success. It supplied chemicals to industry and pharmaceuticals to the retail trade. Howard also supplied ether to John Dalton in Manchester, which the chemist needed for his experiments. The two men began a lifelong correspondence sharing all ideas meteorological. In 1837 Howard published his *Seven Lectures on Meteorology*, with a dedication to John Dalton in recognition of 40 years of friendship.[12]

Like Dalton, Howard kept a daily record of the weather. For 21 years he noted London's temperature, rainfall, air pressure, and wind speed and direction. He realised that urban areas, such as London, maintained a slightly higher temperature than the surrounding countryside, especially at night, and he was one of the first people to develop the idea of an urban heat island. His studies of urban climates resulted in his landmark publication, *The Climate of London* (two volumes published in 1818 and 1820, respectively), for which he was elected a Fellow of the Royal Society in 1821.

Two years later, he was one of the founding members of the Meteorological Society of London. It had something of a fitful existence. It was eventually wound up in 1850 in favour of the newly formed British Meteorological Society, established on 3 April 1850. At its first ordinary meeting on 7 May 1850, Howard, now aged 76, joined and became a member.

* * *

It had been clear to Howard that clouds, far from being 'airy nothings', were subject to the laws of nature. Physics and chemistry, in particular, with their interest in heat and energy, gases and vapours, seemed to offer the best prospects of understanding the weather, in general, and clouds, in particular. Being a good Linnaean, Howard felt that the first thing to do was to classify the clouds into their different types. This was the basis of his famous 1802 paper, 'On the Modifications of Clouds'.

Others were also having a go at trying to bring order to the skies. The French naturalist, Jean-Baptiste Lamarck proposed a cloud classification scheme in 1805.[13] However, he used French nomenclature and, although his types are not dissimilar to some that Howard identified, his list of descriptive terms didn't catch on. With his Linnaean hat on, Howard classified his clouds using Latin nomenclature. Howard's solution to the problem of how to classify short-lived, ever-changing clouds was both appealing and elegant. Very quickly his cloud types and the names he gave them caught on with both scientists and the general public.

Howard said there were three simple cloud types, determined by their appearance. Some clouds had the look of fibres or wisps of hair (*cirrus*), others piled up in heaps (*cumulus*), while some covered the sky in vast layers or sheets (*stratus*). He also argued that each type could change from one to the other; or they could combine, giving rise to intermediate and compound types. This gave him a classification comprising seven types of cloud, the names of which have entered our everyday language. Here are Howard's original descriptions:

> *Cirrus*: parallel, flexuous, or diverging fibres, extensible in any or all directions.
>
> *Cumulus*: convex or conical heaps, increasing upwards from a horizontal base.
>
> *Stratus*: a widely extended, continuous, horizontal sheet, increasing from below.
>
> *Cirro-cumulus*: small, well-defined roundish masses, in close horizontal arrangement.
>
> *Cirro-stratus*: horizontal or slightly inclined masses, attenuated towards a part or the whole of their circumference, bent downward, or undulated, separate, or in groups consisting of small clouds having these characters.
>
> *Cumulo-stratus*: the cirro-stratus blended with the cumulus and either appearing intermixed with the heaps of the latter, or super-adding a widespread structure to its base.
>
> *Cumulo-cirro-stratus* or *Nimbus*: a horizontal sheet, above which the cirrus spreads, while the cumulus enters it laterally and from beneath.

His classification was a landmark achievement in the world of meteorology. It showed that cloud formations were the visible signs of atmospheric processes and were based on the laws of physics. Howard recognised that clouds were made up of particles of water or ice which had condensed from vapour rising and cooling. He adopted John Dalton's idea that the particles descend slowly (because of air resistance) and once they fall below the base of the cloud, they evaporate. So, although the air, vapour and tiny water particles are all in motion, up and down, down and up, the cloud as a whole does not appear to descend at all. Only when the water droplets became too big and heavy to remain suspended do we get rain.

The 1802 paper immediately became popular. It saw order in the turbulent skies. It gave form to the formless. The paper was reprinted in journals, books and magazines; and it began to influence the way artists saw clouds and painted them, and poets wrote about and described them.

* * *

One of Howard's biggest and earliest fans was the German poet, philosopher and weather-watcher, Johann Wolfgang von Goethe. He wrote that Howard, 'was the first to hold fast conceptually the airy and always changing forms of clouds, to limit and fasten down the indefinite, the intangible and unattainable and give them appropriate names'.[14] He talked of creating precision from the imprecise, whether it was seeing shapes in the clouds or order in the weather. It is perhaps no surprise that the Romantics, both poets and painters, developed a fascination with clouds. The ever-changing, indefinite, ungraspable nature of clouds appealed to their sensibilities. The clouds and sky were seen as a source of infinite moods.

In his book, *The Invention of Clouds*, Richard Hamblyn writes that for 'Goethe the identification and naming of the clouds had done nothing less than transfigure mankind's relationship with aerial nature'.[15] With his romantic outlook, Goethe felt that Howard's classification could now inspire and inform both science and art. Howard, he wrote, had mentally grasped what no previous hand could reach or clasp. He not only corresponded with Howard, he also wrote several poems in his honour. There is a translation of Goethe's poem, 'Atmosphäre', by Anthony Howell. It appears on the webpages of Tottenham Clouds, a site that celebrates the achievements of Luke Howard, one-time resident of the North London suburb. It ends with the hope that his 'airborne song' will give 'thanks for the "Namer of the Clouds"'.[16]

In spite of Goethe's efforts, German artists didn't seem that interested in Howard's cloud classification. The painter Caspar David Friedrich went even further in expressing his misgivings. He was concerned that 'to force the free and airy clouds into a rigid order and classification' would damage their expressive potential and even 'undermine the whole foundation of landscape painting'.[17] However, in England, there was more enthusiasm. Indeed, the way clouds were painted after the publication of Howard's paper changed radically.

* * *

Prior to the beginning of the nineteenth century, clouds were often depicted by artists in either a stylised fashion or somewhat generically. There are exceptions, of course. Many seventeenth-century Dutch artists gave clouds and the sky a central role in their paintings. Jacob Isaacksz van Ruisdael's *View of Ootmarsum*, painted between 1650 and 1665, pictures cumulus clouds bubbling darkly above a church spire and windmill. However, although the Renaissance had begun to encourage painters to render clouds and their appearance more faithfully, the eighteenth century saw something of a return to approaches that were thought to be more classical and morally uplifting. Reality was idealised. Paintings of nature and landscapes for their own sake were viewed rather snootily.

Howard's classification coincided with the beginnings of the Romantic Movement in art, music and literature. The arts in the early eighteenth century looked for harmony, balance and calm in nature. However, the prevailing mood of the Enlightenment was one which valued rational thinking. In its applied form, whether in mining, manufacturing or farming, it sought to tame nature: manage it, fashion it, exploit it. By the force and action of fire, air and water, wrote Descartes in part VI of the *Discourse on the Method*, we can 'make ourselves … lords and possessors of nature'.

However, a growing reaction began to take place against this cool, detached, exploitative stance. Romanticism excited artists to run in the opposite direction. It celebrated the individual, the subjective and the emotional. Poetry and painting helped us to recover our relationship with nature. Under the artist's eye, the earth and sky became re-enchanted. Nature began to be viewed as a place of wild, untamed beauty that could arouse the senses and reconnect men and women with the deeper reaches of their conscious selves. The artist's relationship with the world around became experiential rather than descriptive.

The Norwegian artist, Johan Christian Clausen Dahl (1788-1857), was one of the few painters to respond to Goethe's suggestion that the new, scientific studies of clouds should inform art. He worked mainly in Dresden. He was one of the leading landscape painters of German Romanticism as well as being the founder of the Norwegian school of landscape painting. Many of his paintings reveal his interests in geology and meteorology, and his cloud studies bear an uncanny similarity to those produced by John Constable.

In literary Britain, Romanticism began with the publication in 1798 of William Wordsworth and Samuel Taylor Coleridge's *Lyrical Ballads*. In the preface to the second edition in 1800, Wordsworth described poetry as 'the spontaneous overflow of powerful feelings'. Similar sentiments were beginning to be expressed in art. There was a growing appreciation of the transient and dramatic effects of light, colour and atmosphere on the appearance of lakes and mountains, seas and skies.

In his paintings, J.M.W. Turner captured nature in all her dynamic, restless, sublime beauty. John Thornes writes that Turner's skies are 'full of the power of nature' in which mankind's efforts are dwarfed and rendered futile.[18] In his studies of clouds, his paintings of storms, his depictions of rain and rainbows, Turner captured skies in all their wild and wonderful moods. In his essay on 'modern' landscape painting, published in 1856, John Ruskin wrote that 'the first thing that will strike us, or that ought to strike us, is *their cloudiness*. Out of perfect light and motionless air, we find ourselves on a sudden brought under sombre skies, and into drifting wind.'[19] It is when artists capture the changing moods of restless skies that our emotions are aroused and we tremble as we reflect on our own inconstant presence in the world.

Of all the early romantic artists, perhaps no one painted the sky with more understanding and sympathy than John Constable. In his sketches and paintings, clouds were no longer just there and incidental to the subject. Often they were *the* subject. Clouds appeared glorious and centre stage. Even before he came across Howard's classification, Constable had made hundreds of sketches of clouds and their forms. He studied them as carefully as any scientist might. He painted them in oil, and all are dated with the time of day, the direction and speed of the wind, along with other cloudy facts.[20]

His understanding of winds and the weather probably began in his teens. In the late 1780s, for a year or so, the young John worked for his father helping him to mill wheat at their windmill on East Bergholt Common, Suffolk. Studying the skies and having a good sense of wind speed and direction were some of the key skills that anyone operating a windmill would need to learn.

In 1815 Thomas Forster published the second edition of his book, *Researches about Atmospheric Phaenomena*. His first chapter, 'Of Mr Howard's Theory of the Origin and Modification of Clouds', fully acknowledges his indebtedness to Mr Howard, writing that 'I shall always use the terms which he has adopted'.[21] The book sold extremely well. It was the second edition, with a series of plates illustrating the major cloud types, that John Constable first read in 1821. It inspired him to embark further on his own cloud studies. Hundreds of sketches of the sky and the clouds were made from the high ground of Hampstead Heath, near to where he lived. They suggest movement and change. They have a dynamic feel about them.

True to the romantic spirit, he felt the only truth lay in nature and it was this truth he tried to capture in oil, pen and ink. He believed that we can only know the world subjectively, through our feelings. 'Painting is with me', he famously said, 'but another word for feeling'; and, of all that any landscape might offer, the sky, he felt, was 'the chief organ of sentiment'. It is 'the source of light in nature – and governs everything'.[22]

We might mention two of Constable's paintings in particular. *Rainstorm over the Sea* was painted between 1824 and 1828 during his stays in Brighton. It was painted at great speed to capture the turbulent, fast-moving nature of the scene. Thunderous black clouds and torrential rains lash across the waters. The feelings generated in both viewer and painter are ones of awe, danger and excitement. *Salisbury Cathedral from the Meadows* was painted around 1830. Again, there is a stormy sky. The cathedral's spire appears to pierce a black, threatening cloud. Constable's exuberant brush strokes reflect the energy of the moment; and arching across the whole blustery scene is a rainbow.

By the middle of the nineteenth century it seemed that the turbulent skies were finally being tamed by artists and scientists alike.

6

Weather Forecasts and Cloudy Thinking

In 1896, the World Meteorological Organization, with a few minor amendments, adopted Luke Howard's cloud classification. Since then, the science of meteorology has developed by leaps and bounds. Over the last hundred years, our understanding of the physics and chemistry of the atmosphere has become ever more sophisticated. The complex interactions between land, sea and air have shown that, in order to understand the weather, we need to understand the dynamics of the whole planet including the fundamental part that life plays in helping to create, maintain and modify our weather and climate. The oceans, in particular, play a key role in meteorological processes. They are four hundred times more massive than the atmosphere and have a heat capacity more than a thousand times larger. Super-computers and satellites, mathematics and modelling have also transformed the ability of scientists not only to make sense of the weather, but also to predict it with increasing accuracy.

The ability to predict the weather has always been a hope and a dream. Natural philosophers, sailors, farmers, travellers, country folk and city dwellers have all had a fascination with what the weather might have in store. Early attempts by people such Robert FitzRoy, trained by William Beaufort (he of the wind-speed scale), had some success but, in truth, the accuracy of their forecasts was rather hit or miss. Nevertheless, their efforts and growing expertise laid the groundwork for future forecasters. Indeed, it was FitzRoy who first coined the term 'weather forecast'.[1]

Vice Admiral FitzRoy had already enjoyed a busy and successful naval career, including his captaincy of HMS *Beagle*, the ship on which Charles Darwin joined him as they went on their five-year scientific expedition around the world. After a stint as governor of New Zealand and a short spell back on boats, in 1854 he was recommended by the president of the Royal Society to be the chief of a new department to be named the Office of Meteorological Statistics of the Board of Trade, later to be known as the Meteorological Office, or Met Office, for short. FitzRoy's formal title was Meteorological Statist to the Board of Trade and his job was to collect and collate weather data, especially information about the weather out at sea.

The heavy loss of lives and shipping whenever there were storms and high winds was a constant worry. The hope was that, by taking readings on boats out at sea and at weather stations positioned along exposed coasts, bad weather might be anticipated. The new electric telegraph meant that local weather data could be sent to FitzRoy and his small team without delay. It was then up to the team to interpret the information and forecast what the weather might be like at different locations for the next day or so. FitzRoy introduced 'storm warning cones' which could be hoisted aloft at all the major ports whenever they felt bad weather was on its way.

The first weather forecast appeared in *The Times*, predicting the weather for 1 August 1861.[2] Forecasts were made for 24 locations around the coast. For example, on that inaugural day, the temperature in London was forecast to be 62 °F, with clear skies and a south-westerly wind. In Liverpool, the temperature was to be 61 °F, with very cloudy skies and a light south-westerly wind.

Although not all forecasts were successful, the satirical magazine, *Punch*, named FitzRoy the new 'Clerk of the Weather' and 'The First Admiral of the Blew'. Unfortunately, in spite of his scientific and organisational achievements, Fitzroy began to suffer personal financial problems. His health also began to fail and his struggles with depression became increasingly difficult to manage. He took his own life on 30 April 1865 by cutting his throat with a razor. Nevertheless, in recognition of his dedication, hard work, pioneering contributions to meteorology, and concern for the safety of sailors at sea, in 2002, the shipping forecast sea area, Finisterre, was renamed 'Fitzroy' by the UK's Meteorological Office in honour of their founder. It covers a large area of sea west of the Bay of Biscay between Ireland and Spain.

* * *

Throughout the twentieth and twenty-first centuries, with advances in atmospheric physics, mathematical modelling, satellites, and the use of super-computers, forecasting has become increasingly accurate, with good reliability up to five or six days ahead.

A major boost to accuracy was given by the British mathematician and meteorologist, Lewis Fry Richardson.[3] In 1922, he came up with the method that now underpins all modern forecasting. He called it 'Numerical Weather Prediction'. Given the complexity and chaotic nature of the atmosphere, meteorology can never be an exact science but, with the vast amount of data collected from all over the world that now pours into the super-computers from satellites, passenger jets and instruments on land and at sea, high and low, we understand weather and climate better than we ever have done before.

Although the science of the atmosphere has changed beyond all recognition, the clouds above are still there, evolving and dissolving, constantly in motion, shape-shifting and free-floating. Luke Howard's cloud classification remains sound, although a few elaborations and refinements have been introduced over the last two hundred years. His curiosity and wonder allowed him to see order where others were only seeing nature at her most unruly and inconstant. Howard's cloud classification gave rise to the idea that the weather could be studied scientifically, that underlying the bubbling turbulence of clouds, the laws of physics and chemistry were at work.

The World Meteorological Organization now classifies clouds into ten main groups, called genera.[4] There are low clouds, mid-level clouds and high-level clouds, depending at what level in the atmosphere they have formed.

We still talk of stratus – the flat, layered and smooth clouds. Cumulus clouds remain puffy and heaped, fluffy and cotton wool-like. Feathery wisps of cirrus clouds continue to lightly brush the blue, high above. Joining them are their mid-level cousins, the *alto*, and *nimbus*, the rain-bearing clouds. The names can also be combined to give us, for example, *nimbostratus*, a flat layered cloud from which rain might fall.

It is from clouds high and low that we get our ten main groups. They would still be recognised and understood by Howard and Constable, Beaufort and FitzRoy:

> **High clouds** (CH) whose base is usually 20,000 feet or above when over the British Isles:
> cirrus
> cirrocumulus
> cirrostratus.
> **Medium clouds** (CM) whose base is usually between 6,500 and 20,000 feet when over the British Isles:
> altocumulus
> altostratus
> nimbostratus.
> **Low clouds** (CL) whose base is usually below 6,500 feet when over the British Isles:
> stratocumulus
> stratus
> cumulus
> cumulonimbus.

These ten groups make up our familiar, everyday clouds. However, if you are lucky, you might just come across one or other of the rarer, more exotic types. We met the ghostly *noctilucent* clouds at the beginning of Chapter 5. You might also see the low, sometimes shelf-like, sometimes rolling wedges of *arcus* clouds associated with storms. *Mammatus* clouds are unusual and distinctive. They swell, breast-like, beneath the base of large, unstable cumulonimbus clouds, often foretelling heavy rain, hail and thunder. There are the rare and beautiful *asperitas* clouds that seem to ripple like slow motion ocean waves across the sky's deeps. In the planet's icy north and south, you might be transfixed by the soft, pearly opalescent hues of high-level polar *nacreous* clouds as they reflect the sinking sun's fading light.

Nonetheless, whether it's towering clouds of cumulonimbus or the ethereal drift of high altocirrus, clouds continue to inspire poets and painters. In his wheat field paintings, it is van Gogh who catches the turbulence of clouds as they swirl, curl, tumble and roll in the winds. The arrival of photography also meant that clouds could be captured in all their moods. As well as the dramatic and unusual, clouds also leant themselves to the abstract and atmospheric. The 1959, black and white photograph, *Moon and Clouds, Northern California*, by Ansel Adams captures the white, light caresses of cirrus across a night black sky.

Poets are particularly fond of clouds. They lend themselves especially well to the poetic voice. However, it is the transient mutability of clouds, their impermanence, and their ability to appear, reshape and then melt away that gives all artists, musicians and writers one of their richest sources of metaphor. The journalist, Rebecca Rosen, even wonders whether clouds might be 'the most useful metaphor of all time … we can find meaning in them and project meaning onto them'.[5]

It is the very nebulousness of clouds that represents change, diffuseness, inconstancy, possibility. You can't grasp clouds. They are there but they seem to be without substance. Clouds fog the mind. They make thoughts difficult. We are troubled when we see dark clouds looming ahead. Guilty minds live under a cloud. Yet clouds also have silver linings. You can feel on top of the world, on cloud nine.

In 423 BCE, Aristophanes' play, *The Clouds*, had its first performance. It was a comedy in which Aristophanes made fun of what he felt were the airy-fairy ideas of the day's fashionable philosophers, including Socrates. Over two millennia later, in 1802, William Wordsworth wandered 'lonely as a cloud' in his famous celebration of solitude and nature's timeless beauty.[6] David Mitchell's acclaimed novel, *Cloud Atlas*, explores how human nature takes on different forms, across time and place.[7] 'Souls', he writes, 'cross ages like clouds cross skies', taking on new forms, new colours, but, throughout their journeys, they remain souls, they remain clouds. And in her 1960s song, 'Both Sides Now', Joni Mitchell sings about clouds. In their lighter moods they bring brightness and joy but in their blacker moments they block the sun and life feels seems.

* * *

What about the fate of this word document, this computer file, this digital manuscript that I'm writing at this very moment? At some point in its life, it might well enter 'the cloud', that imagined, dreamy place somewhere above, somewhere else, storing our digital lives. Of course, however, the 'cloud' in computer-land is real. Data is remotely stored, via the internet, on *terra firma*, in massive computer servers and data centres that consume enormous amounts of electricity, cooled by air conditioners sitting in discrete buildings located throughout the land and all over the planet. The cloud computing metaphor refers to the diagrams that picture the various interconnected, networked elements of hardware and software that can be accessed by users from desktops, laptops and smart phones. The complex matrix of digital wizardry and virtualised software can be thought of as an amorphous cloud.

On that digital high, we'll float gently down to earth to rest on solid ground and see what people were beginning to think about the land, rocks, mountains and hills.

Part IV

Rocks

7

Down to Earth

The ground we walk on is, by and large, solid. It stretches beneath our feet, sometimes flat, sometimes hilly. There are mountains and valleys. If you walk far enough in any one direction you'll eventually reach the sea. Intuitively, the Earth's surface feels flat, save for its topographical ups and downs. Indeed, many ancient civilisations thought that the world was flat. Moreover, hard as it is to credit, there are modern flat earth societies, some tongue-in-cheek, but some seriously entertaining the idea that the Earth really is flat.

Ancient Greek philosophers were among the first to regard the Earth as a huge sphere. Phoenician sailors knew that as a ship sailed into the distance it would disappear over the horizon, suggesting some sort of curvature of the sea's surface. Ancient astronomers observing lunar eclipses saw that, when the Earth lay between the sun and the moon, the planet cast a circular shadow across the moon, again suggesting a spherically shaped planet.

Perhaps most remarkable of all were the measurements made by the Greek polymath, Eratosthenes, around 240 BCE. He measured the angle of the sun at midday at various locations along the Nile Valley, north to south. He knew the distances between these points. Using his knowledge of angles and mathematics he worked out that the Earth was a sphere with a circumference of around 252,000 Egyptian stadia, which in today's units equals 39,375 kilometres or 24,466 miles. The modern value from pole to pole is 40,008 kilometres and, around the equator where the Earth bulges slightly because of the centrifugal force exerted by the planet's rotation, the circumference is measured at 40,075 kilometres. He was less than two per cent out in his estimation. Extraordinary.

From these ancient of days people had been curious about the nature of rocks and minerals, volcanoes and earthquakes, fissures and fossils. There were ideas around to explain some of them – the work of gods, the gods being angry, changes of sea level, great floods – but there were no systematic enquiries, at least not until the beginning of the second millennium AD. By then, leading thinkers from the Middle East, Iran, India and China were beginning to ask and answer questions about rocks and minerals, but in a piecemeal fashion. Only slowly did questions of a more recognisable geological character begin to be posed. What is the Earth? What is it made of? How old is it? Has it always been the same, or has it changed over time? What would a science of the Earth and its rocks look like?

In Christian Europe, at least until the seventeenth century, the Bible remained the authority when trying make sense of rocks and their various types. In particular, the story of the Great Flood in Genesis seemed to provide a good explanation for the current state of the world. The tale reverses God's original creative efforts described in the book's first verses. On the third day of creation God said:

> 'Let the waters under the sky be gathered together into one place, and let the dry land appear.' And it was so. God called the dry land Earth, and the waters that were gathered together he called Seas. And God saw that it was good.

However, as time slipped by, God was becoming increasingly unhappy with men and their behaviour. There was too much corruption and violence. So He reversed His original act. The floods returned, covering the whole Earth, sweeping away all that was rotten.

> And the LORD said, I will destroy man whom I have created from the face of the earth; both man, and beast, and the creeping thing, and the fowls of the air; for it repenteth me that I have made them.

Of course, he saved the virtuous Noah, his family and all the 'clean beasts' of the Earth. They boarded the ark that the 600-year-old Noah had built to float on the rising waters of the flood. The 'fountains of the great deep' broke. The 'windows of heaven' opened and it rained for forty days and forty nights. The floods were so great that even the tops of mountains were submerged. After 150 days, the floods began to recede. The earth dried; and Noah, his family and all the favoured beasts left the ark, went forth and multiplied.

As natural philosophers looked for evidence of the Great Flood, they began to pay more and more attention to rocks and fossils. At first glance, it seemed that the deluge offered a good explanation for the presence of fossils and the banded nature of many rocks. The idea was that the rising waters wore and washed away rocks and soils. Animals drowned. Then the floods retreated and, as they did, sediments from the worn-away mountains were deposited in layers. The remains of the dead animals slowly sank into the settling sands, silts and muds to be entombed as fossils.

In 1702 William Whiston succeeded his mentor, Isaac Newton, to the Lucasian Chair of Mathematics at the University of Cambridge. Among his many achievements, he wrote a book entitled *A New Theory of the Earth from Its Original to the Consummation of All Things.*[1] Published in 1696, it argued that the biblical flood was probably caused by the Earth's encounter with the watery tail of a comet, resulting in a planetary soaking and the consequent deluge. The force of the comet also ripped open much of the earth's crust releasing 'the great fountains of the deep', adding yet more water to the floods. Whiston believed that, when the waters receded, they left behind strata of rock that stretched across the surface of the whole world. The theory became known as 'flood geology' and in the professor's eyes confirmed the veracity of the Bible story.

* * *

However far off the mark it might have been, 'flood geology' led to a growing interest in rocks, their origins and their age. It was clear than many rocks had a stratified appearance and that their make-up could change from one layer to another, from compacted muds to silts to sands to lime. Many rock types also contained bands of fossils. One of the first people to have modern ideas about the true origins of what we now know as *sedimentary rocks* was the Danish scientist, Nicolas Steno (1638-86). He understood that sediments settling out of water would gradually compact under the weight of sediments above. Higher layers would therefore be younger than the older layers beneath.

Mining for minerals also increased opportunities to see what was going underground as well as on the surface. The presence of minerals that contained copper and lead, iron and tin begged questions about their origins. Abraham Gottlob Werner (1750-1817) lived and worked in Saxony, east Germany. He was employed by the Freiberg School of Mines. He certainly had an interest in minerals. It was his belief that all rocks, including basalt, were laid down in water and that the Earth was once covered by a great ocean. In his theory, even volcanoes could be explained by arguing that deep coal seams could catch fire and melt the rocks around. The molten rocks would rise to the surface and erupt as a volcano. All those who supported theories about the watery origins of rocks became known as Neptunists after the Roman god of the sea.

Opposing the Neptunists were the Plutonists, named after the Roman god of the underworld. They argued that all rocks at one time had been molten magma. When magma cooled and solidified it formed rocks such as granite, basalt and the many veins of mineralised quartzite that can be seen cutting through other rocks. They were happy to recognise that these plutonic, *igneous rocks* would weather and erode, and that the eroded material would be carried away by rivers to be deposited into lakes and seas to form new, sedimentary rocks. The strength of their view was that many granites and basalts can clearly be seen intruding into, and cutting across, often at right angles, the water-lain layers of muds, silts and sands. The Neptunists didn't really have a plausible explanation for how this could happen.

* * *

James Hutton (1726-97) is often acclaimed as the 'father of modern geology', at least in Britain.[2] He was a Plutonist. He was born in Edinburgh and attended various universities, including the University of Leiden where he obtained a degree in medicine, aged 23. By 1750, Hutton was back in Britain, living in London. He soon got into correspondence with an old school friend, John Davie, who was still living in Edinburgh. When they had been students together, they had discovered a way to make ammonium chloride, more commonly known as 'sal ammoniac', from coal soot. On one of his visits to Edinburgh, Hutton caught up with Davie. They recalled their student days and the excitement they felt when they had first made sal ammoniac. Their discussion eventually led to a decision to set up a chemical factory in Edinburgh to manufacture the crystalline salt. The chemical could be used in the welding of metals, particularly soldering processes, dyeing, and as a key ingredient in the reviving qualities of smelling salts. The business was a success and provided Hutton with an income for the rest of his life.

Although his father died when he was only three years-old, Hutton had inherited a lowland farm at Slighhouses in Berwickshire, some 35 miles south-east of Edinburgh, and a nearby hill farm at Nether Monynut. It wasn't until the summer of 1754 that Hutton finally moved back to his homeland. He settled in Slighhouses to begin farming proper. Farmers, of course, tread their lands, know their lie and become familiar with their soils. He dug ditches. He observed the rocks through which the burns and streams had cut. Bit by bit, not only was he accumulating knowledge about the land as a farmer, he was developing a serious interest in the rocks which lay beneath the land. He began to read books on the latest geological thinking. He was familiar with Whiston's Great Flood theory of rock formation.

After thirteen years on the farm, in 1767 Hutton returned to Edinburgh to live in the family home with his three sisters. He let his farms to tenants. This was a time when Edinburgh was becoming one of the leading centres of Enlightenment thinking in all of Europe. The city could boast some of the best minds of the time, including the philosopher David Hume, and the political economist Adam Smith.

In 1770 Hutton built his own house at St John's Hill in Edinburgh. Fittingly, it lay beneath and looked across to Salisbury Crags, which we now know to be a 325-million-year-old intrusion of igneous dolerite. This was an exciting time to be in Edinburgh and Hutton began to play a full part in the city's intellectual life, including helping set up the Oyster Club. The club was founded by Adam Smith, the chemist Joseph Black and Hutton. Scientists and philosophers, national as well as international, met weekly throughout the 1770s to discuss the big ideas of the day, including the Earth and the origin of its rocks. A decade or so later, Hutton also became an active member of the Royal Society of Edinburgh, founded in 1783.

After several decades working the land, touring and exploring Scotland, advising on the building of the Forth and Clyde Canal, and discussing geological matters with his friends, Hutton eventually published the book that established him as one of the founding figures of modern geology.

Theory of the Earth was first published in two volumes in 1795, although he had earlier outlined his ideas in papers first read at the Royal Society of Edinburgh in 1785, and which were later published in the transactions of the Royal Society of Edinburgh in 1788. The book's prose was rather leaden and heavy going so Hutton's friend and champion, the mathematician John Playfair, rewrote it in plainer English and published it in 1802 with a new title *Illustrations of the Huttonian Theory of the Earth.*[3] This more accessible account introduced Hutton's work to a much wider audience and established him as a major figure in the new science of geology.

Hutton believed that close observation of rock formations in the field, coupled with methodical recording of what was objectively seen, were key to the science's development. For him, facts led to theory rather than theory presuming to predict the 'facts', which was the case with 'flood geology' and ideas based on readings of the Bible. In the spirit of Francis Bacon, induction from observation rather than deduction from theory was the way forward.

From his lifelong observations of the natural processes of weathering, erosion and the redeposition of sediments along riverbeds, lake bottoms and sea floors, he understood that, as Charles Lyell later put it, 'the present is the key to the past'.[4] Rock formations could be understood as the consolidated result of past erosional and depositional events. Depending on its exact character, a hillside outcrop of sandstone might once have been the sandy bottom of a deepening sea, or a wind-blown dune of an ancient desert. As obvious as this might seem today, looking at past events in terms of present-day processes was a revolutionary idea when it was first suggested, not just by Hutton but by a growing number of eighteenth-century scientists throughout Europe.

Hutton's observations begged two further questions. How had the soft sediments of mud, silt, sand, broken shells and decaying vegetation ended up as hard rock? How had these soggy, loose deposits turned into mudstones, siltstones, sandstones, limestone and coal? Secondly, how had they been pushed up into hills, or been bent and fractured, tilted and torn into great folds and faults?

It seemed clear that the original soft sediments were the result of pre-existing lands being eroded by ancient rains and rivers, ice and wind. The sediments then spread across lake bottoms and sinking sea floors as ever thickening layers and strata. As they got buried deeper and deeper, the sediments were subjected to growing heat and pressure. Any water in them would be driven out and chemical cementation would gradually turn muds into mudstones, sands into sandstones and so on.

It was Hutton's belief that deep reservoirs of heat lay beneath the earth's crust. The heat was capable of melting rocks and creating huge upward forces that could thrust the 'lithified' beds of sands and silts high and wide, bending and breaking some in the process. He saw volcanoes as a kind of geological safety-valve that helped release some of the heat that constantly built up deep beneath the surface. The highly crystalline granites, he felt, were definitely not the result of chemicals being precipitated from the sea as the Neptunists believed. Rather, they were solidified magmas that in their original molten state had pushed upwards from deep below the crust and intruded themselves into higher, but pre-existing, older rocks. Similar explanations could be given for mineral veins of quartzite, and the sills and dykes that he found cutting through beds of sandstone, bands of silts, and layers of limestone.

For Hutton, the Earth's hot, molten, mobile interior provided the energy and engine to raise mountains, explode volcanoes and intrude granites. As the Earth's surface was repeatedly pushed up and pulled down, so sea levels rose and fell. Over vast periods of time, rocks would form, wear away and re-form in endless cycles to create the complex geological landscapes we see all around us today.

Seeing the world as both dynamic and restless, Hutton was able to explain all the major rock types. Erosion and weathering of older rocks, including granites and basalts, provided sediments that could be compressed and compacted into new *sedimentary strata* that one day might be thrust into a new mountain or a high plateau.

Around the same time, the Swiss scientist, Horace Bénédict de Saussure was entertaining similar ideas.[5] He was a geologist and keen mountaineer. On top of Mont Blanc, he felt the view that opened up before him presented 'the most ravishing and instructive spectacle'. In his 1796 accounts he went on to write that he was suddenly able to make sense of the raised beds of rocks that stretched all around and below him, confirming his own theory that great forces were at play thrusting what was once below the sea up high to create great mountains.

* * *

Solidified magmas accounted for the granites and other *igneous rocks* such as basaltic lavas, andesites and mineral veins of intrusive quartzite. Hutton only had to look out of the windows of his

Edinburgh home to see the intruded sheets of doleritic magma that form the Salisbury Crags. Beyond them rose the basalt lava flows and the volcanic crater that make up Arthur's Seat, the eroded remains of a 340-million-year-old volcano that gave such fine views of the city and so impressed the poet Coleridge. He recorded in a letter to his friend and fellow poet, Robert Southey, dated 13 September 1803: 'What a wonderful City Edinburgh is! ... – I climbed last night to the Crags just below Arthur's Seat, itself ... it was an affecting sight to me!'

Sedimentary rocks that get caught up in some of the more extreme contortions of the Earth's mobile crust can also experience tremendous heat and pressure. These extremes, felt Hutton, could turn muds into slates, limestones into marble, and silts into schists. These are the *metamorphic rocks*. They make up much of the Scottish Highlands which, in their weathered, billion-year-old splendour, give us the wild landscape we enjoy today. Thus, by the early nineteenth century, geologists had identified the three major rock types: igneous, sedimentary and metamorphic.

* * *

One of the clinching pieces of evidence for Hutton – that the Earth's surface was a place of repeated erosion, deposition and mighty upheavals over aeons of time – was on a visit he made to Siccar Point. In 1788 he took a boat trip with John Playfair and Sir James Hall to make observations along the Berwickshire coast south-east of Edinburgh. It was at Siccar Point, a mere eight miles north of his own lowland farm at Slighhouses, that he made his famous observation.

He spotted a group of bare, rough rocks jutting into the sea. He noticed a marked junction between older beds of dark grey, *vertically* tilted rocks resting *below* an almost *horizontal* layer of younger red rocks lying directly above. The older greywackes composed of muds and coarse sands had been deposited at the bottom of a Silurian sea some 435 million years ago. They had then been buried, folded and tilted. Some time later, they were thrust to the surface. There, they suffered erosion which wore them to a flat plane. Although the exact time gap wouldn't have been known by Hutton, 65 million years later, river-borne, wind-blown, red sands of the Devonian period were deposited over a tropical landscape, the rocky base of which was the weathered surface of the up-ended, vertically tilted Silurian greywackes.

The distinct change from one rock type and orientation to another is known as an *unconformity*, a break in geological time, missing time if you like. It illustrated beautifully all that Hutton was arguing. Erosion, deposition, sinking, compaction, rock formation, upheaval, folding, faulting, weathering, more erosion, fresh sedimentary deposition, newer rocks, different angles – slow, repeated cycles taking place over immense periods of time. Playfair would later comment that at Siccar Point 'the mind seemed to grow giddy by looking so far into the abyss of time', which echoed Hutton's own breathtaking conclusion to his 1785 paper: 'The result, therefore, of our present enquiry is, that we find no vestige of a beginning, no prospect of an end.'

Siccar Point is now a place of pilgrimage for geologists from all over the world.

However, before the full import of many of Hutton's ideas gained ground, he fell ill and died on 26 March 1797, aged 70 years. He was buried in the historic churchyard of Greyfriars, Edinburgh, not far from his house on St John's Hill, beneath the volcanic rocks of Arthur's Seat and the Salisbury Crags. He didn't live to see the success of his book, rewritten by Playfair, but his ideas lived on and inspired the next generation of young geologists and scientifically aware novelists. 'It's not what is upon this island, but what is underneath that interests me', says Professor Lidenbrock in Jules Verne's *Journey to the Centre of the Earth*.[6] It is with that same thought in mind that we'll continue our own journey into deep time and the rocks below.

8

Mary Anning and 'Strata' Smith

During the early decades of the nineteenth century, geology rapidly established itself as a major, indeed popular science. Throughout Europe and America, geologists vigorously debated their ideas about the Earth, its make-up and evolution. Increasing fieldwork and careful observations confirmed geology's empirical credentials.

Artists and poets were also taking an interest in the new science. German Romantics were particularly inspired by the drama of rocks and mountains. Johann Christian Reinhart was one the founders of romantic landscape painting. His pen, ink and wash drawing of the *Entrance to the Muggendorf Cave near Streitberg, 1786* contrasts the massive rock formations with the diminutive human figures. Human existence appears insignificant compared to nature's awesome presence. The Austrian painter, Joseph Anton Koch was a contemporary of Reinhart. He also took an early interest in geology. He studied rocks and the forces of nature in his attempts to understand how they shaped and fashioned the landscape. As a result, his paintings of mountains became more rugged, more heroic. Also, standing on the 'stupendous summit, rock sublime' of Beachy Head's sheer chalk cliffs, the poet Charlotte Smith felt ecstatic as she contemplated the boundlessness of land and sea.[1]

Beneath John Constable's skies, the land was also revealing nature's earthly rhythms. To complement his study of clouds, Constable was taking an interest in geology. In his examination of Constable's letters, the German historian, Kurt Badt, records that on 17 July 1832 the painter took his sons to a lecture on volcanoes. Constable wrote that it was 'most interesting indeed'. This was followed by a later letter, dated 10 November 1835, in which he wrote that the study of geology satisfied his mind more than any other science.[2]

The art critic John Ruskin had a lifelong interest in rocks and their origins. His biographer Andrew Hill quotes Ruskin's father as writing that, 'from Boyhood he has been an artist, but he has been a geologist from Infancy, and his geology is perhaps the best part of his Art'. Indeed, it was Ruskin who chose to be painted by John Everett Millais against a backdrop of a tumbling burn and a cliff face of gnarled gneiss in Scotland's Glen Finglas in the Trossachs.[3] Hill goes on to say that Ruskin understood nature as a whole, spiritually, artistically, emotionally and scientifically.[4]

* * *

Throughout the early days of the Enlightenment, natural philosophy, including geology, was primarily a gentleman's game, the pursuit of men who had more often than not attended one of the universities of Oxford, Cambridge or Edinburgh. Many were relatively well-off and could afford to self-fund their scientific interests. Yet there were a few notable exceptions; and one of these wasn't even a man. Mary Anning collected fossils and *she* was a woman.

It was clear that, in general, rocks lower down in a sequence were older than rocks higher up in that formation. However, it was difficult to compare the ages of different rocks in different locations. One way to make a chronological comparison presented itself. Fossils found in rocks seemed to change over time, often quite radically, but what if you found the same types of fossil in different places, even in different rock types? Might this suggest a way of comparatively dating rock strata, even if they were miles apart? Up until the eighteenth century, fossils had been collected as either curiosities, or proof that life forms had been different in the past. There were even those who were beginning to entertain the idea that life had not only been different in the past, but that maybe it was evolving in some fashion. Whatever the collector's motives, fossils were becoming of increasing scientific interest both to geologists and biologists.

Mary Anning was born in 1799 in Lyme Regis, Dorset.[5] Her family were poor. She was one of nine children but only Mary and her older brother survived into adulthood. Their father was a cabinetmaker but, living on a coast where the Jurassic rocks stretch mile after mile as sea-worn cliffs, he also became an amateur fossil collector. As a young girl, Mary would often join her father and help him look for fossils. When they got home, they would clean and sell them in their little shop. The most common fossils, and the ones which sold well to the growing tourist trade, were the curly-swirly ammonites and bullet-shaped belemnites.

Mary had little formal education. However, she could read and managed to get hold of books on geology and animal anatomy. Then tragedy struck. When she was only eleven years old, her father died from tuberculosis. Money was in short supply. Mary continued to collect fossils, but their sale became even more critical in supporting the family's finances.

However, it would not be Mary's success as a collector of ammonites, as beautiful as they are, that eventually made her famous. It was her joint find with her brother Joseph of an ancient marine reptile that brought her to the attention of the scientific community. This would earn her an esteemed place in the history of palaeontology. It was less than a year after their father died that Joseph found a strange-looking fossilised skull buried in the cliff face. He mentioned it to his sister. Aged only twelve and on her own, Mary slowly and carefully dug around the rest of the creature's fossilised remains, gradually revealing the outline of a 5.2-metre-long skeleton. The whole excavation took her several months. When scientists came to examine it, they thought it might be a species of crocodile.

The strange fossil was studied and debated for years. It was eventually named *ichthyosaurus*, or 'fish lizard'. Today we know it as a long extinct marine reptile that lived around 200 million years ago in the Jurassic Period. Mary's finds continued to be many and remarkable. In 1823 she discovered a complete skeleton of a *plesiosaurus*, meaning 'near to reptile'. This was followed in 1828 by her discovery of a *pterosaur*, a flying reptile, perhaps better known today as a pterodactyl. She was even a pioneer in the collection and examination of *coprolites*, that is to say, fossilised animal faeces, including dinosaur poo. Coprolites can tell you a surprising amount about where animals lived and what they ate. In a recent example, the fossilised faeces of a sea-living ichthyosaur revealed the shelly remains of ammonites, belemnites and many fish scales, indicating it enjoyed a rich and varied seafood diet.

However, although her finds were extraordinary, her humble origins and female sex made the male, gentrified scientific community reluctant to recognise her knowledge, skills and talents, or, in some misogynistic cases, even acknowledge that the fossils were found, excavated and cleaned by her before other scientists could admire, appreciate and study them. In spite of her growing reputation as a palaeontologist, the Geological Society of London, only recently founded in 1807, refused to admit her to its gentlemanly ranks. In fact, it would be another 97 years, in 1904, before that body of men finally agreed that women could become members.

Throughout her life, and in spite of her extraordinary success as a fossil collector, Mary's finances continued to be under strain, even though she was becoming universally recognised as a fossil hunter *extraordinaire*. She received visits from most of the great geologists of her day, even taking some of them out with her collecting. Henry de la Beche, Charles Lyell, Adam Sedgwick, William Buckland, Roderick Murchison and his wife, Charlotte, with whom Mary became friends, all made their way down to Dorset to see Mary. She died in Lyme Regis of breast cancer in 1847, a few days short of her forty-eighth birthday.

Although famous as a collector of fossils, she never earned the medals, membership or plaudits that came so readily to the professors, the well-off and the gentlemen amateurs. She would have to wait well over a hundred years before her achievements as a working-class woman advancing scientific knowledge in a privileged, rich man's world finally gain recognition.

Today the Natural History Museum in London has showcases displaying several of Mary Anning's most spectacular finds. The cliffs where she found most of her fossils are now known as the Jurassic Coast, designated a UNESCO World Heritage Site. She has been the subject of many biographies. Francis Lee's 2020 film *Ammonite* is about her. She is the inspiration behind Tracy Chevalier's 2014 novel, *Remarkable Creatures*;[6] and, although it would be wonderful if true that the tongue twister 'She Sells Sea Shells' is all about Mary Anning and her collection of ammonites, sadly the evidence remains rather thin:

> She sells seashells by the seashore.
> The shells she sells are seashells, I'm sure.
> So, if she sells seashells on the seashore
> Then I'm sure she sells seashore shells.

From their fieldwork, Mary and her fellow geologists were getting a good sense of the relative ages of different rock strata. Fossils were proving to be particularly good indicators. James Hutton and others had even intimated that the Earth was of a very great age but quite how old was still not clear.

* * *

It was now generally understood that sedimentary rocks must have accumulated at the bottom of seas and lakes, along river flood plains and ocean shorelines, desert basins and tropical swamps. It was also agreed that, unless the geological forces had been extremely disruptive, the general view was that older layers of rock would lie beneath younger layers of rock. Furthermore, if a strata of rock contained a particular and distinctive assemblage of fossils and those same fossil types were found in another rock band many miles away, it might reasonably be deduced that the two rock outcrops were of a similar age, even if they were of different sedimentary rock types.

Those who studied and mapped these layers, these strata, became known as stratigraphers and supreme amongst these early mappers of rocks and where they could be found across the landscape was William Smith. He was even referred to as William 'Strata' Smith, such was his geological skill.[7] Like Mary Anning, his origins were humble and working class.

William Smith was born in the village of Churchill, Oxfordshire, in 1769. His father was the village blacksmith but died when his son was only eight years old. For the next couple of years until their mother remarried, William and his three younger siblings, went to live with their uncle who farmed nearby. William proved to be a bright, sharp-eyed boy. When he was seventeen, he got a job as a surveyor's assistant working for Edward Webb of Stow-on-the-Wold, Gloucestershire. Webb was also an excellent teacher.

As his skills as a surveyor improved, Smith found himself becoming more and familiar with the land over which he was measuring and mapping. He got to know the changing character of the soils and rocks beneath the fields and along the cuttings. He seemed to have that rare skill of being able to visualise things in 3D. This gave him an intuitive sense of what was going on both above and below the ground. He could imagine different bands of rock rising and dipping beneath the surface. So, knowing the vertical sequence and pattern of rocks in one area, he had a good idea of what he might find in the next valley or over the next hill.

There are Carboniferous coal seams beneath Somerset. In the late eighteenth century, landowners were keen to mine this resource. To help them exploit the coal, they needed surveyors who knew how to map outcrops on the surface and make sense of the rock sequences below. From his work for Webb, Smith already knew something about the geology of the area. He had also inspected many of the coal mines, making detailed drawings of the vertical rock sections he encountered in the pits. From this work, he soon realised that the order of rocks seen in one shaft could generally predict the order in another nearby shaft. Moreover, he recognised that the fossils peculiar to a particular band of rock or seam of coal would be found in the same strata in other pits.

His reputation as a surveyor grew considerably over these early years. So, when a group of Somerset coal owners, faced with the rising costs of transporting coal by horse and increasing competition from the South Wales pits, decided to support the idea of building a canal from their coalfields to the city of Bath, the newly formed Somersetshire Coal Canal Company found itself in business. It also found itself in need of a good surveyor. In 1794 it appointed the 25-year-old William Smith as its official surveyor for the project.

The canal-cutting work provided Smith with a wonderful opportunity to slice through virgin land and examine the newly exposed rocks in all their fresh detail, fossils included. Although in 1799 he was sacked from the Somerset Canal Company for reasons that are not clear, he continued to find employment as a surveyor. The work allowed him to examine quarries, road and railway cuttings, collect ever more fossils, and draw maps and sections of the geology he encountered.

His collection of fossils, particularly those from the Jurassic Period, grew larger and larger, and confirmed his idea that fossils could be used to compare and age rocks across wide areas of the country. They also allowed him to formulate 'The Principle of Faunal Succession', which is to say that fossil assemblages changed over time as you went up and down a rock sequence. This, along with his appreciation that rock strata had a recognisable and regular order of succession, and that they could rise and dip beneath the landscape, meant that his talent to visualise what was going on beneath the surface became increasingly sophisticated. 'Strata' Smith was born.

The discovery that certain fossils were unique and peculiar to certain beds of rock meant that whatever the sedimentary details of a particular rock strata, or whether they were found in Dorset, Oxfordshire or Whitby in Yorkshire, if they contained exactly the same mix of fossils the rock would be the same age and from the same geological period. Smith could therefore show, for example, that the shallow Jurassic marine muds and silts, sands and limestone that were found in the coastal cliffs of Dorset stretched as a continuous band north-eastwards all the way to the coast of North Yorkshire.

* * *

By the end of the eighteenth century, Smith was beginning to think horizontally as well as vertically about how to represent the geology of an area. In 1799, he produced a large-scale geological map of the region around Bath. The design of his maps were partly inspired by the work of the Somerset County Agricultural Society. They had produced colour-coded maps of soil types and vegetation. Smith adopted the idea and used different colours to show, on a map, the extent and boundaries of different rock types as they appeared on the surface.

Smith's work as a mineral surveyor was beginning to take him all over the country. He was rapidly gaining a good sense of the geology of large parts of England and Wales. By 1801, he was able to draw a rough geological map of most of Britain. This was a first. However, it would be 1815 before he was able to produce and have printed the first colour-coded geological map of the whole of England and Wales, and parts of southern Scotland.

Although there had been a few earlier attempts to outline the broad character of a country's geology, none were as colourful, detailed or clear as that published by William Smith. Each major geological period and rock group was represented by a particular colour. The map was geologically accurate. It was also rather beautiful with its subdued, pale bands of pinks and greens, blues and browns, purples and greys. In her poem celebrating the map, Maura Dooley evokes its fading, settled colours: 'Like oil on a puddle, both muted and blending.'[8]

Although around 400 of the maps were originally published, fewer than forty have survived. One of them hangs, behind blue velvet curtains, above one of the marbled staircases of Burlington House on Piccadilly, London, the home of the Geological Society. The map measures 2.6 metres by 1.8 metres. Smith dedicated it to Sir Joseph Banks, the then president of the Royal Society and the project's most patient, influential and financial supporter. The map's full title is:

> A Delineation of the Strata of England and Wales, with Part of Scotland; Exhibiting the Collieries and Mines, the Marshes and Fen Lands Originally Overflowed by the Sea, and the Varieties of Soil According to the Variations in the Substrata, Illustrated by the Most Descriptive Names.

It is remarkably similar to modern geological maps of the British Isles. A geological cross-section of the country from Snowdon to London accompanies the map. The section shows various rock strata including the Jurassic limestones and Cretaceous chalk as they dip gently south-eastwards across the Midlands and South-East England, with younger beds lying on top of older ones.

Smith's cross-section is also a journey in time. In broad terms as you head north-west from London to Snowdon in Wales, the rock strata, hills, valleys and mountains you cross take you back in geological time, from the 35-million-year-old beds of the London clays, over the Cretaceous, Jurassic, Triassic, Devonian, Silurian, Ordovician and, finally, to the Cambrian rocks of Snowdonia, around 500 million years old. Moreover, if you carry on in the same direction, over the Menai Straits to Anglesey you can meet even older rocks of Pre-Cambrian age. In a little over 200 miles you can time travel a billion years.

That one man, without much formal education, a man who had to work for his living, could produce such an accurate map of the whole country, beautiful in design and execution, was extraordinary. Smith's knowledge and skills as a surveyor paved the way for all future makers of geological maps. His concept of using fossils to identify sedimentary rocks and their relative ages remains sound up to the present day. What he conveyed with his astounding achievement was not only a three-dimensional picture of the world, but also a sense of the enormity of geological time and the immense age of the Earth. His great map was a philosophical wonder and an aesthetic masterpiece.

* * *

In 1824 Sir John Johnstone appointed Smith as land steward to his estate in Hackness, five miles north-east of Scarborough. Between 1824 and 1834 Smith lived and worked in Hackness, during which time he produced a wonderfully detailed and accurate geological map of the Hackness estate on a scale of six and a half inches to the mile, published in 1832.[9]

Sir John Johnstone was also president of the Scarborough Philosophical Society. The society raised funds for the building of the Rotunda Museum in Scarborough. The museum was built to Smith's design using Hackness stone. It opened in 1829. The museum housed a collection of fossils and rocks arranged in stratigraphic order. The geologist and nephew of William Smith, John Phillips, produced a coastal geological section of Yorkshire which was drawn inside the dome of the building. The museum is still going strong today and is well worth a visit.

In spite of his extraordinary achievements as a stratigrapher, like Mary Anning, William Smith had been treated rather shabbily by the gentleman of the Geological Society. He had not even been invited to be a member.

However, things were changing. The old guard was on its way out and a new generation of talented geologists was in the ascendency, both in the society and in the country at large. The new president of the Geological Society was the Reverend Professor Adam Sedgwick of the University of Cambridge. He had a sincere admiration for the journeymen of geology. During his own mapping expeditions to the Lake District, he had consulted regularly and respectfully with Jonathan Otley,[10] the Keswick clock repairer, amateur geologist, maker of some of the earliest geological maps of Cumbria, recorder of Lakeland's daily weather and friend of the chemist, John Dalton.

With the enthusiastic support of two other giants of mid-nineteenth-century geology, Sir Roderick Impey Murchison and the dean of Westminster, William Buckland, Sedgwick proposed that the society honour William Smith as the very first recipient of the society's most prestigious award, the Wollaston Medal. Later recipients would include Charles Darwin and James Lovelock, the author of Gaia theory.

William Smith was thrilled to receive such a high-profile recognition. Now aged 62, he was home at Hackness when he received the news. In February 1831, he was invited down to London to receive the medal and join the members for their anniversary dinner. Some 90 people attended the award ceremony, including not only Sedgwick, Murchison and Buckland, but also his Yorkshire patron, Sir John Johnstone, and the astronomer William Herschel. In a generous, perhaps somewhat hyperbolic address, Sedgwick said it was a privilege for the society to place its first honour 'on the brow of the father of

English geology', one of the first people to appreciate the importance of fossils in helping geologists date, compare, correlate and sequence rocks up and down the geological column, and from one end of the country to the other.

Smith's final years were good to him. In 1832 he was granted a yearly pension from the Crown. He became an enthusiastic member of the newly formed British Association for the Advancement of Science. In 1835 he joined the Association on a trip to visit Trinity College, Dublin, where, to his surprise, he was awarded an honorary doctorate of laws.

A few years later, on his way to attend the annual meeting of the British Association in Birmingham, he decided to stop off and spend a few days with a friend of his in Northampton. He caught a cold which settled on his chest. His nephew, John Phillips, already in Birmingham for the meeting, was summoned to visit his uncle. Not many hours after his nephew's arrival, William Smith died on 28 August 1839, aged 70. He was buried in the nearby church of St Peter's. The *Scarborough Herald*, 5 September 1839, gave him the following obituary, with a clear dig at those gentlemen scholars of British science who for so long failed to appreciate William Smith and his remarkable talents:

> Simple minded, of a heaven born temper, warm hearted, kind and cheerful, and instructive, no man however great his talents, ever spent an hour in his society without being enriched in knowledge, and elevated and inspired with a new ardour and energy in the pursuit of truth. If England had known how to nurture her gifted sons, instead of leaving them to pine away in neglect, what advantages to her might have resulted from his employment in her service.

The parents of John Phillips, Smith's nephew, died when he was young. He was raised in London by his uncle William, brother of his deceased mother. As a young man John helped his uncle with surveying, map making and fossil collecting. The experience taught him the business of being a field geologist. Phillips would go on to have a distinguished career as a geologist in his own right, enjoying appointments as professor of geology at King's College, London, followed by a post at the University of Oxford. He became an authority on developing a global timescale for the major geological periods, work partly inspired by his uncle's recognition that fossils could be key to dating rock strata. In 1845 he followed further in uncle William's footsteps when he, too, was awarded the Wollaston Medal by the Geological Society, of which, unlike his uncle, he was a member.

* * *

The mid nineteenth century was an exciting time for geologists. Their subject was extremely popular with the public, with its hints of deep time, strange creatures and other climates. Charles Lyell's three-volume book, *Principles of Geology*, published between 1830 and 1833, was a bestseller. It was the book that Charles Darwin read on the *Beagle* as he was voyaging round the world. With its theories of immense passages of time, it certainly influenced the young naturalist's thinking about life's variety and the origin of species.

Even the poet Wordsworth recognised that people were fascinated by rocks, fossils and their history. Knowing that it would help boost sales of the 1835 edition of his popular *Guide to the Lakes*, Wordsworth invited the geologist, Professor Sedgwick, to add a few brief 'letters' on the geology of the Lake District. The two men had met on occasion, usually when Sedgwick was visiting either Jonathan Otley or Wordsworth's friend and fellow poet, Robert Southey, over in Keswick.

Professor Sedgwick was one of the major players busy working out the order of the rocks. Which were the oldest? Which the youngest? Vigorous discussions were taking place between Sedgwick, Roderick Murchison, Charles Lyell and Charles Lapworth, about what to call the different rock formations and where to draw the time boundaries between one group and another. Gradually, over the final decades of the nineteenth century, a consensus was emerging across Europe about how to order the major geological periods and what names to give them.

Many of the rocks found in Wales were recognised as amongst the oldest. Sedgwick named the period in which these rocks were laid down the *Cambrian*, after the Latin name for Wales, Cambria. Initially, anything before the Cambrian (which later turned out to be most of Earth's history) was simply described as the Pre-Cambrian.

Along the borders of Wales can be found rock sequences that are slightly younger than the Cambrian. Lapworth[11] named these the *Ordovician* after the Celtic Welsh border tribe, the Ordovices. Next up the sequence came the even younger rocks studied and mapped by Murchison in South Wales. He named them the *Silurian* series after another Welsh Celtic tribe, the Silures who lived in the area. A quick run through the nomenclature of the remaining major geological periods reveals similar thought processes based on classic examples of rock groups, their location and character.

In remaining order, from oldest to youngest: following the Silurian we have the Devonian, named after the county; the Carboniferous, so called because within its layers are the main, coal-bearing seams found across many parts of the world; the Permian named by Murchison after Perm, an area in Russia some 700 miles east of Moscow; then the Triassic, named after three very different rock types of that period found throughout Germany. The Triassic is followed by the Jurassic, named after the Jura mountains which run along the French-Swiss border. Next up is the Cretaceous, from the Latin, *creta*, for chalk, a rock formation that stretches across much of Europe from Britain, across the Paris basin and further east. For a long time, the youngest geological period was known as the Tertiary, but more modern stratigraphical systems have renamed this most recent era the Cenozoic, from the Greek meaning 'new life', a time which includes the Quaternary Period and takes us up to the present day.

Today's geological maps of the British Isles are kept up to date by the British Geological Survey. The Geological Survey of Great Britain was founded in 1835 by the Board of Ordnance as the Ordnance Geological Survey. Henry De la Beche was appointed its first director. He was a geologist and palaeontologist. He spent part of his childhood living with his mother in Lyme Regis where he first met and got to know Mary Anning. In later years when Mary was struggling financially he helped her out by selling lithographs of his watercolour sketches of Mary collecting fossils and donating the monies to her.

The Geological Survey was the first such national service in the world. In 1984 it was renamed the British Geological Survey. It provides the government with advice about a wide range of geological matters including mineral resources, hydrological matters and tunnelling. It also prints a wide range of geological maps including one of the whole of the British Isles. The map bears a remarkable similarity to the one produced by William Smith, even remaining faithful to many of the colours he first used to denote each of the major rock groups.

* * *

The early earth scientists had done a brilliant job ordering the world's major rock series and outlining their relative ages. However, they still

Geological Time Chart

Era	Period	
CENOZOIC	Quarternary	
	Neogene	
	Palaeogene	
		66 mya
MESOZOIC	Cretaceous	
		145 mya
	Jurassic	
		201 mya
	Triassic	
		252 mya
PALAEOZOIC	Permian	
		299 mya
	Carboniferous	
		359 mya
	Devonian	
		419 mya
	Silurian	
		444 mya
	Ordovician	
		485 mya
	Cambrian	
		541 mya
PROTEROZOIC		
		2500 mya
ARCHAEAN		
		4000 mya
HADEAN		
		4560 mya

didn't know their absolute ages. The evolutionary biologists, including Charles Darwin, were also beginning to think about how much time they would need to make sense of the evolution, appearance and variety of new species in the fossil record. So, although everyone suspected that to talk of geological time was to contemplate millions and millions of years, no one knew for sure how old the Earth actually was. Thus, having established a stratigraphical order for the geological periods, the next challenge was to establish their exact ages and, if possible, the age of the planet itself.

9

Geological Time and the Restless Planet

The speculation about the vast amount of time needed to explain rocks and fossils was a far cry from the calculation that had been made by the Very Reverend James Ussher (1581-1656). Ussher was the archbishop of Armagh in Ireland. In 1650, based on a very careful reading of the biblical book of Genesis, the archbishop worked out that the Earth was created on Sunday, 23 October 4004 BCE. Yes, he was that precise.

The idea that the Earth was a mere 6,000 years old seemed ludicrous to nineteenth-century geologists and biologists. Their challenge was to try to estimate the age of the Earth scientifically rather than theologically. If, they argued, the planet is slowly cooling from its molten beginnings, then knowing the rate of heat loss and the current condition of the Earth, it should be possible to calculate the age of the planet.

One of the key figures to have a go at this sum was another Irishman, William Thomson, who later became Lord Kelvin, a title he took from the River Kelvin, a northern tributary of the lower Clyde which flowed not far from his laboratories at the University of Glasgow.[1] Born in Belfast in 1824, he went on to study at the University of Cambridge before spending the rest of his academic career in Glasgow. He enjoyed extraordinary fame and success as a mathematician, physicist and engineer.[2]

Kelvin was one of the nineteenth century's great physicists. His contributions to the study of heat and electricity were outstanding. He was held in high regard. It was no surprise, therefore, to find that he got drawn into the debate about the age of the Earth. Using his expertise on the rates at which heat flows from hot to cold bodies, and making the assumption that the Earth was once a very hot body but was now much cooler, he had a go at calculating the likely age of the planet. After several stabs and many qualifications about the melting point of rocks and the state of the earth's interior, in 1897 he eventually estimated that the planet must be between 20 and 40 million years old. However, in spite of the esteem in which Kelvin was held, geologists and biologists still thought this figure to be far too small. For their processes to take place, they needed the Earth to be much, much older. A none-too-friendly debate followed, in which Kelvin stuck by his calculation.

When the debate was at its fiercest, Kelvin was well into his seventies. He was famous, distinguished, and it seemed more than a little presumptuous to disagree with so great a man. If his calculations said the earth was only 40 million years old, then the geologists were wrong and they would have to rethink their ideas.

However, it was Kelvin's fate to end his final days during one of science's more exciting times. In 1896 Henri Becquerel discovered radioactivity in uranium. By 1898 Marie and Pierre Curie had added radium and polonium to the list of elements that were radioactive. As they decayed, these radioactive elements emitted various sub-atomic particles and electromagnetic radiation releasing huge amounts of heat and energy in the process.

It soon dawned on geologists that this was a powerful way to explain where the Earth gets a lot of its internal heat from. If the radioactive minerals deep inside the Earth, of which there would be vast amounts, were decaying and generating heat in the process, this would explain how the planet was able to sustain high internal temperatures over millions of years. It is now realised that at least half of the earth's internal heat comes from radioactive decay. Most of the other half of the heat present is from when the planet first formed, accreted and melted under the force of gravity. A small amount of heat is also generated by tidal flows and movements in the Earth's molten, outer, iron-nickel core.

So, yes, heat is being continuously lost, but huge amounts are still being generated by radioactive decay. Modern-day calculations give an age for the Earth of about 4.6 billion years, more than a hundred times older than the venerable Lord Kelvin's date based on the idea that the once very hot planet had simply cooled. The newer calculations meant that there was more than enough time to explain rock formations, rock deformations, fossils and evolution.

* * *

The radioactive decay of some elements also provided twentieth-century geologists with another trick, one which allowed them to work out an absolute age for each of the major geological periods. It is known as radiometric dating.[3]

The nucleus of every chemical element, with the exception of the most common isotope of hydrogen, is packed with two types of sub-atomic particles – protons and neutrons. In the case of the radioactive elements, the packing of the protons and neutrons is inherently unstable. To achieve stability, at some point in its life, the atom of a particular radioactive element will break down into two lighter, more stable elements, releasing a huge amount of energy in the process. This is called nuclear *fission* (as opposed to nuclear *fusion*). Nuclear fission is the basis on which nuclear power stations currently work. The rate at which any mass of a radioactive element decays into two or more stable elements is known as its *half-life*, that is, how long it takes for half the atoms of a body of radioactive elements, also known as radioactive isotopes, to turn into two or more new, more stable elements.

Even more useful is the discovery that each radioactive element has a unique half-life. For example, for uranium 238 (one of whose final break-down elements is lead) the half-life is 4.5 billion years. The half-life of carbon 14 (breaking down into an isotope of nitrogen) is only 5,700 years. By measuring how much of the original element is still present in a rock or fossil or archaeological artefact and comparing it with how much of the new break-down element is present, it is possible to calculate the age of a particular rock, fossil, organic remain or artefact, give or take a few years.

Using these techniques along with some support from the fossil record, geologists are now able to calculate the ages of the rocks in each of the geological periods. So, for example, we now know that the Cambrian period began 540 million years ago and lasted about 50 million years. The Jurassic period, so expertly explored and investigated by William Smith and Mary Anning, began around 201 million years ago before passing into the Cretaceous Period which started some 145 million years ago. The end of the Cretaceous is famously marked by an asteroid striking the Earth and contributing to the rapid decline and death of the dinosaurs 66 million years ago. This event didn't lead to the complete extinction of this group of reptiles. A sub-group of dinosaurs known as maniraptoran therapods – the avian dinosaurs – survived and evolved into today's birds. You only have to look into their eyes to see the resemblance!

Radioactive decay had provided a tool to calculate the age of rocks. It has also explained how the Earth continued to maintain a hot, molten interior. This set the stage for geology's next revolutionary idea and the thoroughly outlandish thought that the continents, whole continents, could actually drift across the face of the planet.

* * *

The residual heat from the Earth's original accretion coupled with the energy continually being released by radioactive decay mean that not only is the interior of the planet hot, but also much of it is either molten or 'plastic', which is to say, the rocks can move and flow, albeit very slowly, rather like a thick, heated, sticky tar. At the centre of the planet is a solid, iron-nickel, inner core. It has temperatures that range between 5,000 °C and 6,500 °C. The outer, iron-nickel core is molten with temperatures that lie between 4,500 °C and 5,000 °C. Being molten, the outer core can flow and move, generating electric currents which in turn give rise to the Earth's magnetic field.

Above the core is the mantle. It lies between the core and the base of the Earth's crust and is 2,900 kilometres thick. It makes up 84 per cent of the planet's volume. The rocks here are certainly hot, ranging between 500 °C and 4,000 °C. Although these temperatures at these pressures are not great enough to melt the rocks of the mantle, they are sufficient to make them soft and viscous. As a result, mantle rocks can flow, very, very slowly like hot plastic or heated glass. These flowing, glowing properties of the mantle turn out to be very important for the final part of our Earth story.[4]

Above the mantle sits the Earth's crust, a thin skin of relatively light, less dense, solid rocks that make up the continents and the ocean floors. The boundary between the crust and mantle is known as the Mohorovičić discontinuity, or Moho, for short. It is named after the Croatian seismologist, Andrija Mohorovičić, who first identified the boundary in 1909 from his examination of the shock waves that rang through the earth whenever and wherever an earthquake took place.

Oceanic crust is typically around five to ten kilometres thick and made of rocks such as basalt and gabbro which are slightly denser than continental crust. Continental crust ranges in thickness from 30 to 50 kilometres and is mainly made of less dense rocks such as igneous granites, sedimentary rocks and metamorphic rocks including gneisses, slates and marbles. Being less dense, continental crust rides above both the mantle and oceanic crust.

For several centuries, it struck a number of people that, when looking at maps of the world, the continents, particularly the west coast of Africa and the east coast of South America, had an uncanny fit. Push them closer, and they seem to slot neatly together like pieces of a giant jigsaw. Wilder speculations even wondered whether the continents actually moved across the surface of the planet. However, these outrageous ideas were not taken seriously. The fit between continental boundaries was just a quirky coincidence. Although geologists appreciated that seas rose and fell, and that lands got worn away in one place and thrown up into mountains in another, there seemed to be no conceivable force or mechanism that could physically shift whole continents around the face of the planet. Yet, the idea never quite went away.

Alfred Wegener was born in Berlin in 1880.[5] His university studies included physics, meteorology and astronomy. His participation in several polar expeditions allowed him to develop an expertise in meteorology. Sailing the seas and exploring lands also meant that he had a good sense of the geography of the planet and so, like others before him, Wegener became struck by the jigsaw-like appearance of many of the world's continents.

In 1912 he published his ideas. They were supported not only by the apparent fit between the great landmasses, but by emerging evidence that similar rocks and fossils could be found along the same latitudes on either side of the Atlantic Ocean in South America and South Africa. To explain this, Wegener suggested that at one time the rocks formed a continuous block of the same landmass which then rifted and split, allowing the continents to drift to their present positions. He called the phenomenon *continental drift*. The proposal was that the continents slowly glided over the denser oceanic crustal rocks, possibly driven by some kind of centrifugal force generated as the Earth rotated. Nonetheless, again, the scientific community wasn't convinced; and Wegener not being a geologist didn't help.

* * *

Arthur Holmes *was* a geologist, through and through.[6] Born in 1890 in Hebburn, County Durham, the son of a cabinetmaker, he went on to enjoy a rich and varied career as a mining and academic geologist. He became professor of geology at the University of Durham, before later taking up the chair in geology at the University of Edinburgh in 1943, where he stayed until his retirement in 1956.

His expertise lay in the radiometric dating of rocks. He suggested that the heat generated by radioactive decay, added to any of the planet's residual heat, meant that the mantle beneath the Earth's crust would be a hot, dynamic place where things were constantly, albeit slowly, on the move. Here, in the viscous, but mobile, mantle was the mechanism, he believed, that could explain continental drift. He first presented his ideas in 1931 but, once again, strong doubts greeted the theory. Nevertheless, over the following few decades, the evidence slowly began to mount that indeed, the geography of the Earth's surface was ever-changing and that maybe there was something in this idea of continental drift.

The top of the mantle, just beneath the crust, has temperatures ranging between 500 °C and 1,000 °C. However, the lower reaches of the mantle towards the molten outer core can exceed 4,000 °C. This heat difference sets up mighty, slow-moving, convection currents in the hot, viscous rocks.

When water is heated in a pan, the lower layers warm first and, as a result, their density decreases. With their lower density, the bottom layers begin to rise to the surface. Once at the surface, this warmer water cools slightly, becomes a little more dense, and so once again sinks to the bottom, only to be reheated and sent in upward motion all over again. This cycle of bottom heating and surface cooling sets up circulating convection currents in the pan of water.

In exactly the same way, but on a planetary scale, huge, slow-motion, convection cells are generated in the hot, viscous rocks of the Earth's plastic mantle. As the tops of these cells flow slowly beneath the Earth's solid outer shell, they drag the crustal rocks, known as 'plates', along with them.

The whole process of massive slabs of crust being dragged this way and that is now known as *plate tectonics*.[7] The Earth's crust, or lithosphere, comprises both continental crust and oceanic crust. Both types are dragged by the mantle currents. So, while the idea of continental drift triggered the search for a force that could move mountains, it was the realisation that not only plates of continental crust could be shunted around the surface but also oceanic crust could be dragged by mantle currents. It was this that led to the term 'plate tectonics' being preferred to continental drift.

The lithosphere, that is the earth's relatively thin, crustal, outer shell, is made up of seven very large continental and ocean-sized plates: the South American, Pacific, Australian, African, Eurasian, North American and Antarctic Plates. There are also a number of smaller plates including the Caribbean and Indian plates. These crustal plates slip and slide, push and pull relative to one another, typically at rates of between three and ten centimetres per year.

When the rising currents of two, adjacent, mantle convection cells reach the top of the mantle and flow in opposite directions, they *diverge*, pulling apart the crust above them. This creates a 'rift' in the crustal plate along which magmas can ooze and erupt to form volcanoes, new basaltic crust and oceanic ridges thousands of miles long. The African Rift Valley is one example. The mid-Atlantic Ridge and its many volcanic islands, including Iceland, is another. Jules Verne was clearly tuned in to the scientific ideas of his day. In his 1864 novel, *Journey to the Centre of the Earth*, Axel, the young narrator, on arriving in Iceland with his geologist uncle, says, 'This extraordinary island clearly emerged from the watery depths at a relatively recent period. It is perhaps rising imperceptibly. If indeed so, its origin can only be attributes to the work of underground fires.'[8]

As the diverging currents pull the crust apart in a process known as sea-floor spreading, they also open up new seas and widening oceans. Around 180 million years ago, during Jurassic times, the vast plate known as Pangea began to rift and split. Heading off west away from the Eurasian plate, roughly at the rate of five centimetres per year, was the North American Plate and into the gap flooded the Atlantic Ocean, still widening at the stately rate of five centimetres per year, five metres a century, five kilometres every million years.

In contrast, when two adjacent cooling mantle convection currents *converge*, cool and descend, they drag the opposing crustal slabs towards each other. This results in a planetary crash site where two crustal plates plough into one another.

In a process known as *subduction*, the denser oceanic crust of one advancing plate is thrust *beneath* the less dense, more buoyant continental crust of the other. As it dives into the mantle, the subducted oceanic crust and the compacted seabed sediments begin to melt. Some of the molten rocks make their way to the surface where they erupt as volcanoes, many of which tend to be violent and explosive. Examples occur all along converging plate boundaries, including Indonesia, Japan, New Zealand, the Andes, Italy and Turkey. These subduction zones also put colliding rocks under great stress. The stress is periodically released giving rise to earthquakes. Rain and rivers begin to wear away the volcanoes and rising crust, pouring sediments of sand, silt and mud into the sinking sea basins that lie above the subduction zones along the plate boundaries.

The collision zone is also a place where the rocks and accumulated sediments of the converging plates, including the vast sedimentary deposits of the sinking sea basins, get cemented and compacted, crumpled and crushed, pummelled and pushed, folded and fractured into great mountain chains. This is why we can find marine fossils and sedimentary rock bands on the tops of mountains. The Alps, even today, continue to buckle and bend as the African plate bulldozes into the European plate. The Indian plate is another chunk of crust grinding north, riding on the slow flowing mantle currents beneath. As India drives into and beneath the Eurasian plate, the crustal rocks have been, and continue to be pushed high, in this case to form the Himalayas. In South America, the Nazca plate in the eastern Pacific is slowly but inexorably, at the rate of about 3.7 centimetres per year, ploughing into and plunging under the South American plate pushing up the Andes in the process.

Crustal rocks and sediments deep beneath these rising *orogenic*, or mountain-forming, belts continue to melt. The molten plumes then make their way upwards into the heart of the mountains where they slowly cool to form granites with their big and beautiful crystals of feldspar and quartz. Above and around the rising molten granites, mineral-rich, hot, hydrothermal fluids flow, fracture and force their way into the fissured rocks of the rising mountains above. The hot, mobile, molten fluids eventually cool and form veins rich in minerals and metals.

Radioactive decay. A hot dynamic Earth. Tectonic plates drifting and shifting on viscous seas of mantle magma, slowly gliding over the earth's surface, constantly reconfiguring the continents and re-arranging the geography of the planet. It seems – no, *it is* such a wonderful, outrageous idea, but the scientific evidence in favour of the theory is now overwhelming. It is marvellous that there have been men and women gifted with such imaginations that they could dare to wonder on such a scale and see a whole planet, restless, never still, forever changing.

* * *

Plate tectonics explains so much of the Earth's geology and behaviour. Mountains rising and being weathered away. Oceans coming and going. Rift valleys and ocean trenches. Seas sinking and filling. Island arcs and volcanoes, lavas and earthquakes. The carbon cycle, in which atmospheric carbon dioxide dissolves in the oceans, helping to form the shells of tiny foraminifera and coccoliths, whose remains fall to the sinking sea floor to become limestones, which eventually get subducted and heated, producing volcanoes as two plates converge, releasing carbon dioxide back into the atmosphere for the cycle to begin all over again. Minerals of silver and lead, tungsten and copper crystallising in rich metalliferous veins. Sedimentary rocks caught up in tectonic crumple zones suffering great heat and pressure being transformed into metamorphic slates, gneisses and marbles. The tropical remains of fossilised plants being mined hundreds of millions of years later in coal seams that now lie in the cold far north. Fossilised seashells, marine reptiles and scaley fishes crumbling out of sedimentary shales and limestones a thousand metres up a mountainside. Folded rocks, faulted rocks. The whole of planet Earth was beginning to make narrative sense.

From biblical floods to a whole Earth engine, from a 6,000-year-old biblical world to a 4.6-billion-year-old planet, all in less than three hundred years is a remarkable scientific journey, a wonderful story and an extraordinary achievement.

* * *

Geologists explore deep time, fragments of which are briefly captured in whichever rocks manage to survive and offer up their clues to whoever chances upon them and has eyes to see.

Introducing his poems about time during the Geological Society's Geopoetry Day held in Edinburgh on 1 October 2020, the geologist Neil Hodgson reminded his audience that most of what gets eroded and washed away never survives, never gets preserved. It gets lost in the past. Erosion eats time. However, said Hodgson at the conference, the 'sediments that are preserved are collecting and recording little bits of time. So, as most moments in time are not recorded, each piece of rock is special, it is a captured moment of time.' Fossils, rocks, strata and beds are time capsules, each telling whoever finds them something about our world and our place in it. Hodgson calls them a 'silent library'[9]. For geologists, poets, painters and writers of prose, the purpose of rocks is to tell their stories of times past. Rock strata are like pages of a book; they can be read as a story of geological time and change. But there are many missing pages. Rocks that don't get deposited are missing time.

* * *

I'm going to end this rocky journey on a parochial note. Britain has a truly amazing variety of rocks, of every type, from every geological period. Given its small size, the country is fairly unusual in this respect. For early geologists, there was a lot to see, much over which to puzzle and a lot to fire the imagination. This partly explains why Britain produced so many of the science's early pioneers: Hutton, Smith, Anning, Buckland, Sedgwick, Murchison, Lyell, Phillips and Holmes. So here's the tectonic story of the British Isles over the last half-billion years in a nutshell.[10]

Earth scientists have worked out that just over 450 million years ago, Scotland and England were south of the equator but on different continents and on different plates. They were separated by the Iapetus Ocean. As the two plates began to converge, the Iapetus Ocean closed up, and England and Scotland became geologically united, fused for the first time along what is known as the Iapetus suture. Rather wonderfully, this geological stitch follows, more or less, the current administrative divide between Scotland and England running from the Solway Firth in the west to Lindisfarne on the Northumberland coast in the east.

Since that original union, most of the area we now call the British Isles (except the very north-west of Scotland), along with the rest of Europe, has been on a slow, steady tectonic journey from roughly 50 to 60 degrees *south* of the equator to their present position 50 to 60 degrees *north* of the equator. At different times as it has drifted north, Britain has been a weathering land, a deepening sea, a filling-up sea, a shallow sea, a drying-up sea, a mountain range, a desert, a tropical forest, a river delta, a land of volcanoes, a land of ice and snow, before finally finding itself where we are today, a temperate maritime land suffering increasing pollution, decreasing biodiversity and global heating.

All this can be seen in the remarkably varied geology of our island: granites that were once the deep roots of rising mountain chains, basalt lavas that flowed across the unstable margins and island arcs of advancing plates, red sandstones that were once deserts, yellow and orange sandstones that accumulated in river estuaries and sinking seas, the coals that were once tropical forested swamps, grey-blue slates that began life as muds and oozes on the beds of ancient, deep oceans, and limestones and chalks that slowly accumulated at the bottom of warm, tropical Cretaceous seas long, long ago.

Some of the most recent deposits to cover the bedrocks of the British Isles are the boulder clays and sands left behind by the retreating glaciers and ice sheets of the last Ice Age. As the ice slid its way over the mountains of Scotland and the North of England before spilling out across the bleak tundra plains, it slowly chiselled and ground the rocks beneath its frozen rasp. The advancing ice sheets carried their heavy cargoes of eroded pebbles, boulders, clays, silts and sands far and wide. However, when once again the climate warmed, the ice retreated. The pebbles, boulders, clays, silts and sands were dumped along valley bottoms and river plains, and piled into ridges and low, rounded hills. The Birtley Clay is one such deposit. It lies between Durham and Newcastle-upon-Tyne and it formed during the Quaternary, also known as the Pleistocene Ice Age, which first advanced around three million years ago. The Pleistocene Ice Age, with its warmer 'interglacial periods', is the geological age in which we find ourselves today, although human-induced global heating is upsetting nature's icy rhythms.

Birtley Clay has been used for making bricks for hundreds of years. It is also prized by the sculptor, Anthony Gormley. In a short piece for BBC Radio 4's *Today* programme on 21 November 2020, he talked about the clay and how it affects him, artistically, physically, sensually:

> It is the smell of the stuff that really gets to you. It smells time. It is black … black, black, black. It is just wonderful what just touching the earth gives you. … I've been working with clay that's been dug out of the ground in the North of England in between Durham and Newcastle. I've been making these life-size, sleeping bodies. … There is something incredible about touching the earth of this age. And it's been giving me such pleasure. This is clay that's been dug out of the ground about 25 metres down. It's a very thick seam. It's called the Birtley Clay seam, not very far from the Angel of the North … the joy is feeling and

> touching something that formed between the end of the Pleistocene Ice Age and the beginning of the Holocene. … And just being with it, allowing it to work on me just as much as I work on it … [the clay] tells us about time, about history, but also about how very small we are in the scheme of things. You might say that's frightening but actually it's freeing.

Gormley's reflections on geological time, his sensuous relationship with the earth and his creative spirit are a fine note on which to end our own earthbound story.

Part V

Life

10

Plants and Animals

Intuitively, we divide the world around us into things that are either alive or dead, animate or inanimate. Living things are bounded physical entities and they do a number of things that non-living don't do. They move, respire, grow, reproduce, excrete and react to their surroundings. They evolve through natural selection.

Within each living organism, vast numbers of complex chemical reactions are taking place every second, breaking down molecules, releasing energy, maintaining life. This chemical activity is known as metabolism. Life is a continuous chemical reaction. By using energy from the sun or burning foods of one kind and another, life makes more of itself by converting the environment into itself. The whole business of how complex gatherings of atoms and molecules become self-perpetuating life forms remains fundamentally baffling. One of the key principles that defines life, thinks the Nobel laureate, Paul Nurse in his book, *What Is Life?*: 'is that living entities are chemical, physical and informational machines. They construct their own metabolism and use it to maintain themselves, grow and reproduce. These living machines are coordinated and regulated by managing information, with the effect that living entities operate as purposeful wholes.'[1]

So that's life. But how do we order it, differentiate it, name it?

* * *

We learn to name plants and animals, particularly animals, as soon as we learn to talk: 'doggie', 'pussy cat', 'moo cow', 'birdie'.

For children, animals provide a good illustration of what psychologists call 'declarative pointing'. This ties up nicely with children's development of social understanding, the thing that makes us a frighteningly successful social species. By pointing at a dog and saying 'doggie', the child seeks to draw the parent's attention to what interests the child. This demonstrates an early understanding that other people have minds and that what goes on in them is different to yours. However, you can also influence the mind of the other person. By pointing at the dog and saying 'doggie', the child learns to influence the behaviour of another so that it lines up with the child's interests. The other person looks and says, 'Yes, it's a doggie!' A connection is made, mind to mind.

As you see the world from the other person's point of view, he or she can also be made to see it from yours. Psychologists call this whole remarkable developmental achievement 'theory of mind' and it's a defining feature of being human. Throughout this exchange, the child is also beginning to see difference and recognise types as it engages with the buzzing, bustling living world, a world of doggies, pussy cats and birdies.

Differentiating and naming living things is one of the oldest examples of human beings imposing order on the natural world. It seems obvious that birds are different to fish, which are different to insects. The categories feel intuitive. They are based on observing differences and using these differences to put each animal type into a category. Birds have wings, lay eggs and most of them fly. Fish have fins and live under water. Insects are small, have six legs and emerge from larvae.

The Bible's opening chapter, Genesis, offers its own explanation of how God-ordained, natural orders were created. On the third day, the book of Genesis says, the 'earth brought forth grass, and plants yielding seed after his kind, and the tree yielding fruit'. On the fifth day:

> Let the waters bring forth swarms of living creatures, and let birds fly above the earth across the firmament of the heaven. ... And God said, Let the earth bring forth the living creature after his kind, cattle, and creeping thing, and beasts of the earth after his kind: and it was so.

Finally, and appropriately, on the sixth day, with no hint of the sixth mass extinction likely to be caused by humanity's rapacious appetite, 'man' appeared on the scene and God said: 'let them have dominion over the fish of the sea, and over the birds of the air, and over the cattle, and over all the earth, and over every living thing that moves upon the earth'. Not the wisest commandment if we wish to preserve biodiversity.

Aristotle's approach to understanding the natural world was much more reasoned, more systematic, and less theological.[2] He was born in Greece in 384 BCE. His ideas about the biological world remained dominant for over two thousand years. From his own observations, he distinguished hundreds of types of birds, mammals and fish which he then classified hierarchically.

Aristotle was aware that most larger animals had a physiology based on blood and most smaller ones, such as insects, he thought, didn't. Each side of this broad division could then be broken down into further groups. There were animals with four legs that were warm blooded and gave birth to their young. These roughly equate with our modern-day idea of mammals. However, because dolphins and whales didn't have legs even though they were warm blooded and gave birth to live young, they were placed in a different group. Then there were birds. They laid eggs, had feathers and had two legs. There were reptiles that also laid eggs but were cold-blooded and had four legs. This meant that snakes, without legs, were placed in a different group. Fish had blood, laid 'wet' eggs, although some, like sharks, had skeletons made of cartilage instead of bone. The animals that Aristotle thought didn't have blood included, amongst others, shellfish, spiders, insects, worms, scorpions, corals and star fish.

Aristotle's ideas about the natural world were sophisticated, holistic and, in many ways, quite modern. Underpinning much of his thinking was the belief, first propounded by Empedocles, that the four elements of earth, fire, water and air combined and interacted in different ways giving rise to all that we see in the natural world, both organic and inorganic. The four elements roughly equate with matter being in its solid, liquid or gaseous form, with fire as an energetic extra.

One result of this way of thinking was Aristotle's belief that all things – animal, vegetable and mineral – could be arranged in a hierarchy of increasing perfection, with minerals at the bottom and, inevitably, men and women at the top. This was known as the *scala naturae* in Latin – the *Ladder of Nature*, or the *Great Chain of Being* – with the hottest, wettest and most energetic placed at the top of the hierarchy and the coldest, driest, most earthy and least active at the bottom:

Men and Women
Live-bearing tetrapods (e.g. dogs, cats, cows)
Cetaceans (e.g. whales, dolphins)
Birds
Egg-laying tetrapods (crocodiles, chameleons)
Snakes
Egg-laying fishes (e.g. sea bass)
Sharks, skate and rays
Crustaceans (e.g. crab, shrimp)
Cephalopods (octopus, squid)
Hard-shelled animals (cockles, snails)
Larva-bearing insects (ants, cicadas)
Spontaneously-generated (worms, sponges)
Plants
Minerals

Ordering the living world in this way stayed pretty much the same for the next two thousand years, such was Aristotle's authority and reputation. Indeed, strong echoes of his hierarchical classification still reverberate around modern ways of tidying up nature. However, there was a downside to the idea of a ladder of perfection. Throughout the centuries, the religious elite, the rich and powerful have endorsed the idea that the world is naturally ordered and that one's station in life is, indeed, divinely ordained.

For example, Christian theologians in medieval Europe believed that the Great Chain of Being was decreed by God. The chain begins with God at the top with the angels immediately below. These are disembodied, unchanging and eternal beings. Beneath the angels are humans who do change and eventually die. Men and women are then followed by animals, plants and, finally, the inert, lifeless mineral world. Each link in the chain is divided into finer distinctions. This is where the whole idea, when translated into human affairs, becomes invidious as it cements social inequality into the very fabric of society.

Feudalism was based on the Divine Right of Kings, with the king (or, if it really couldn't be avoided, the queen) at the top, followed by aristocratic lords, landowners and the clergy, and, at the very bottom of the social pile, the peasants. Everyone had their station in life.

Everyone had to know their place. It even filtered down into family life where fathers were deemed to be head of the household. Because the order was supposedly divinely ordained, any criticism of the arrangement was tantamount to heresy. However, dissatisfaction did begin to grow. The fourteenth-century priest, John Ball, dared to ask:

> When Adam delved and Eve span
> Who was then the gentleman?

The peasants, of course, did occasionally revolt but it was not until the Age of Enlightenment, towards the end of the seventeenth century, that reason began to challenge clerical edict, religious dogma and bigoted belief. In France it culminated in the French Revolution and the establishment of secular forms of government.

* * *

In spite of the use and social abuse of a purported ordained hierarchy of all living things, Enlightenment scholars did retain an interest in thinking about how nature might be classified. Taxonomies were in. Ladders of perfection, if not altogether out, were less in evidence. Georges Cuvier, the early nineteenth-century French naturalist, said that in his classification there was no in-built 'superiority' of one group over another. He divided animals into four great groups: Vertebrata, Articulata, Mollusca and Radiata (such as starfish and sea urchins).

Even earlier than Cuvier was one of the Enlightenment's great classifiers: the Swedish naturalist, Carl Linnaeus.[3] He was born in the village of Råshult in Småland, Sweden, on 23 May 1707. Although Carl's father's surname was originally Ingemarsson (Sweden then used the patronymic system of naming), Carl's father, a Lutheran minister, later adopted the Latinate name, Linnaeus after the lime tree, or *lind* in Swedish. It was Carl's father who taught his son Latin as a child.

When Carl was just a year old, the family moved into the rectory in the village of Stenbrohult, southern Sweden. Carl's interest in plants took hold at a young age. He grew them, collected them and in his teens began to study them as a botanist might. By his late teens he was already becoming an expert on plants of all kinds.

When he was seventeen, and with the permission of his father, Carl went to live with the regional doctor, Johan Rothman and his family in the town of Växjö, 30 miles north-east of Stenbrohult. Dr Rothman taught the young lad physiology and botany. A few years later, his mentor advised the 20-year-old Carl that he should attend Uppsala University where he would have an opportunity to further his knowledge of both botany and medicine. That is not such an odd combination as it might sound to the twenty-first-century ear. In the eighteenth century most doctors would be familiar with those herbs and plants that had medicinal properties.

In Uppsala, Linnaeus went to live with Olof Celsius, professor of theology, amateur botanist and, as it happens, uncle of Anders Celsius, an astronomer, who invented the temperature scale, now named after him. However, for Carl, the real bonus of living with the professor was access to his library, reputed to be one of the best botanical libraries in all of Sweden.

By age 23, the young Carl was giving lectures about botany at the university. Two years later, he went on a plant-collecting journey north to Lapland. He travelled by foot and on horse, eventually reaching the Arctic Ocean before heading back south along the coast of the Gulf of Bothnia, north of the Baltic Sea. He returned with hundreds of specimens. He described his collection in his first, and highly original book, *Flora Lapponica*.

It was while he was writing his book that Linnaeus puzzled how best to name all his plants. Using local names was no good because they wouldn't mean much outside Sweden. You wouldn't know in France whether what he was describing in Sweden was the same or a different flower, shrub or grass to those found growing in French soil. He needed something that could be used, agreed and recognised anywhere and everywhere. Moreover, the naming problem wasn't only true for plants, it applied to animals too.

This is where Linnaeus's knowledge of Latin came in useful. Latin was still the international language being used by many European scholars and it made sense to base any nomenclature on classical grounds. This would provide taxonomists with a common language.

Beginning with plants, Linnaeus's genius was to pick a few key traits and note any shared features as well as significant differences. The recent discovery that flowers had sexual organs was an obvious characteristic to home in on. The male organs, the stamens, hold the pollen. Insects and wind can pick up the pollen and when they brush and breeze across another flower, they can fertilise the pistils, the female organs. He reasoned that reproduction was central to life. So

Linnaeus used the number and size of stamens and pistils to organize *species* into larger groups, called *genera*. This twin strategy led to his *binomial system* for naming plants.

For example, he named the common European daisy *bellis perennis* – an 'everlasting' species (perennial) of the genus *bellis* (pretty), 'bellis' being the generic name for all species of daisy.

Today's taxonomies have grown considerably more elongated and elaborate. Above and beyond the specific level, the genera go into *orders*, orders into *classes* and so on until we reach the level into which all plants find themselves, that of the *Plant Kingdom*. Here is the English oak (*Quercus robur*, the 'mighty oak') in its full, modern, taxonomic glory:

Kingdom: *Plantae*
Phylum: *Magnoliophyta*
Class: *Magnoliopsida*
Order: *Fagales*
Family: *Fagaceae*
Genus: *Quercus*
Species: *Robur*

If it seemed a logical way to distinguish and classify plants, what about the rest of nature – animals, minerals, rocks? Again, Linnaeus identified what he thought were key characteristics for animals and minerals and, again, he came up with a system of classifying them, once more using Latin as his preferred language of nomenclature. He was only 28 when first he reported his ideas in 1735.

Over the next few years, Linnaeus expanded and refined his system until it eventually led to what is now regarded as his definitive work, the tenth edition of his *Systema Naturae*, published in 1758. This is the book which became the basis of all modern taxonomies, at least for plants and animals. However, he was on the wrong track when it came to ordering the inanimate world of rocks and minerals, and fairly quickly geologists needed to think about ordering their world in an entirely different way. As far as plants and animals were concerned, however, it was Linnaeus who gave us the first rules for naming and classifying all living things. The rules and names were easily understood and internationally meaningful, and so the system soon caught on.

* * *

Let's bring the classification hierarchy closer to home and up to date and look at ourselves, human beings, *homo sapiens.*

Homo is the Latin for man. However, in the fossil record there have been several types, or species of 'man' dating back over the last few million years. They all belong to the genus *homo.* Each type has its own 'species' name, for example, *homo erectus, homo habilis, homo neanderthalensis.* However, with the exception of ourselves, all the other species of 'man' have died out. We're the only ones left, which may or may not be clever of us but, nevertheless, we have chosen, immodestly, to classify ourselves as *homo sapiens*, 'wise man', 'sapiens' being the Latin for 'wise'.

Anatomically, we're not so different to apes and chimpanzees – and even not too distant from gibbons and orangutans. Modern classificatory systems place apes and chimps, gibbons and humans as members of the 'superfamily', *Hominoidea.*

We can continue to climb the taxonomic ladder. Man, apes, monkeys, lorises, lemurs and many others are all members of the 'order' *Primates.* Beyond that, we look for even broader characteristics to capture and classify whole populations of animal types. Does the animal give birth to and suckle live young; have hair or fur; have three middle-ear bones? Then it's a member of the 'class' *Mammals*, as distinct from other classes such as *Reptiles*, *Birds*, *Amphibians* and *Fish.* Beyond class, we have all animals with a backbone (the vertebrate *phylum*) and animals without a backbone (the invertebrate *phylum*); and they're all members of the *Animal Kingdom.*

From bottom to top, from the very specific to the most general, up through the taxonomic ranks, isn't that an extraordinary feat of acute observation, careful analysis, and tidy thinking? Species, genus, family, order, class, phylum, kingdom, domain.

However, modern thinking and our understanding of life at the cellular, genetic and molecular level has complicated the picture even more. Woven into these elaborate systems, modern taxonomists have recognised the enormously diverse world of the very small, the world of bacteria, cryptozoa, moulds, fungi and many, many more living things.

* * *

And yet, and yet, wondered the Romantic artists. Might we be missing something when we carve up nature into neat and tidy slices of generalised and mounting order? Shouldn't we just lose ourselves in nature's munificence?

In her autobiography, the novelist P.D. James tells us about the time when she watched a butterfly, a Holly Blue, settle.[4] Butterflies, of course, are that most beautiful and yet symbolically ephemeral of things. Their moment can be as brief as a day, but what a glorious day:

> The butterfly fluttered to a leaf close to me and rested motionless. It was one of those rare moments in which fugitive beauty, briefly contemplated, untouchable, is experienced with peculiar intensity, the sense of being a privileged spectator of a life which, however brief, is part of a mysterious whole.

It's cats that do it for John Gray.[5] He is a philosopher who has cats. Cats, he believes, unlike most humans, live simply for the sensation of life. They don't struggle to be happy. Too much striving robs us of the pure joy of life. In the last sentence of his book, *Straw Dogs*, he asks: 'Can we not think of the aim of life as being simply to see?' This is what the best artists and the most perceptive scientists seem able to do. Simply to see.

Scientists also see, but their gaze takes in a different view. They may see beauty but they also look for order in the world of butterflies and cats, animals and plants. Order and classification is often their first step in making sense of nature and the miracle of life; and it was Linnaeus who taught us how to make some of those first, bold strides.[6]

* * *

By 1741 Linnaeus and his family had moved to Uppsala where Linnaeus took up a post at the university. The job gave him an opportunity not only to employ his medical know-how but, more particularly, to indulge his love of botany. He soon became responsible for running the city's botanical garden which he promptly reorganised and expanded.

More collecting expeditions and books followed. His success and fame continued to grow and. in 1747, the king of Sweden, Frederick I, granted Carl Linnaeus the title *Archiater*, or Chief Physician. In 1750 he was appointed rector of Uppsala University.

Always a man to be led by science and his own observations, Linnaeus also began to campaign against upper-class women farming out their babies to wet nurses. He wanted to promote breast-feeding by children's own mothers. He saw how Lapp mothers breast-fed their babies and believed that this promoted good health and robust children. What was good enough for animals in the wild and Laplanders in the north was surely good enough for all human infants; indeed, it was the natural thing to do. It is thought that his role in this campaign led to his choice of the term *Mammalia* for his class of all breast-feeding animals.

More books and more success followed, resulting in the king of Sweden granting him the rare honour of becoming a knight of the Order of the Polar Star. This allowed him to wear the order's insignia, which he did on every possible occasion.

By all accounts Linnaeus wasn't a modest man – on the contrary. He adopted the motto 'Deus creavit, Linnaeus disposuit', which translates as 'God created, Linnaeus classified'. Nevertheless, his supreme self-confidence also allowed him to put forward ideas that were radical at the time. For a while he thought whales were just very large fish, but his anatomical skills and recognition that they nursed their young made him realise that they were in fact marine mammals. This was at odds with much of the thinking of his day but he held his ground. Moreover, if classifying whales as mammals was bold, he was even braver when he suggested that human beings, apes and monkeys should all be seen as primates. Anticipating the trouble that Darwin would get into a century later, this did not go down well with the church authorities.

There was one final royal honour. In 1761 Carl Linnaeus was ennobled by the king of Sweden, Adolf Frederick. Thenceforth, he became known as Carl von Linné. His coat of arms featured his favourite flower, *Linnaea borealis*, a sub-arctic, woodland sub-shrub, commonly known as the twinflower. The shield in his coat of arms is divided into thirds: red, black and green for nature's three great kingdoms: animal, mineral and vegetable.

Linnaeus's fame began to spread world-wide. He received many international honours. In 1769 he was elected to the American Philosophical Society for his work. By now, however, in his sixties, his health was beginning to suffer. Strokes left him partially paralysed and his memory was no longer reliable. He died, aged 70, on 10 January 1778 and was buried in Uppsala Cathedral.

His library and most of his specimens were eventually sold to the English botanist, James Edward Smith, who in 1784 bought the whole collection, comprising 14,000 plants, 3,198 insects, 1,564 shells, about 3,000 letters and 1,600 books. Possessed of a remarkable collection, in 1788 Smith founded the Linnean Society of London, now the oldest biological society in the world. Its offices are to be found in Burlington House, Piccadilly.

The society offers a forum for the discussion and advancement of the life sciences. Indeed, it was at a meeting of the Society in 1858 that papers presented on behalf of Charles Darwin and Alfred Russel Wallace, outlining the theory of evolution by natural selection, were first delivered. Their papers marked the beginning of the next revolution in the life sciences. The theory of evolution explained why there are similarities and differences between the species, why we have such a huge variety of life forms, and why similar but distinct species occur in different places and at different times.

11

On the Origin of Species

Charles Darwin was born in Shrewsbury, Shropshire, on 12 February 1809. He was the fifth of six children. When he was only eight years old, his mother died. His family was wealthy and well-connected. His paternal grandfather was Erasmus Darwin, philosopher, poet, naturalist and one of the founding members of the Lunar Society of Birmingham.[1] Erasmus was fond of writing poetry, albeit of a not particularly distinguished kind. Nevertheless, uncannily anticipating his grandson-to-be's ideas about evolution, in 1803 he published *The Temple to Nature*, a long poem in four cantos. Here are a couple of extracts:

> With finer links the vital chain extends,
> And the long line of Being never ends. …
> Each new Descendant with superior powers
> Of sense and motion speeds the transient hours;
> Braves every season, tenants every clime,
> And Nature rises on the wings of Time.
>
> (Canto II, ll. 19-20, 33-36)

Charles Darwin's early career offered a few hints that he might realise his grandfather's poetic predictions. His father, Robert, originally hoped his son would follow in his footsteps and become a doctor. In 1825, aged sixteen, Charles enrolled as a medical student at the University of Edinburgh but medicine failed to fire his interest and he wasn't too keen on the sight of blood. However, what he did enjoy was natural history, including biology and geology. Botany held a particular fascination and he soon became familiar with the work of Carl Linnaeus and his classification of all living things.

Not happy with his son's poor progress in medicine, in 1828 Charles's father decided to send him to Christ's College, Cambridge to study for an arts degree with a view to the young Darwin becoming an Anglican parson. At Cambridge, Charles was able to continue and develop his interest in natural history. He befriended botanists and entomologists. He collected beetles. He read widely. He attended Adam Sedgwick's geology classes and went on the professor's mapping course to Wales. These interests taught him how to observe and see, work and think scientifically.

Aged 22, with an ordinary arts degree under his belt, Charles Darwin was all set to train for the priesthood and lead the life of a country parson. Then fate intervened. Out of the blue, an opportunity presented itself that he could hardly have dared hope for.

After returning from his geological field trip in Wales, he received a letter inviting him to join Captain Robert FitzRoy[2] on an expedition to chart the coastline of South America. Although it would be understood that Darwin, as a young naturalist, would wish to collect various fauna and flora, he would also be expected to act as a 'gentleman' companion for FitzRoy. At the time of sailing FitzRoy was only 23. After some initial reluctance by his father to support the venture, another family member, Josiah Wedgwood II,[3] persuaded Robert Darwin to allow his son to join the expedition; indeed, Josiah volunteered to fund his nephew's trip. This support gave him financial independence, which meant that the young Darwin enjoyed some freedom to pursue his own interests as well as retain ownership of all the specimens he collected on the adventure.[4]

The survey ship, HMS *Beagle*, set sail from Plymouth Sound on 27 December 1831. The expedition lasted nearly five years. While FitzRoy and his men were busy charting coastlines, Darwin spent much of his time on land and by the sea, collecting plants, animals, marine invertebrates, rocks and fossils. Whenever he could, he packaged up what he had collected and had it shipped back to Cambridge.

As well as writing up his observations and recording his thoughts, there was also plenty of time to read. FitzRoy was not always the most congenial of companions and Darwin would later recall a number of quarrels between the two men. Nevertheless, when he was in a good humour, the captain could be sociable and considerate. Well into the voyage, FitzRoy gave Darwin the recently published first volume of Charles Lyell's *Principles of Geology.* In the book, Lyell argued that the surface of the Earth was ever-changing. Over immense periods of time, ice, water and volcanoes were constantly shaping and fashioning the landscape, adding and taking away clays and sand, muds and pebbles, ash and lava.

It was clear from Lyell's theories that the Earth was very old, much older than the Bible suggested and much, much older than most people had previously imagined. Over enormous periods of time, it appeared from the geological record that the Earth and all living things were constantly changing. Indeed, Lyell was one of the first to introduce the idea of evolution as it applied to natural geological processes. Lyell's book greatly influenced Darwin's thinking.

In 1835, the expedition visited the Galápagos Islands. Darwin observed subtle differences and similarities between particular species on different islands. On Chatham Island, for example, he noted that a mockingbird was similar to those he had seen in Chile. He then found another type of mockingbird on Charles Island, again similar to, but different from those he had observed on the other islands. He also collected finches from each of the islands but didn't make much of their differences at the time.

From the Galápagos Islands, the *Beagle* sailed west across the Pacific, calling at Tahiti, New Zealand and Australia before heading home via South Africa, Brazil and the Azores. On 2 October 1836, the expedition finally docked at Falmouth whence Darwin made his way home to Shrewsbury.

* * *

The success of the voyage of the *Beagle* helped launch Robert FitzRoy as a scientist and pioneer weather forecaster and, of course, it provided Darwin with a large and exotic collection of specimens. The collection got him thinking about life and what he saw as the instability of species. The thought that species could change and adapt to their environment over time began to take shape in his mind.

On his return, Darwin presented the finches and other specimens to the Zoological Society of London.[5] The finches from the Galápagos Islands were examined by the famous ornithologist, John Gould. Gould concluded that what Darwin had found was an entirely new family of ground finches, comprising many different species. Although Darwin hadn't been particularly assiduous at the time he was collecting the birds, with the help of other expedition members, he managed to work out on which island each species of finch had been caught. Gould also concluded that the mockingbirds from each island were also of different species. It gradually became apparent to Darwin that from a common South American mainland ancestry, over time, each species of finch, or mockingbird, had gradually adapted to the particular conditions and environmental opportunities present on its island.

Darwin's finches are a classic example of what these days we would call 'adaptive radiation'. The finches had arrived on the Galápagos from the South American mainland about three million years ago. As they adapted to the habitat and resources particular to each island, they evolved specific characteristics to take advantage of the local conditions, in the process of which they began to differ in things such as beak size and shape. Over time, they continued to adapt and evolve until eventually their differences became great enough to distinguish them as separate species, albeit of the same family.

Armed with his knowledge of the vastness of geological time, his experiences of collecting fossils from different time horizons, and his understanding that a species could adapt and change over time, Darwin began to formulate his revolutionary idea: that life can and does evolve. Species were not immutable. In one of his notebooks he drew a tree in which each branch stretched out from an ancestral trunk to evolve into a new species – the tree of life.

It was also possible to make sense of the taxonomic hierarchy of Linnaeus's system – species, genus, family, order and so on – if you recognised that each species was more closely related to other members of their shared genus than they were to species in another genus. Linnaeus had rejected evolution as an idea. However, in Darwin's mind, it seemed that the traits that Linnaeus used to put species in a family or genus could be seen to have been inherited from a common ancestor. So, for example, although whales swim in the sea, unlike fish they are warm blooded and nurse their young. Their anatomies are fundamentally mammalian. They need to surface in order to breath. If evolution is a fact, then it seemed entirely plausible that the distant ancestors of whales were land mammals, and that whales are mammals that have gradually adapted to living a sea life. Indeed, as the biographer Richard Holmes[6] notes, it was the poet Coleridge who recognised taxonomies as useful but static, while scientific principles such as evolutionary theory could be explanatory and dynamic.

Taxonomies appear midway between the particularities of things and cases, and the universal laws of nature. First, scientists observe, sometimes experiment and always describe. Then they seek patterns and go on to classify and order what they have seen and described. Beyond that, they try to find some underlying logic that generates the patterns that account for the order. Finally, if possible, explanations are sought and theories, such as the theory of evolution, put forward to make sense of everything observed, described, ordered and conceived. Each science has its grand projects. Each science needs men and women who can wonder and imagine.

* * *

Back in Britain, Darwin's life became increasingly busy. He moved from Cambridge to London. He wrote papers on the *Beagle* expedition, corals, volcanic islands and barnacles. He gave lectures. In 1838 he was elected to the Athenaeum Club, quickly followed in successive years with election to the Royal Society of London, and the council of the Royal Geographical Society. In 1839 he married his first cousin, Emma Wedgwood. They would go on to have ten children together.

By 1842 he had written a 35-page piece sketching out his ideas on his theory of evolution by natural selection, sharing the paper a couple of years later with a small number of close friends. The year 1842 was also when Darwin moved his young family to Down House, Kent, about fifteen miles south-east of central London. This was to be his home for the rest of his life.

* * *

Although Darwin continued to think about and refine his theory, he still hadn't got round to publishing anything public on the subject. However, in April 1856 he invited the biologist Thomas Huxley and several other naturalists to a weekend party, where they discussed Darwin's ideas on the origin of species. Spurred on by these discussions and encouraged by the geologist Charles Lyell, he decided to put pen to paper and write something more substantial for publication. However, events began to overtake him.

For a while, Darwin had been corresponding with Alfred Russel Wallace,[7] a young explorer and fellow naturalist. In 1858 Wallace was in Indonesia, observing and collecting specimens. It began to strike him that only the fittest members of a species survived, and only those which survived would go on to mate and reproduce, passing on their adaptive characteristics to the next generation. He outlined an idea that a species might evolve as its environment changed. He knew that Darwin was interested in the subject and, in all innocence, wrote to him explaining his thoughts, enclosing an essay entitled 'On the Tendency of Species to Depart Indefinitely from the Original Type'. Without him realising it, Wallace's ideas were along the same lines as those of the still unpublished Darwin.

Of course, Darwin had been working on the very same ideas for the last twenty years, sharing his thinking and papers with close friends, but he still hadn't formally published anything about his theory. Having discussed the situation with a number of his associates, it was collectively decided that the thoughts of both men, Darwin and Wallace, should be presented at an extraordinary meeting of the Linnean Society to be held on 1 July 1858. This is an extract from the letter sent by Charles Lyell, the geologist, and Joseph Hooker, botanist and close friend of Darwin, requesting the meeting at which the papers by Darwin and Wallace were to be read;[8]

> MY DEAR SIR, – The accompanying papers, which we have the honour of communicating to the Linnean Society, and which all relate to the same subject, viz. the Laws which affect the Production of Varieties, Races, and Species, contain the results of the investigations of two indefatigable naturalists, Mr. Charles Darwin and Mr. Alfred Wallace.
>
> These gentlemen having, independently and unknown to one another, conceived the same very ingenious theory to account for the appearance and perpetuation of varieties and of specific forms on our planet, may both fairly claim the merit of being original thinkers in this important line of inquiry; but neither of them having published his views, though Mr. Darwin has for many years past been repeatedly urged by us to do so, and both authors having now unreservedly placed their papers in our hands, we think it would best promote the interests of science that a selection from them should be laid before the Linnean Society.
>
> We have the honour to be yours very obediently,
>
> CHARLES LYELL.
> JOS. D. HOOKER.

Having finally gone public, Darwin now moved quickly. Within a year he wrote a book for a non-specialist audience titling it, *On the Origin of Species by Means of Natural Selection*, published in 1859, priced fifteen shillings.[9] The initial print run of 1,250 copies soon sold out. Darwin corrected and revised the book before the second edition was published in 1860.

* * *

The basic thesis was simple yet revolutionary. Darwin proposed that individual organisms of a particular species vary a little from each other in a myriad subtle ways. Some that have a particular combination of characteristics might be marginally better suited to the environment in which they happen to find themselves. This means that they are more likely to thrive and survive and, if they survive, they have more opportunities to breed and pass on some of their adaptive characteristics to their offspring. In turn, the new generation that has inherited some of these parental variants will be better adapted to the prevailing environment. As environments change, so will the most adaptive characteristics. Life is struggle. 'Nature', as the nineteenth-century journalist, John Heraud wrote in his poem, 'Descent into Hell', 'yearns to rid her imperfections.'[10] There is constant competition for limited resources. Only those species possessed of traits that are best suited to take advantage of the world around them will survive, reproduce and pass on their advantages to their offspring.

Over prolonged periods of time, the incremental adaptive changes that increase the chances of survival may become sufficiently great to warrant the recognition of a new species. Hence the title of Darwin's book – the *Origin of Species by Natural Selection* – and it was natural selection that explained how the branches on the 'tree of life' gradually grow apart, leading to the extraordinary variety of life forms that we see today.

If the branches of the tree of life are traced back in time towards the main trunk, then similar species will have shared a common ancestor of the same genus; animals (or plants) in similar genera will have had a common ancestor of the same family; and so on. The further you go back in geological time, says the evolutionary biologist Richard Dawkins, the more you trace the common ancestry of all living things.[11]

Environments can change in any number of ways. Birds might be blown off course and find themselves on a different island. A lake might become more saline. Your main predator might get faster. The climate might change. Omnivores might cope better than carnivores when food sources become scarce. Your behaviour or appearance might be more attractive to potential mates.

Although Carl Linnaeus had ordered and classified nature's biological kingdoms, the challenge of how to make sense of life's extravagant variety hadn't been explained, unless you accepted the living world and all its creatures as being ordained by God. Darwin's theory provided a powerful explanation, one that did not rely on divine action. Not surprisingly, Darwin's theory did not go down well with church authorities and 'creationists', hostilities that have echoed down the years right up to the present day.

The very idea of the evolution of species over vast aeons of time was heresy to those who read the Bible literally. Matters got particularly heated at the suggestion that human beings had probably evolved from an earlier species of ape. This led to the infamous jibe by the Lord Bishop of Oxford, Samuel Wilberforce, directed at Darwin's friend and fierce defender, Thomas Huxley. The bishop wondered whether Huxley was descended from an ape on his mother's side or his father's side.

However, the power and potency of Darwin's theory was too great for any cheap quip to hold it in check. More recently, the philosopher Daniel Dennett in his 1995 book, *Darwin's Dangerous Idea: Evolution and the Meanings of Life*, wrote:

> If I was to give an award for the single best idea anyone has ever had, I'd give it to Darwin. ... In a single stroke, the idea of evolution by natural selection unifies the realm of life, meaning, and purpose with the realms of space and time, cause and effect, mechanism and physical law.[12]

Some accolade.

* * *

Darwinism, as it became known, quickly began to influence the views of some members of the British Association for the Advancement of Science. The theory was a brilliant way of linking the vastness of geological time, the constant and sometimes radical changes found in the fossil record, the Linnaean classification of all plant and animals, and the extraordinary variety of species to be found in nature. Linnaeus had successfully looked at nature, saw order, and described *how* things are. Darwin looked at nature and wondered *why* there is such variety and order, and then asked how the living world got to be the way it is.

Darwin continued to refine his theory. In 1868 he published *The Variation of Animals and Plants under Domestication.*[13] He knew that breeders of 'fancy' pigeons could create hundreds of varieties that looked dramatically different to wild pigeons. He also knew that they all come from one species, *Columba livia*. Darwin decided to breed his own pigeons. By crossing birds with different characteristics, he could generate offspring with different traits. By artificially selecting in this way, he gathered valuable evidence for his theory of evolution by natural selection. If breeders could manipulate the way a single species looked in captivity, then it seemed logical to expect that different environments, across place and over time, could manipulate all species naturally in the wild.

In 1871 Darwin published *The Descent of Man.*[14] He also extensively rewrote *On the Origin of Species*. It was in this sixth and last edition that he personally used the word 'evolution' for the first time. His last major work, *The Expression of the Emotions in Man and Animals*, appeared in 1872, completing his great cycle of evolutionary writings.[15] However, he retained a soft spot for earthworms. He'd been interested in them ever since he returned from his round-the-world expedition. Their part in keeping soils fertile, plants healthy and making life possible caused him to wonder 'whether there were many other animals which have played so important a part in the history of the world'. In a final paean to worms, in 1881 he published *The Formation of Vegetable Mould through the Action of Worms*, a surprising bestseller.[16]

In his later years, Darwin's health was not good. Over Christmas 1881 he suffered a heart attack, followed by a series of seizures. He died on 10 April 1882 at Down House. He was finally buried in the nave of Westminster Abbey, not too far from Isaac Newton and his friend, the geologist Charles Lyell. Darwin's descendants live on. Splendidly in keeping with his ideas about the living world and endless change, in 2008 his great-great-granddaughter, the poet Ruth Padel, published *Darwin: A Life in Poems*, a miniature biography of her relative's remarkable life.[17] In his 2009 review of the book, Richard Holmes writes fittingly that 'Darwin's descendent has evolved a new species of biography'.[18]

12

Genetics

While all the hoo-hah was going on around Darwinism, an Augustinian monk by the name of Gregor Johann Mendel was quietly working away growing peas in the garden of his abbey in Brno, a town in what is now the Czech Republic, but was then part of the Austrian Empire.[1] However, he wasn't growing peas simply to feed his fellow friars. As a keen scientist, trained in maths and physics, he was carrying out an experiment. Between 1856 and 1863, he set about growing peas in a rigorous and systematic way. In some of his experiments he grew as many as 10,000 pea plants.

Mendel chose to look at seven characteristics of his pea plants. He observed and noted the plants' height, pod shape and colour, seed shape and colour, and flower position and colour. He repeatedly bred and cross-bred them, noting what had changed and what hadn't changed over each generation. For example, he showed that, when a true-breeding yellow pea and a true-breeding green pea were cross-bred their offspring always produced yellow seeds. In this *first-generation* crop, there were no green peas, only yellow, even though half the 'parental' generation peas had been green.

However, in the next, *second generation*, when the first-generation yellow peas had been cross-bred with each other, green peas *reappeared* in the ratio of one green pea to three yellow peas.

To explain the findings, Mendel coined the terms 'recessive' and 'dominant' for each particular trait. All the cross-bred *first-generation* peas would, of course, have a dominant yellow pea trait inherited from the original yellow pea parent, that's why they were all yellow, yellow being a dominant trait and green recessive. But, when the yellow, cross-bred, first-generation peas were further cross-bred with each other to produce a *second generation* of cross-bred peas, there were four possible trait combinations inherited from the cross-bred first-generation crop:

dominant yellow/dominant yellow
dominant yellow/recessive green
recessive green/dominant yellow
recessive green/recessive green.

Whenever the dominant yellow trait was present, the pea would be yellow. Only when the combined traits were both recessive green would the pea be green, a combination that statistically could occur only one in four times.

Mendel published his research in 1866. Not knowing what lay behind these regular but predictable breeding outcomes, he simply referred to them as invisible 'factors'. Today we know them as genes. However, at the time, the significance of his work remained largely unappreciated. He died in 1884, aged 61, only two years after Darwin's own death.

* * *

It was not until the beginning of the twentieth century that Mendel's laws of heredity became more widely recognised. The originality and relevance of his research slowly began to dawn on the scientific community. It allowed biologists to make sense of the mechanisms that lay behind much of Darwin's theory of evolution. The idea of dominant and recessive traits meant that a given characteristic would not simply get diluted over successive generations as many who began to doubt Darwinism were beginning to think. A trait, or gene as we know it today, could pass unchanged from parent to offspring without losing any of its effect. These laws of inheritance entitle Mendel to be regarded as the founder of modern genetics.

Linnaeus saw order in all living things. Darwin saw that all living things are connected and have a common ancestry. Mendel provided the mechanism that could explain how change was possible and might account for Darwin's argument that similar species had common ancestors. Between them, these three radical pioneers laid down the foundations of modern biology.

* * *

Building on the combined efforts and insights of Linnaeus, Darwin and Mendel, twentieth-century life scientists developed what has become known as the *Modern Synthesis*. Today, this synthesis includes not only Darwinism and Mendelian genetics, but an understanding of the part that genes and DNA play in the whole wonderful story of life and its 'endless forms most beautiful'. We'll take a brief look at our own species, *homo sapiens*, to outline the role that DNA, genes and chromosomes play in modern genetics. In our own case, every one of our genes exists as a pair. We inherit one from each of our biological parents, originally the result of a sperm and egg fusing together.

First observed in the 1870s by the German physician, Walther Flemming, *chromosomes* are thin strands of the tightly coiled molecule *DNA* (deoxyribonucleic acid) located within the nucleus of each cell in our body. We have 46 chromosomes in each of our non-reproductive cells. We inherit one set of 23 chromosomes from our mother and one set of 23 chromosomes from our father. So we have two sets of 23 chromosomes or 23 pairs.

The DNA molecule itself has a very long coiled, double-helix-shaped structure. Each chromosome is sub-divided into sections known as *genes*. A gene is therefore a short length of the molecule DNA. Different threads of chromosomes vary in how many genes they contain, ranging from a few hundred to a few thousand arranged in long chains. Each gene codes for the production of a specific protein. Together, our genes provide the instructions – our genetic code – to make all the proteins which our bodies need to grow, function and maintain themselves in a healthy state. Genes are therefore the basic unit of genetics. The sum of all the genes in any organism is known as its *genome*; and a genome is nothing less than an instruction manual to make and then maintain that organism. In the case of human beings, we have over 20,000 protein-coding genes in our genome which can combine in an almost infinite number of ways. The geneticist Paul Nurse reminds us that: 'our genomes, each three billion DNA "letters" long, are very similar across genders, ethnicities, religions and social classes. This is an important equalizing fact that societies across the world should appreciate.'[2]

Genes in each of the body's cells initiate and control the complex business of protein synthesis. Proteins are the building blocks for membranes, muscles, nerves, connective tissues, skin and most other structures. Enzymes are particularly complex proteins which act as biological catalysts that affect all aspects of a cell's metabolism. They control and carry out most of the chemical processes and reactions within an organism. Complex living entities produce thousands of different enzymes. Thus, the entire structure and function of an organism's body is governed by the different amounts and types of proteins the body synthesizes.

There are many types of cells in an animal's body. There are muscle cells, heart cells, kidney cells, nerve cells, liver cells. In an extraordinary and wonderful way, DNA also encodes instructions about when and at what age, where and at what location in the body certain genes get switched on or off, what type of cells should be being made, what functions they serve and how many of them there should be. In other words, DNA, and what are known as 'hox' genes, in particular, control the timing and location of all *gene expression*. For example, when we reach puberty, genes begin to instruct our bodies to sprout pubic hair, grow breasts or beards, ovulate or develop deeper voices. Older still, and genes kick in that tell our bones to stop growing longer.

Another surprise lay in store for 1970s geneticists. It was assumed that the greater the difference between two species, the bigger would be the difference in their genetic makeup. One of the favourite animals used to study genetics and growth, change and mutation, was the fast-reproducing fruit fly, obviously vastly different and far removed from any mammal, especially human beings. However, researchers were in for a shock, albeit an exciting one. This is how the geneticist Sean Carroll sums up the story:

> contrary to the expectations of any biologist, most of the genes first identified in governing major aspects of fruit fly body organization were found to have exact counterparts that did the same things in most animals, including ourselves. The discovery was followed by the revelation that the development of various body parts such as eyes, limbs, and hearts, vastly different in structure among animals and long thought to have evolved in entirely different ways, was also governed by the same genes in different animals.[3]

This comparison of developmental genes between species gave birth to a new discipline that combined embryology and evolutionary biology. It became known as evolutionary developmental biology, or 'evo-devo', for short.[4] So although the number of genes and the differences in the genetic make-up between species is not as great as we once thought, an organism's construction and complexity ultimately rests on how and when those genes get switched on and off in the course of development, the character of the environment in which they operate, the proteins they produce, and the interactions between those proteins.

Evo-devo explains how complexity is constructed from a single embryonic cell into a whole animal. Modifications in development further increase complexity and expand diversity. Thus, continues Carroll, 'the discovery of the ancient genetic tool kit is irrefutable evidence of the descent and modification of animals, including humans, from a simple common ancestor' going back billions of years.[5] These discoveries provided further powerful support for Darwin's theory of evolution, captured nicely in Thomas Hardy's poem, 'Heredity', in which the timeline of life stretches back to the very beginning of the tree of life:[6]

I am the family face;
Flesh perishes, I live on,
Projecting trait and trace
Through time to times anon,
And leaping from place to place
Over oblivion.

The years-heired feature that can
In curve and voice and eye
Despise the human span
Of durance – that is I;
The eternal thing in man,
That heeds no call to die.

Even more thought-provoking, the external environment, lifestyle, diet and, in the case of human beings, our emotions and levels of stress can also affect how and when certain genes get expressed, get switched on or off, for good or ill. This fascinating relationship between gene expression and the environment, both internal and external, has given rise to the new science of *epigenetics*.[7] Gene expression is therefore not only affected by what we eat and breathe, but also how we live and how we feel. For example, smoking thirty cigarettes a day seriously affects your risk of cancer; but smoking thirty cigarettes a day *and* having a childhood history of abuse and neglect, trauma and stress increases that risk even further.[8,9]

We also have to remember that the trillions of cells, the huge number of their types, their myriad functions, and the complex, living structure that is the adult body, all arose from a single fertilised cell with its cargo of DNA and instructions how to build a living, self-sustaining entity. Every cell in an animal's body is the descendant of that single fertilized egg cell. That single cell begins to divide and the divisions continue billions of times over until there is a complete new, viable living being. Although during the early stages of this process the dividing cells look very similar, nevertheless they each have their own destiny and part to play in the final make-up of the living organism.

* * *

As cells reproduce by dividing in two, each new cell requires a complete set of DNA to ensure the continued synthesis of vital proteins. DNA molecules in the original cell therefore must replicate themselves during each cell division. Various mechanisms are built into a gene's make-up to ensure that the DNA is copied accurately. So huge and complex is the business of replicating the DNA, occasionally mistakes occur. These result in *mutations* in the replicated DNA molecule. Most minor mistakes and their resulting variations in DNA don't have any discernible effect, although all subsequent cells and their mutated DNA will inherit the change. This only becomes a major problem, for example, in the case of cancer cells.

However, DNA mutations do become relevant for our story of natural selection and life's rich variety when they effect the reproductive cells – the egg and sperm cells. In this case, the mutations and the coding changes they contain will be passed on to the organism's offspring.

Inherited mutations may be unique to an individual or family. Fortunately, the more harmful ones are relatively rare; but this is the point in our journey where, after our excursion into the complex world of modern genetics, we need to reconnect with Darwin and Mendel and their insights into natural selection, evolution and the origin of species.

An inherited characteristic might be fine for each successive generation, until, let's say, the environment changes. At that point the adaptation might no longer be a survival asset and instead become a survival liability. The organism and the DNA that sponsors its traits become less adapted as the world around it begins to change. It will either die, fail to compete, or have fewer opportunities to reproduce. Natural selection predicts that the inherited variation and its characteristics will gradually die out in the population as the individuals which possess those variations fail to pass on their genes.

However, the opposite is also true. Every now and again, a mutation introduces a change that produces a survival advantage or opportunity. Being healthier and fitter increases the chances of being able to reproduce and every reproduction leads to a new generation in which that beneficial mutation is passed on. The genetic change, however minor, if it increases an organism's fitness to adapt and ability to survive, will gradually become more common in successive generations.

It is these slow changes that occur over aeons of time, caused by small mutations and the processes of natural selection, that in an interbreeding population we call evolution. There is no underlying purpose driving evolution. Nevertheless, evolution by natural selection can bring about great variety, huge complexity and the rich and wonderful biodiversity we see all around us. Evolution explains how new species arise, new classes emerge, new phyla are created. Over geological time, the leaves on Darwin's tree of life multiply and multiply until their numbers are beyond imagination.

No matter how tiny and slow are the changes, geologists have taught us that there is more than enough time for mammals to evolve from primitive Pre-Cambrian life forms, and for trees to evolve from ancient oceanic algae, and everything in between. Follow Darwin's tree of life far enough back in time, back nearly four billion years, and at root we are all one, related to every other form of life on the planet.

The life sciences have often inspired more dystopian outlooks on the human condition. This is especially true of novels, including science fiction writing. Evolutionary theories, social Darwinism and the idea of 'survival of the fittest' have given us fiction that tackles the more brutal and dubious sides of human nature. *The Time Machine* and *The War of the Worlds* by H.G. Wells, Joseph Conrad's *Heart of Darkness*, R.L. Stevenson's *Dr Jekyll and Mr Hyde* and Margaret Atwood's *The Handmaid's Tale* all explore Darwinian thinking in its darker moods. Genetic theories have also prompted novelists to travel down bleaker, more morally complex roads. Margaret Atwood's

MaddAddam Trilogy and A.S. Byatt's *A Whistling Woman* are just two examples given by Paul Hamann-Rose in his book, *Genetics and the Novel: Reimagining Life Through Fiction*.[10]

However, at the more particular and specific level, the living world has provided musicians, writers and artists with brighter, more joyous thoughts. From Robert Burns' 'Wee, sleeket, cowran, tim'rous beastie' to William Blake's 'Tyger Tyger, burning bright, In the forests of the night'; from Beatrix Potter's Peter Rabbit to C.S. Lewis's lion Aslan; from larks ascending to swans dancing; from hosts of golden daffodils to vases of glorious sunflowers: life of every kind has been used by artists to amuse, moralise and uplift the spirits.

In 2009, in the course of a single summer, Patrick Barkham set out to find and see, in the wild, every one of Britain's 59 species of butterfly.[11] The mission was triggered by the childhood adventures he had had with his dad. They shared a love of butterflies. They hatched a plan to try to see as many different British species as they could, believed then to number 58. Eventually they 'ran out of summers, or steam' and got stuck at 54. However, the lepidopteral lure didn't go away. Approaching his fortieth year, Patrick decided that he must complete the 'unfinished business' and so in that early summer he started his quest to 'unlock the ordinary, everyday beauty of the natural world'. It was after a long search, that he finally came across the small, misty, Wood White – in a wood, of course, in Surrey. It was hanging on a leaf and was 'the shape of a droplet of water'. But what the find also did was give Patrick an understanding, an insight. The delicate, fragile, still butterfly with its wings closed, he thought, has 'the ability just to be, and live fully in the present', and maybe that is the living world's most precious gift: the ability just to be, and live fully in the present.

Part VI

Elements

13

The Philosopher's Stone

When I was in my mid-teens, I read a book on the periodic table of the elements. I remember it began with a definition of a chemical element that went something like: *A chemical element is any substance that cannot be decomposed into simpler substances by ordinary chemical processes.* Elements are the fundamental materials of which all matter is composed including stars, clouds, living things and rocks. Most of us have heard of the more common, everyday elements including oxygen, carbon, gold, iron and tin but there are more exotic and much rarer elements such as krypton and iridium.

Elements can combine with one another to form a huge variety of more complex substances called compounds. When two or more elements combine to form a compound, they lose their separate identities. The compound has characteristics that are different from those of its constituent elements. For example, when two parts of the gas hydrogen combine with one part of the gas oxygen, we end up with a liquid compound, water. No one realised this until the 1780s.

Altogether, there are 92 naturally occurring elements. Hydrogen is the lightest, uranium the heaviest. Many elements occur naturally in only very small trace amounts, although modern technological devices often rely on them to perform their wonders. For example, indium is one of the elements involved in making your smart phone's screen touch-sensitive.

* * *

One of the recurring themes of this book is the amazing realisation that there have been people, throughout the ages, who didn't just take the natural world for granted but looked at it with curiosity, and then wonder. Around 600 BCE, the Greek philosopher, Thales of Miletus believed that the origin of all matter was ultimately down to one essential principle, or element. He said that this element was *water* which could be transformed into all types of matter. A few decades later, Anaximenes (also of Miletus) suggested that *air* was the primary elemental material, while not long after him Heraclitus thought it was *fire*.

The next logical step seemed to be to suggest that maybe all three 'elements' were necessary to make matter. A century and a half after Thales first suggested water as the primary element, another Greek philosopher, Empedocles, did take this logical step, adding *earth* to his elemental mix to give matter some solidity. For Empedocles, these four elements seemed to account for the entire make-up of the world. Earth is a solid. Water is a liquid. Air is a gas. Fire is energy.

Empedocles then went on to argue that everything in the world was made of various combinations and proportions of air, water, earth and fire. These were the four basic elements. They were indestructible. They couldn't be changed. Nothing in the world could be created or destroyed. This meant that nothing fundamentally new could come into being, only the constant reworking and reconfiguring of the four elements as nature endlessly processed them, creating fresh combinations along the way. Plants grow out of the damp earth, die and decay. Wood burns, releasing fire, soot and smoke and leaving behind a residue of ash. From the earth, the green mineral malachite can be heated by fire to release copper. Cows eat grass and produce milk. Empedocles and his theory held sway for the next two thousand years, partly as a result of receiving a boost a century later from the great Classical Greek authority, Aristotle.

Aristotle added further refinements. He said that each of the four elements bore qualities that affected our senses. Matter could be experienced as *hot* or *cold*, *dry* or *wet*. So fire, for example, was both hot and dry. Water was cold and wet. The earth was cold and dry. The air was hot, moist and wet – and, just for good measure, he added a fifth element, *aether*. Aether was a divine element that made up the stars and planets, the realm of the gods.

* * *

It was not until the Middle Ages that the four-element theory began to be questioned. Such was Aristotle's authority, even after two thousand years, that it seemed presumptuous, even heretical, to challenge the great man's ideas. Nevertheless, doubts began to be cast by a new breed of thinkers and experimentalists. These included the alchemists and some very early eighth-century Arabic philosophers.

It might seem ironic that the challenge came from men who thought there was a way of turning base metals into gold, to change, as Milton wrote, the 'drossiest ore to perfect gold'.[1] The alchemist's belief drove them to experiment with matter. They would mix, burn, dissolve, distil, filter any number of materials in their search for the secret of turning lead into gold. However, even as they were failing to make gold, they were learning many things about the material world, its properties and characteristics, how it was made, how it could be combined and how it could be taken apart.

A number of substances known to ancient civilisations we now know to be elements, defined in the modern sense. They were mostly metals, including copper, iron, tin, silver and lead, but the ancients still thought that these metals were composed of some combination of the four classical 'elements'. So, still believing this, the early medieval alchemists began to experiment with many of these metals thinking that by adding things and taking away things, by heat and distillation, they could alter the balance of the metal's natural elemental make-up and turn it into pure gold.

On the face of it, their ideas weren't entirely mistaken. After all, you could heat certain rock types and minerals to release molten metals. Heat the mineral malachite and you get copper. Burn the mineral galena in a crucible and beads of liquid lead appear. Indian, Chinese and Islamic alchemists also believed that there existed a special catalyst that would help pull off the trick of transmuting base metals into gold. Islamic philosophers called this elusive compound *al-iksir*, which translated to *elixir*, a remarkable substance that could not only act as a catalyst, but could also cure diseases and bestow immortality on whoever drank it.

When medieval European alchemists first heard of the astounding properties of the elixir, they also went on a quest to discover it. They began to refer to the purported elixir as 'the philosopher's stone'. The writer Paul Strathern quotes the fourteenth-century Spanish alchemist, Arnold of Villanova, who defined the philosopher's stone as follows: 'There exists in Nature a certain pure substance, which when discovered and brought by Art to its perfect state, will convert to perfection all imperfect bodies that it touches.'[2]

In their search for the stone, alchemists ransacked, pulverised, interrogated and analysed all manner of rocks, minerals, compounds, liquids, substances, plants and powders; and, in doing so, they gradually built a huge knowledge base about the physical world and its chemical properties. A surprising number of the great minds of the age had a go at trying to convert base metals into gold, including Albertus Magnus, Roger Bacon, Paracelsus, Robert Boyle and Isaac Newton.

Of course, they never found the philosopher's stone. It doesn't exist. In the end, all their ennobling efforts proved unsuccessful, but what they did discover along the way were any number of new substances, including sulphuric, nitric and hydrochloric acids, which were corrosive, highly reactive and chemically very interesting. The alchemists were gaining chemical insights and experimental know-how. They learned observational rigour, scientific methods and new ways to think about matter. These were the beginnings of chemistry as a practical science. Most of their efforts were still by trial and error. There was no real understanding of what was actually going on. They lacked any conceptual framework.

* * *

By the seventeenth century, experimentalists were beginning to understand the difference between a mixture and a chemical compound. Adding sugar to salt gives you a mixture. No chemical reaction takes place. No new compound is produced. It's still a mixture of sugar and salt. In contrast, in the Netherlands, the physician and chemist, Franciscus Sylvius recognised that many salts are precipitated when acids and alkalis react. A chemical reaction takes place. If you add hydrochloric acid to the alkali, sodium hydroxide, you get sodium chloride (common salt) and water – two new compounds:

$$HCl + NaOH \rightarrow NaCl + H_2O$$

Salts are not a simple mixture of any two or more chemicals but entirely new substances. They are chemical compounds created out of reactions between acids and alkalis.

Experiment by experiment, alchemy was being left behind and chemistry as we know it today was beginning to take shape – and what the chemists were doing with the elements, the poets, said Jorge Luis Borges, were doing with base words, turning them into literary gold.[3] Under the imaginative gaze of both scientists and artists, nature was yielding more and more of its depths and wonders.

14

The Rise of the Chemist

Robert Boyle was born in 1627.[1] Perhaps he is most famous for his gas law, now known as Boyle's Law, which states that, if the temperature remains constant, a decrease in the volume of a given amount of gas will result in an inversely proportional increase in its pressure. Or, if you pump more gas into a given volume, its pressure will rise. This is what happens when you add more air into your car tyre. However, Boyle's fame also rests on his book, *The Sceptical Chymist*, first published in 1661.[2] Boyle not only dismissed alchemy, but he also took aim at the Aristotelian theory of the four elements. The elements, he argued, are primary particles. Elements are: 'certain primitive and simple, or perfectly unmingled bodies; which not being made of any other bodies, or of one another, are the ingredients of which all those called perfectly mixt bodies are immediately compounded, and into which they are ultimately resolved.'

Boyle went on to say that elements *could* combine to form compounds. Here he was anticipating the idea of molecules in which atoms of one or more types of element bond together. For example, when two hydrogen atoms bond together, we get a molecule of hydrogen (H_2). Combining the two insights, it was possible to make sense of many chemical reactions. For example, when iron is dissolved in a weak solution of sulphuric acid, a pretty blue-green salt of iron sulphate is precipitated, releasing hydrogen in the process. It is then possible to recover the original iron by subjecting the iron sulphate compound to various chemical processes.

However, we have to remember that, at the time, Boyle wasn't entirely sure which substances were truly elemental. Chemical techniques were still being developed. It was still possible that many substances that were thought to be elements were in fact compounds, made up of two or more elements. It would take a few more centuries to establish which substances were and were not true elements.

It was at this point in his own scientific story that Boyle went astray. He thought metals were *not* elements. True, he couldn't break them down into simpler substances, but he thought this was due to a failure of chemical know-how and technique. It would be only a matter of time before chemists, he thought, would discover what the metals themselves were made of. Unfortunately, this gave the alchemists all the ammunition they needed to rebuke Boyle's dismissal of their efforts. If metals were not elements but compounds, then it seemed entirely plausible to believe that maybe lead or copper or tin did contain gold and that they could be coaxed into releasing it. He hadn't yet managed to kill off the dreams of the alchemists and their hopes of getting extremely rich by turning cheap lead into expensive gold.

Nevertheless, Robert Boyle is now seen as one of the founders of modern chemistry and the scientific method. He also helped set up the Royal Society in London. The very first meeting of this 'learned society' took place on 28 November 1660. The meeting was followed by a lecture given by the architect, Christopher Wren. Other leading figures of the day joined Boyle and John Wilkins, an Anglican clergyman and natural philosopher, to found their 'invisible college'. It was not long before the group received royal approval, and from 1663 it became known as 'The Royal Society of London for Improving Natural Knowledge' before its eventual abbreviation to the Royal Society, the oldest scientific society in the world. Its motto is *Nullius in verba*, translated as 'take nobody's word for it'. Facts not beliefs.

* * *

Up until this point, only around a dozen substances were known to be likely candidates for being elements, including sulphur and gold, iron and lead. However, as chemists began to get into their experimental stride, many more were about to be discovered.

Born around 1630, Hennig Brand lived and worked in Hamburg. He was a merchant and perhaps one of the last people to have a serious interest in alchemy. Like so many before him, he was on a search to find the philosopher's stone. Human urine was yellow; gold was yellow: therefore, he reasoned, perhaps if he experimented with urine, he might find gold, or at least the elusive ingredient that could turn base metals into gold. He collected fifty buckets of pee and left them to evaporate. The stench in his laboratory must have been overwhelming.

The evaporation left him with a thick, syrupy residue. He then subjected this to a series of elaborate chemical processes which eventually left him with a distillate which he collected in a beaker containing cold water. What he had produced was a transparent waxy substance. When he removed it from the water, it glowed in the dark. In air it was prone to ignite spontaneously, giving off dense, white fumes. He named his substance *phosphorus* from the Greek *phos* (light) and *phorus* (bringing). It wasn't gold, but it was a new substance that had remarkable properties.

Five thousand five hundred litres of urine had yielded just 120 grams of the element phosphorus. What Brand hadn't realised was that, if he had kept more of the residue rather than discard it, his yield would have been much greater. Nevertheless, however inefficient this first effort proved to be, he had discovered phosphorus. Modern analyses show that one litre of human urine contains about 1.4 grams of phosphorus salts, which amounts to around 0.11 grams of pure white phosphorus. Even though phosphorus doesn't occur in its isolated state in nature, it plays a key part in organic life and it would only be a matter of time before phosphorus and its compounds would be used to make matches, fertilisers, and be added to foods.

As the eighteenth century progressed, more new elements were found. Swedish scientists, including Carl Wilhelm Scheele, were often at the forefront of these discoveries. Scientists across the continent were finding more and more new substances that had the potential to be identified as elements including cobalt, molybdenum, manganese, platinum and tungsten. The gases hydrogen, oxygen, chlorine and nitrogen were also discovered and isolated.

* * *

Claims about who actually discovered an element first are often not straightforward. A chemist might have produced and described a new substance without realising that it was a new element. For example, Scheele had produced oxygen in 1771, but didn't publish his results. In 1774, the Yorkshire chemist, Joseph Priestley prepared what in fact turned out to be oxygen by focussing the sun's rays on mercuric oxide but he called the gas released 'new air' or 'dephlogisticated air'. It was the French scientist, Antoine Lavoisier, three years later, who prepared his own oxygen and he was the first to recognise that the gas was a new substance, an element in its own right. He named it oxygen.

However, of the many scientific understandings and breakthroughs achieved by Lavoisier, perhaps his lasting legacy was to tidy up the way we named the elements and, in turn, name their compounds. We have already seen how developing a universally agreed language for naming natural phenomena gave a boost to biology, meteorology and geology. Linnaeus had paved the way with his 1735 publication, *Systema Naturae*. Using Latin as the scientific *lingua franca*, he developed a binomial system for naming plants. Luke Howard adapted the idea when he named his clouds. In similar fashion, Lavoisier came up with his own scheme for naming chemical compounds after the elements of which they were composed.

In 1787, along with a number of colleagues, he published *Méthode de nomenclature chimique* ('Method of Chemical Nomenclature'), in which he explained his system and its rational underpinnings. For example, hydrochloric acid was a compound of hydrogen and chlorine. Lead oxide was a compound of lead and oxygen. Common salt is sodium chloride.

For chemists at least, there was no longer any need to call a particular compound by its local name which might not mean anything to another chemist working in a different country, in a different tradition. So, no longer 'vitriol of Venus' but copper sulphate; sulphuric acid and not 'oil of vitriol': Lavoisier's new naming system quickly caught on and remains the basis of chemical nomenclature to this day.

In his later book, *Traité élémentaire de chimie* ('Elementary Treatise on Chemistry'), published in 1789, Lavoisier offered his own definition of an element, which was not very different to that made by Robert Boyle 128 years earlier. Lavoisier states that, if a body is subjected to a process of systematic analysis and it finally proves impossible to decompose it any further into two or more simpler bodies, then that body probably is an element. As a good scientist though, he did add that even then there was always the possibility that new techniques and future chemists might reveal the body to be composed of two or more substances, in which case it would be a compound and not an element.

With this proviso, in his book Lavoisier drew up a list of 33 substances which he believed to be true elements. In the event, eight of these proved to be compounds, including 'lime' and 'magnesia', and two were just plain wrong. Lavoisier thought that 'light' and 'caloric' (heat) were elements. Later, scientists would identify them as forms of energy. Nevertheless, given that chemistry was only just getting going as a science, this was a remarkable achievement by the French scientist.

Unfortunately for Lavoisier, 1789 was also the year of the French Revolution. It was his fate to have had too many links to the hated *Ancien Régime* of Louis XVI, including collecting taxes on the king's behalf. For a while he managed to keep on the right side of the new republic, but as the revolutionary Terror got into full swing, and in spite of his reputation as a scientist of international distinction, he was tried for defrauding the state and watering down tobacco. He was found guilty and guillotined on 8 May 1794, aged fifty.

A further 49 elements would be discovered over the course of the nineteenth century, beginning with vanadium in 1801 and finishing with two radioactive elements – radium, discovered by Marie and Pierre Curie in 1898, and the gas radon, first observed by, amongst others, Ernest Rutherford in 1899. Leading the way in the century's chemical charge was a young Cornishman, Humphry Davy.

15

In Their Element

One of the most successful scientists of the nineteenth century to prepare and isolate new elements was the English chemist, Humphry Davy. We first met Davy at the beginning of this book when he was climbing Helvellyn in the company of William Wordsworth, Robert Southey and Walter Scott. The year was 1805.

Davy was born in Cornwall on 17 December 1778. He was educated at his local grammar school in Penzance. As well as an interest in science, he also wrote poems. Davy's early poems gave strong hints that the sixteen year-old clearly had scientific ambitions. In the poem 'The Sons of Genius' he aspired:

> To scan the laws of Nature, to explore
> The tranquil reign of mild Philosophy;
> Or on Newtonian wings sublime to soar
> Through the bright regions of the starry sky.
>
> To teach, on rapid wings, the curious soul
> To roam from heaven to heaven, from pole to pole,
> From thence to search the mystic cause of things
> And follow Nature in her sacred springs.[1]

And scan the laws of nature he did. In 1800, Davy was recommended to William Wordsworth by his friend Samuel Taylor Coleridge to proof-read their anthology *Lyrical Ballads*.[2] Davy first met Coleridge and another poet, Robert Southey, when he was living in Bristol.

In 1798 he had taken a job working for Dr Thomas Beddoes at the Pneumatic Medical Institute. The institute was experimenting with various gases including nitrous oxide, better known as laughing gas, still used in anaesthetics today. All three friends had inhaled the gas. They obviously enjoyed the experience. Southey wrote to his brother saying:

> O Tom! Such a gas has Davy discovered, the gaseous oxide. Oh, Tom! I have had some; it made me laugh and tingle in every toe and finger tip. Davy has actually invented a new pleasure, for which language has no name. Oh, Tom! I am going for more this evening. It makes one strong and happy! So gloriously happy![3]

Although there was clearly fun to be had with nitrous oxide, Davy was establishing himself as a competent research chemist. In 1799 a number of leading scientists founded the Royal Institution. It was housed in grand premises at 21 Albemarle Street, Mayfair, London. It was to be an organisation devoted to scientific education and research. In 1801 Davy was invited by the founders to join the institution. He was appointed as an assistant lecturer in chemistry, director of the chemical laboratory and assistant editor of the journals to be published by the institution. He had his own room, 'furnished with coals and candles', and was paid a salary of £100 per annum. So successful were Davy's lectures that at the age of 23 he was appointed to be a full lecturer. He became a Fellow of the Royal Society in 1804 and in 1807 he helped found the Geological Society.

As well as his highly popular lectures, many of them attended by his friend, the poet Coleridge, Davy was cementing his reputation as a brilliant chemist. He pioneered new techniques including the use of electricity to split compounds into their constituent elements. The process was known as electrolysis.

It was his expertise as an electrochemist that helped him discover and isolate many new elements, including potassium (1807), sodium (1807) and calcium (1808). Although not the first to produce some elements, he was the first to recognise and isolate them. These included magnesium (1808), barium (1808), boron (1808) and strontium (1808). In 1808 Humphry Davy tried but failed to decompose aluminium oxide (alumina) in an attempt to isolate an element that he and Antoine Lavoisier predicted to exist. Davy named the suspected element 'aluminium' but it would be the Danish chemist Hans Christian Ørsted who would be the first to isolate metallic aluminium in 1825.

Although these days many people best remember Davy as the inventor of the miner's 'safety lamp', his discovery and isolation of so many elements remains astonishing. Edmund Clerihew Bentley thought so too. Bentley was an English novelist and humourist. He invented the 'clerihew', an irregular form of humorous verse on biographical topics. In 1905 he penned this frequently quoted clerihew about Davy:

Sir Humphry Davy
Abominated gravy.
He lived in the odium
Of having discovered sodium

Davy's experiments with chemicals and gases meant that he often found himself working in environments that were noxious, even poisonous. By his late forties his health was beginning to fail. In 1827 he left for continental Europe in the hope that the change of air and scenery would do him some good. He returned briefly to England but was soon back in Rome where he described himself as 'a ruin amongst ruins'. He had been partly paralyzed by a stroke but carried on writing.

Published posthumously in 1830, *Consolations in Travel, or the Last Days of a Philosopher* was an odd mix of poetry, autobiographical sketches, descriptions of dreams, and philosophical musings on the afterlife. In February 1829 he suffered another stroke. Sir Humphry Davy died in his hotel room in Geneva, Switzerland, on 29 May 1829, aged only 50.[4] He is buried in the Cimetière des Rois, Geneva where he finds himself in highly distinguished company. Also buried in the cemetery are the Protestant reformer, John Calvin, the Argentinian author, Jorge Luis Borges and the French child psychologist, Jean Piaget.

* * *

As well as Davy's 1805 ascent of Helvellyn in the company of Wordsworth, Southey and Scott, Chapter 1 also made mention of another chemist and Helvellyn enthusiast, the Quaker John Dalton who was twelve years older than Davy.

Although Dalton and Davy never met on their respective visits to the Lake District, they were familiar with each other's work, although not always in agreement. By the time Davy was at the Royal

Institution, Dalton was already recognised as a leading figure in the world of chemistry. He was based in Manchester where he lived, experimented and lectured for all of his adult career.

In 1803 Dalton was chosen to give a series of lectures at the Royal Institution. He delivered a second series of lectures in 1809-10. Dalton, born and bred in Cumberland, retained his local accent. Some attendees described his London lectures as being a bit dull, indistinct and hard to follow. However, it was for his scientific achievements that Davy suggested in 1810 that Dalton put himself forward as a candidate to become a fellow of the Royal Society. Dalton declined, possibly for financial reasons. However, a few years later in 1822, and without Dalton's knowledge, a proposal was made on his behalf. This time Dalton, a modest, retiring man, with regular habits and daily routines, accepted the honour.

Dalton enters our story of the elements as the scientist who proposed the atomic theory of chemistry.[5] The theory explicitly recognised the atomic and elemental nature of matter. It was his early insights that helped lay the foundations of the Periodic Table of the chemical elements which we shall come to in the next chapter.

Modern-day definitions of the atom describe it as the smallest constituent of matter. Each element – whether hydrogen or sodium, carbon or gold – is made of atoms each of which have chemical and physical properties characteristic of that element. Dalton called atoms 'ultimate particles'. He suggested that each atom of a particular element had its own unique size, atomic weight and other defining properties. Atoms of different elements therefore differ from each other in size, mass, physical and chemical properties. What Dalton was proposing was revolutionary: that an atomic theory should form the basis of chemistry. He wanted to impose order on the increasingly populated world of the elements.

On 21 October 1803 Dalton read a paper to the Manchester Literary and Philosophical Society. It was on this occasion that he first made the original suggestion that each element has its own defining properties, including a unique atomic weight. He said that all atoms of the same element are identical and can combine with other elements to form compounds. A few years later, in 1808, he published his book, *A New System of Chemical Philosophy (Part I)*, followed a couple of years later by *Part II*. These volumes were the first application of atomic theory to chemistry. They were groundbreaking. His work on the atomic theory of chemistry made him world famous, certainly among fellow scientists.

Dalton, following Lavoisier, also proposed that chemical compounds are combinations of two or more different types of atom. However, when different atoms combine, they do so in the same proportions, no matter how they are composed. For example, the solid metal sodium (Na) and the gas chlorine (Cl) can combine to form sodium chloride (NaCl) or common salt. The proportions of sodium and chlorine in the compound are always the same, however manufactured. One atom of sodium for every one atom of chlorine.

Thus, Dalton was able to say that, when atoms of different elements combine to make a particular compound they do so in simple, whole number ratios. Therefore, all chemical reactions are just re-arrangements of atoms in fixed whole number ratios forming new chemical compounds. When two atoms of hydrogen combine with one of oxygen, we get water whose chemical formula is, of course, H_2O. When two oxygen atoms combine with one of carbon, the result is carbon dioxide (CO_2); and in the case of Davy's laughing gas, nitrous oxide, it is two atoms of nitrogen and one of oxygen (N_2O).

Dalton's understanding of atoms, compounds and their reactions fundamentally changed the way we think about chemistry. When chemists grasped his ideas of chemical atomic theory, not only did it help them make sense of what happens when different substances combine, re-combine or separate, but it also opened up the possibility of making many more new compounds and substances. The emerging chemical and pharmaceutical industries now had a clear scientific logic to support their activities.

Having established that individual atoms of each of the elements had a particular weight relative to the atoms of other elements, the next logical step was to create a list of the elements starting with those with the lightest atomic weight and progressively work up to those with heavier atomic weights. Hydrogen was known to be the lightest element so an atom of hydrogen was given the notional atomic weight of 1. The atomic weight of all subsequent elements could therefore be calculated relative to hydrogen.

Dalton chose water as an example. He knew it was a compound of hydrogen and oxygen with the weights of the two elements present in the proportion of 1 to 8. He therefore assigned oxygen an atomic weight of 8. What Dalton didn't know at the time was that water in fact is made up of two atoms of hydrogen and only one of oxygen (H_2O), therefore oxygen should be given an atomic weight of 16. Later discoveries of atomic isotopes would lead to even more refined ways of assigning atomic weights to each element and its isotopes. Nevertheless, the underlying logic of organising and classifying the elements by their atomic weights was sound. A potential method of achieving order in the otherwise seemingly random world of the elements had been introduced.

Dalton died in 1844, aged 77, fifteen years after Davy's own death. Forty-thousand people lined the streets of Manchester to pay their respects as Dalton's funeral cortege made its way to the cemetery, such was his fame and scientific standing.

* * *

The various pieces of the elemental jigsaw were beginning to come together. New elements continued to be discovered. The great Swedish chemist, Jöns Jacob Berzelius was born only a year after Humphry Davy in 1779. Like Davy, Berzelius was a pioneer of chemical electrolysis. He, too, discovered and isolated a number of new elements including cerium and selenium. He also isolated the elements silicon and thorium.

As we noted in Chapter 14, Antoine Lavoisier had introduced a universally agreed system for naming the elements. Berzelius took this a step further. He developed a system of chemical notation in which each element was given a simple label. So, for example, we have H for hydrogen, O for oxygen and N for nitrogen. Other notations appealed to an element's Latin nomenclature: Fe (*ferrum*) for iron, Au (*aurum*) for gold, and Pb (*plumbum*) for lead.

It then became straightforward to represent the proportions of each element in any molecule or compound. In order to do this, Berzelius added the number of atoms of the element present as a superscript. However, the superscript notation was soon abandoned in favour of a subscript. Water is two parts hydrogen to one part of oxygen, hence H_2O. Copper sulphate is a compound of copper (Cu), sulphur (S) and oxygen (O) in the proportions of 1:1:4, hence $CuSO_4$. This system of chemical notation is the one we use today.

This mathematical way of representing molecules and compounds could also be used to predict and represent what new compounds could appear as a result of a chemical reaction in the form of a *chemical equation*. For example, if we burn the gas methane (CH_4)

in the oxygen (O_2) of the air, we get carbon dioxide (CO_2) and water (H_2O) represented by the equation:

$$CH_4 + 2O_2 \rightarrow CO_2 + 2H_2O$$

Methane is the main constituent of natural gas. Burning natural gas produces huge quantities of the greenhouse gas, carbon dioxide, hence the worries about its continued use to heat homes, fire blast furnaces and power cement kilns.

* * *

By the middle of the nineteenth century, upwards of 50 elements had been discovered. Their atomic weights were known, some being very light such as hydrogen and some very heavy such as gold. However, there was still a strong feeling that there must be some kind of underlying logic to this increasingly busy and heavily populated world of the natural elements. A pattern or order of some kind must surely be there. But what was it? And how many more elements might be discovered?

So, what could be done with what was known? Well, you could list the elements in order of their increasing atomic weights as proposed by Dalton. Or you might divide them into metals and non-metals. Some metals resisted corrosion (gold, platinum), while others were highly reactive (sodium, potassium). There were gases, liquids and solids. Surely it was possible to find some pattern that lay behind and accounted for these various properties?

Bromine had been discovered in 1825. At room temperature it is a fuming, red-brown liquid. The German chemist, Johann Wolfgang Döbereiner noticed that it had physical and chemical properties half way between those of the greeny-yellow gas chlorine and the solid iodine.[6] Moreover, bromine's atomic weight also lay half way between those of chlorine and iodine. He saw a similar pattern between calcium, strontium and barium. All three had similar properties and strontium, in the middle, had an atomic weight half way between the other two. He called these groups of three similar and related elements 'triads'. Many of his fellow chemists dismissed the so-called triadic patterns as mere coincidences.

The next to have a go at arranging the elements into some kind of order was the French geologist, Alexandre-Émile Béguyer de Chancourtois.[7] In his 1862 paper, he observed that similar elements with similar properties seemed to show a regular pattern in the way their atomic weights increased. Once again, however, the chemists of his day largely ignored his work.

In 1864, the young English chemist, John Newlands came up with his own pattern of arranging the elements.[8] Like the others, he sorted the elements according to their atomic weights with those having similar properties appearing along the same line. The result was a table of seven rows in which there were eight elements, each with similar chemical properties and increasing atomic weight. Newlands said the arrangement was rather like the way musical notes repeated themselves every eight notes as the pitch increased. He therefore called his own system 'the Law of Octaves'. Few people took his ideas seriously. Again, the apparent pattern was dismissed as just a coincidence.

Yet there was the nagging feeling that something interesting was going on in this elemental zoo. Increasing atomic weights, similar chemical properties, the hint of some kind of order – all the ingredients were there. Surely something deeper and more fundamental lay beneath this elemental profusion? Chemists were just waiting for someone inspired to make sense of it all.

16

The Periodic Table

Dmitri Ivanovich Mendeleev was born on 8 February 1834 in Tobolsk, western Siberia, over a thousand miles east of Moscow.[1,2] In 1847, Mendeleev's father died and, two years later, his enterprising mother decided to head west to Moscow with Dmitri and her other two remaining dependent children. She recognised Dmitri's burgeoning brilliance and was determined to get him the best education possible. However, Russian bureaucracy and the Moscow University quota system denied Dmitri any of the available places. So, once again, the family went west, to St Petersburg. Again, there was red tape and problems. It was only a personal connection of his mother that finally saw Mendeleev enter the Central Pedagogical Institute to study mathematics and natural science. The year was 1850 and Dmitri was sixteen years old.

Ten weeks after he began his studies, his mother died, aged only 57. Mendeleev records that her dying words to him were: 'Refrain from illusions, insist on work and not words. Patiently seek divine and scientific truth', words he said he took to heart and never forgot.

In 1855, not long after he had graduated, Mendeleev caught tuberculosis. For health reasons, he decided to move to the Crimean peninsula on the northern shores of the Black Sea. Two years later, with his health improved, he returned to St Petersburg and the Institute. He soon established himself as an original and talented chemist, although he was not always the easiest person with whom to work. He had a gift for seeing order and patterns, and making sense of complex observations.

Between 1859 and 1861 he joined the prestigious University of Heidelberg as a doctoral student working with the celebrated German chemist, Robert Bunsen, inventor of the bunsen burner. However, Mendeleev fell out with Bunsen and returned to St Petersburg to take up a post at the St Petersburg Technological Institute. Then, at the age of 32, he was appointed professor of general chemistry at the St Petersburg State University, receiving full tenure in 1867. Over the next few years he established St Petersburg as an internationally recognized centre for chemistry research.

* * *

In 1869, while he was writing the second volume of his highly successful book, *The Principles of Chemistry*,[3] he began to realise that he needed to discover some logic in the way he was presenting his descriptions of the elements and their properties.

As others before him had suspected, he felt the key to the order of the elements lay in understanding the relationship between ascending atomic weights and elements that possessed similar chemical properties; but what was this link? He began to scribble possible ideas on the back of a letter he'd received in that morning's post. He became obsessed with the problem. A friend reported that he worked almost non-stop for the next three days and nights trying to figure out a pattern.

His next step was to write out on separate cards the names of each known element, adding their atomic weight and chemical properties. Mendeleev was fond of playing the card game, Patience. He noticed the similarity between the way one had to place the card of each suit in four columns of descending value and the fact that elements with similar properties could be placed in groups with ascending and descending atomic weights. Maybe this was a way to think about ordering the elements? He called his efforts 'a game of chemical patience'.

By this stage he was exhausted. He had to sleep and, famously, he had a dream.

In his dream, Mendeleev was later to say, he saw that, when the elements were laid out in order of their atomic weights, their properties repeated in a series of regular *periodic* intervals. A strong pattern began to emerge. He named his discovery the Periodic Table of the Elements. Two weeks later he published his landmark 1869 paper outlining his discovery. He titled it 'A Suggested System of the Elements'.

Unlike modern presentations of the table, in which elements with similar properties are arranged in vertical columns, Mendeleev laid them out horizontally. So, for example, in one row, running from left to right in order of increasing atomic weight but with similar chemical properties he had the halogens: fluorine, chlorine, bromine and iodine. Notwithstanding the horizontal orientation, the organising principle was sound.

In 1869 there were 64 known elements; and this is where Mendeleev showed both his genius and confidence. There were gaps in his pattern. There were no known elements that possessed the right atomic weight or chemical properties to fit into the gaps. In a bold move, Mendeleev predicted that one day future chemists would discover elements that would slot into the table's missing cells. Moreover, he predicted their atomic weights and chemical properties.

Specifically, Mendeleev predicted that elements would be found with atomic weights and chemical properties intermediate between aluminium and uranium in one case, and between silicon and tin in another. Critics at the time felt that there were just too many gaps in the table for his 'law' to be credible.

However, support for the Periodic Table slowly began to grow. The scientist Julius Lothar Meyer,[4] who had also worked with Robert Bunsen, published papers and books in which he tentatively proposed a similar table to that designed by Mendeleev. The publication dates of Meyer's key tables postdated that of Mendeleev's 1869 paper by a year or two and, as is the custom in science, Mendeleev gets recognition as the one who first came up with the idea of a Periodic Table of the Elements. In 1882 both men later received the Davy Medal from the Royal Society of London in recognition of their work on the Periodic Law.

And what of Mendeleev's predictions? For the first few years after the table's publication, no new elements were discovered. Doubts began to grow about the plausibility of the table's arrangement of the elements. Then in 1875 the Académie des sciences in Paris announced that it had received a letter from the French chemist, Paul-Émile Lecoq de Boisbaudran.[5] He wrote that he had discovered a new silvery, white metal similar to aluminium in a sample of the mineral zinc sulphide, known as sphalerite. He named the element *gallium*, possibly in honour of France, which the Romans called Gallia, or maybe as a vain, mischievous nod to his own name, Lecoq, the Latin for cockerel being *gallus*. This new element had an atomic weight of 69 and chemical properties mid-way between aluminium and uranium, just as Mendeleev had predicted.

The Periodic Table of Elements

H 1																	He 2
Li 3	Be 4											B 5	C 6	N 7	O 8	F 9	Ne 10
Na 11	Mg 12											Al 13	Si 14	P 15	S 16	Cl 17	Ar 18
K 19	Ca 20	Sc 21	Ti 22	V 23	Cr 24	Mn 25	Fe 26	Co 27	Ni 28	Cu 29	Zn 30	Ga 31	Ge 32	As 33	Se 34	Br 35	Kr 36
Rb 37	Sr 38	Y 39	Zr 40	Nb 41	Mo 42	Tc 43	Ru 44	Rh 45	Pd 46	Ag 47	Cd 48	In 49	Sn 50	Sb 51	Te 52	I 53	Xe 54
Cs 55	Ba 56	La* 57	Hf 72	Ta 73	W 74	Re 75	Os 76	Ir 77	Pt 78	Au 79	Hg 80	Tl 81	Pb 82	Bi 83	Po 84	At 85	Rn 86
Fr 87	Ra 88	Ac** 89	Rf 104	Db 105	Sg 106	Bh 107	Hs 108	Mt 109	Ds 110	Rg 111	Cn 112	Nh 113	Fl 114	Mc 115	Lv 116	Ts 117	Og 118

*	Ce 58	Pr 59	Nd 60	Pm 61	Sm 62	Eu 63	Gd 64	Tb 65	Dy 66	Ho 67	Er 68	Tm 69	Yb 70	Lu 71
**	Th 90	Pa 91	U 92	Np 93	Pu 94	Am 95	Cm 96	Bk 97	Cf 98	Es 99	Fm 100	Md 101	No 102	Lr 103

*La (57) – Lu (71) The lanthanides are often called the rare earth elements. They actually sit in the sixth period between barium and hafnium. They are usually shown as a separate row below the rest of the periodic table to make it easier to display the whole table.

** Ac (89) – Lr (103) The actinides actually sit in the seventh period between radium and rutherfordium. They are usually shown as a separate row below the rest of the periodic table to make it easier to display the whole table. The actinides include plutonium.

For an excellent, colour-coded, interactive version of the Periodic Table visit The Royal Society of Chemistry webpage: https://www.rsc.org/periodic-table.

A few more years went by. Then in 1886, the German chemist Clemens Winkler[6] was analysing a mineral collected from a mine near Freiberg when he discovered another new, silvery white, brittle, semi-metallic element. Patriotically, he named it *germanium* and, just as Mendeleev predicted, it had an atomic weight and chemical properties that lay between silicon and tin. The Periodic Table was vindicated and Mendeleev's brilliance and reputation sealed. 'Mendeleev had classified the building blocks of the universe', wrote Paul Strathern in his book, *Mendeleev's Dream*, and with that the Russian's genius heralded a new era of science.

Today we know all 92 of the naturally occurring elements. A further fifteen elements have been synthesised in high-energy physics laboratories. They all fit logically and periodically into the modern rendition of the table. In 1955 at the Berkeley Radiation Laboratory, California, a team of scientists produced element 101, a metallic radioactive element. It was given the name 'mendelevium' in recognition of the Russian chemist's pioneering genius. Mendeleev died of influenza in 1907 in St Petersburg, aged 72.

* * *

What nineteenth century chemists didn't know, including Mendeleev, was that the atoms of each element had a nucleus, and in that nucleus would be a defining, fixed number of sub-atomic particles with a positive electric charge known as *protons*.

Hydrogen, the lightest element has just one proton in its nucleus. It is therefore given the atomic number 1. The next element in the sequence is the gas helium and it has 2 protons in its nucleus. It therefore has the atomic number 2 and so on in an ascending, straightforward numerical sequence until we reach the heaviest naturally occurring element, uranium with a massive 92 protons in its nucleus and a corresponding atomic number of 92. Modern Periodic Tables arrange the elements in horizontal rows of rising atomic numbers, with elements in any one vertical column having similar chemical properties.

The visual appearance of the modern, colour-coded Periodic Table is a beautiful thing. The logic of its order and the principles that underlie its design are truly wonderful. When read horizontally there is an orderly progression by atomic number. When read vertically the elements are seen to share similar chemical properties. The halogens (fluorine, chlorine, bromine, iodine, astatine) occupy one vertical column, the inert gases (helium, neon, argon, krypton, xenon, radon) another. There is a column in which copper, silver and gold appear, and another in which the more reactive metals of sodium, potassium, rubidium and caesium are found. The table's logic helps us to understand why each element has the properties and chemical characteristics that it does and why it is similar, but not quite the same as those above and below it in each of the table's columns.

Celebrating the Periodic Table's 150th anniversary in 2019, Eric Scerri wrote:

> The periodic table has come a long way since it was first introduced some 150 years ago. It has seen off several challenges. … It continues to challenge theoreticians and to evolve into increasingly comprehensive forms. Most of all, it has succeeded in unifying all the chemical elements, and their periodic relationships, into one iconic infographic that is without parallel in the whole of science.[7]

Moreover, it's not only chemists who gaze at the table in awe. The Periodic Table regularly crops up in popular culture.

In 1959 the American singer, humourist and mathematician, Tom Lehrer, wrote *The Elements*, a song in which he named all 102 then-known elements, though not in table order. He sang it at breakneck speed to the tune of the 'Major-General's Song' from Gilbert and Sullivan's comic opera, *The Pirates of Penzance*.

The table's iconic status has appealed to artists, musicians and writers alike who have interpreted it visually, musically and poetically. Primo Levi was an Italian chemist, poet and writer. In 1975 he published a book titled, *The Periodic Table*.[8] The Royal Society gave the work a glowing review although it isn't a science book in any conventional sense. The book is a collection of twenty-one meditations, each one inspired by a particular chemical element, each one a reflection on the human condition, each one based on Levi's own experiences and remarkable life story. The elements he considers range from argon to mercury, zinc to sulphur.

When he was sixteen years old, Levi and a friend electrolysed water to produce hydrogen. They ignited the hydrogen collected. It exploded in the jar with a sharp, angry report, shattering the glass. Levi concluded his encounter with hydrogen saying:

> We left, discussing what had occurred. My legs were shaking a bit; I experienced retrospective fear and at the same time a kind of foolish pride, at having confirmed a hypothesis and having unleashed a force of nature. It was indeed hydrogen, therefore: the same element that burns in the sun and stars, and from whose condensation the universes are formed in eternal silence.[9]

The final chapter of his book considers carbon, the element of life. Whereas other elements say something personal to every individual, carbon 'says everything to everyone'. Levi follows the story of just one carbon atom over millions of years as it courses through the animal, vegetable and mineral kingdoms.

Levi's story begins with the carbon atom bound up in a molecule of calcium carbonate, itself a tiny component of a limestone (calcium carbonate) rock outcrop 'congealed in an eternal present'. The rock is quarried and roasted in a lime kiln where this particular atom escapes with two oxygen atoms into the atmosphere as a molecule of carbon dioxide. It is inhaled by a falcon, but immediately exhaled. For eight years it blows in the winds, high and low. In 1848 the carbon dioxide molecule is captured by a vine leaf where it becomes 'nailed by a ray of the sun' by that miracle of nature, photosynthesis, and enters 'the chain of life'. Our carbon atom becomes involved in a series of complex organic processes before ending up as part of a glucose molecule in a ripening grape. The grape is harvested and turned into wine. The wine is drunk and the carbon atom eventually ends up in the liver of the wine drinker. From there to a muscle, from the muscle to the blood stream, to the lungs where it gets oxidised once more before finally being exhaled as a new molecule of carbon dioxide and returned to the atmosphere. Years later the carbon atom once more gets absorbed and becomes part of the cellulose of the trunk of a cedar tree. Some years later the cellulose, with our atom of carbon, gets eaten by the pupa of a moth which emerges the following spring. The moth dies, and its carapace decays, becomes part of the humus of the soil, oxidises once more and takes to the skies in its third incarnation as yet another molecule of carbon dioxide. Photosynthesis once again captures our atom of carbon in a blade of grass. The grass is eaten by a cow, the cow is milked, and the milk with our carbon molecule in its chemistry is drunk by our author, ingested, absorbed, transported, and ends up in Levi's brain as part of a nerve cell:

> The cell belongs to a brain, and it is my brain, the brain of the me who is writing; and the cell in question, and within it the atom in question, is in charge of my writing, in a gigantic miniscule game which nobody has yet described. It is that which at this instant, issuing out of a labyrinthine tangle of yeses and nos, makes my hand run along a certain path on the paper, mark it with these volutes that are signs: a double snap, up and down, between two levels of energy, guides this hand of mine to impress on the paper this dot, this one.[10]

And on that dot the book ends.

17

Sentient Stardust

Throughout the nineteenth century, many chemists and physicists assumed that elements were composed of atoms, but no one had actually seen an atom or unequivocally proven their existence or had a clue what they might look like. The idea of an atom helped make sense of the elements and their periodicity, the idea of molecules and compounds, and what was going on in chemical reactions. Nonetheless, a few scientists were still not convinced and debates continued until the 1890s.

Several ancient civilisations, including the Greeks and Indians, believed that matter was discontinuous, which is to say that it is made up of extremely tiny, individual, indivisible particles. It wasn't until 1803 that John Dalton attempted a more scientific definition: everything is composed of atoms. They're the indivisible building blocks of matter and cannot be destroyed. All atoms of a particular element are identical. The atoms of different elements vary in size and mass. A chemical reaction results in the rearrangement of atoms in the reactant and product compounds.

In 1827 the Scottish botanist, Robert Brown had observed under the microscope that tiny grains of pollen in water were in constant motion. They jiggled and danced about randomly. He repeated the experiment with fine rock dust and water. Again, he saw the restless, ceaseless jiggle of the particles. In recognition of the Scotsman's findings, the random movement of any microscopic grain in a liquid became known as Brownian motion.

The observation hinted strongly at the presence of atoms, but it would take Albert Einstein in his famous 1905 paper, 'On the Movement of Small Particles Suspended in Stationary Liquids Required by the Molecular-Kinetic Theory of Heat', to show mathematically that the particles were in restless, random motion because they were constantly crashing into millions of even tinier jiggling molecules of water, and these water molecules were made of atoms. Over the next few years, conclusive experimental evidence supporting Einstein's theory of Brownian motion became so compelling that the existence of atoms was now beyond doubt.

The physicist J.J. Thomson was also in no doubt that atoms existed.[1] In 1897 he discovered that the atom itself appeared to be made up of even smaller sub-atomic particles. In particular, he discovered the negatively charged *electron*, for which, nine years later in 1906 he was awarded a Nobel Prize. In later years, it was realised that the chemical characteristics of an element are related to the number and arrangement of electrons in the atom. By 1908, further experimental observations backed by calculations irrefutably confirmed that atoms were real. Within a decade, physicists went even further. By pulling apart individual atoms they began to get a sense that they too had an internal structure made up of even smaller sub-atomic particles just as Thompson had suspected.

* * *

The first couple of decades of the twentieth century ushered in a series of revolutionary changes in the way atoms were structured and understood. First, we must remember that atoms and molecules are very, very small. At normal room temperature and pressure just one cubic centimetre of air contains trillions of molecules.

Ernest Rutherford was a physicist and a New Zealander working with Thompson at the University of Cambridge.[2] He found that at the centre of the atom was a tiny nucleus that held a positive charge. A model of the atom began to emerge in which a small, positively charged nucleus of protons was surrounded by one or more electrons. Like all elementary particles, electrons behave as both particles and waves. It is the exchange and sharing of electrons between two or more atoms that gives rise to chemical reactions and bonds. This provides an understanding of chemical reactions at the atomic level. The nucleus of an atom contains nearly all of its mass. The mass of an electron is a mere 1/1836 that of a proton. For his work, Rutherford received a Nobel prize in 1908. He has become known as the 'father of nuclear physics'.

Rutherford's work confirmed the finding that an element's atomic number corresponded to the number of protons in its nucleus. This in turn governed its place in the Periodic Table. However, this didn't explain the difference between an element's atomic number and its atomic weight.

Further work at the sub-atomic level revealed that as well as protons, the nuclei of atoms also contain electrically neutral particles known as neutrons (with the exception of hydrogen's most common isotope which has just one proton and no neutrons in its nucleus). A neutron has a mass very similar to that of a proton. Thus, the atomic mass (as opposed to atomic number) of an element is the sum of the mass of its protons and neutrons. For example, the most abundant form of oxygen has eight protons and eight neutrons in its nucleus. Its atomic mass is approximately 16, bearing in mind that the mass of a neutron is very slightly greater than that of a proton. Iron has 26 protons and 30 neutrons in its nucleus. Its atomic number is therefore 26 and its atomic mass is approximately 56.

When you look at a modern colour-coded Periodic Table, the whole story of the elements, their atomic weights, atomic masses, atomic numbers and chemical properties is there to read in all its beauty.

We won't follow developments much further except to say that Einstein's papers on the equivalence of mass and energy ($E = mc^2$) and Neils Bohr's introduction of the strange world of quantum mechanics revealed a subatomic universe even stranger than anyone dared imagine.[3,4] Trying to make sense of atoms and light, matter and energy, gravity and galaxies, quarks and quasers, nuclear fusion and nuclear fission suddenly became even more exciting, even more daunting, even more extraordinary. The quantum world turned out to be downright weird and, as Bohr himself is reported to have said, 'Those who are not shocked when they first come across quantum theory cannot possibly have understood it.'[5]

* * *

There is just one more set of questions to ask about the elements, the answers to which take us neatly back to where we began this journey, up amongst the stars. Where do the elements come from? What are their origins? How are they created? To answer these questions, we need to go right back to the very beginning: the Big Bang.[6]

Cosmologists believe that, if we extrapolate backwards, there was a time about 13.8 billion years ago when all the matter and energy in the universe – planets, stars, galaxies – was concentrated at a single point. For reasons that are still being theorised and debated, this singular point suddenly expanded in what the astronomer Fred Hoyle, never a fan of the idea, mockingly described as a 'big bang'.

After a fluctuation in the void, within billionths of a second there followed an initial phase of cosmic super-inflation – the 'big bang' – followed by a relative cooling of the primordial plasma, then the first sub-atomic particles began to appear. Within the next three minutes the phase dubbed Big Bang nucleosynthesis took place. Over the next few hundred thousand years sub-atomic particles of protons, neutrons and electrons begin to bond to form predominantly atoms of hydrogen along with a few of the lightest elements, including helium and smatterings of lithium and beryllium. It's a heady thought that most of the hydrogen nuclei in the universe were produced in the first few minutes. Then add to that thought that 62 per cent of the atoms in your body (9.5 per cent by mass) are hydrogen; we carry the beginnings of the universe in our very make-up.

Then very slowly, over the next few hundred million years, gravity began to exert its influence. Hydrogen and helium atoms began to cluster to form vast gas clouds and, eventually. out of the collapsing elemental dust, the first stars were born. They were many times more massive than our sun and blue-white hot in colour. Deep in their cores, nuclear fusion was underway and the stars began to shine. For the first time in the universe, there was starlight. A cosmic dawn had begun.

Stars shine because the temperatures and pressures reached in their fiery hearts are so great that the lightest atoms, hydrogen and helium, begin to fuse to form heavier elements. In this nuclear fusion process some mass is lost and converted into energy, including heat and light radiation. In the case of our sun, we experience this as warmth and sunlight. Again, this is Einstein's famous equation, $E = mc^2$, in action which tells us that mass (m) multiplied by the speed of light (c) squared can be converted into tremendous amounts of energy (E).

As stars fuse lighter elements into increasingly heavier elements, they burn their nuclear fuel, slowly at first but at increasingly faster rates as they approach the end of their lives. First proposed by Fred Hoyle, the process in which many of the elements are created is known as *stellar nucleosynthesis.*[7] Over the aeons, more and more new elements are forged in these stellar furnaces. From the fusion of hydrogen and helium we get carbon. Then in a chain of ever more energetic and complex fusion processes we get oxygen, neon, magnesium, silicon and all the elements in the Periodic Table until we reach iron with atomic number 26.

The physicist Lawrence Krauss calculated that it takes 100,000 years of nuclear fusion for the carbon to burn and fuse to make oxygen, 10,000 years for the oxygen to burn and fuse to make silicon, and one day for the silicon to burn and fuse to make iron. Iron has such a tightly packed nucleus that no more fusion can take place after its appearance. Without the heat released by nuclear fusion, the star collapses and explodes into a supernova blasting its nursery of new elements, from hydrogen to iron, out into the deep cosmos.

This still leaves the question of how elements heavier than iron are created. For their formation, we need even more cosmic energy and stellar violence. For lead and gold, uranium and mercury to be fashioned we need stars even more massive than those that explode as supernovae.

When these super-massive stars die and explode, they leave behind an extremely dense core made of neutrons. Other than black holes, neutron stars are some of the smallest, most dense objects in the universe. They measure as little as twelve to twenty miles across. However, as we saw in Chapter 4, just one cubic centimetre of their mass would weigh a billion metric tonnes. Moreover, very occasionally, from time to time, somewhere in the vast universe two of these neutron stars will collide. The explosive power is so great and the energy levels so high that astronomers believe that this is when and where many of the heavier elements in the Periodic Table are first created.

The debris and stardust from supernovae and neutron star collisions disperse to join the interstellar gas clouds of hydrogen and helium. Gravity exerts its inexorable pull on all this thinly scattered matter. Slowly the dusty clouds of gas collapse forming new, *second-generation stars* such as our own sun. Surrounding these emerging newborn stars is a disc of dust and gas out of which planets begin to coalesce, again as gravity pulls matter together into larger and larger clumps. The elements in the swirling disc, including many of the heavier ones, condense and form the rocky planets closest to the star, which in the case of our own solar system include Mercury, Venus, Earth and Mars.

It is these self-same elements, the scattered ash of long dead stars, that now enter the theme of this book, from the heavens above to the earth below. They are the stuff of the clouds and the air, the rocks and the sea, the forests and flowers, and all living things, including you and me. As the cosmologist Carl Sagan famously said, 'We are made of star stuff', before going on to add the mind-bending thought that, 'We are a way for the cosmos to know itself.'[8] This is such a beautiful thought that many artists, poets and singers have been inspired to reflect on humanity's deep embeddedness in the universe as well as our cosmic insignificance as we live out our brief lives.[9,10] It is Wordsworth who said:

> The stars are mansions built by Nature's hand,
> And, haply, there the spirits of the blest
> Dwell, clothed in radiance.[11]

We are stardust and to stardust we return.

Specifically, by mass we are 65 per cent oxygen, 18.5 per cent carbon, 9.5 per cent hydrogen, 3.2 per cent nitrogen, 1.5 per cent calcium and one per cent phosphorus. In other words, 99 per cent of the mass of the human body is made up of just six elements. Carbon is the element around which most of the other elements arrange themselves. Carbon has more compounds by far than any other element. We are a carbon-based life form, and the molecules of which we are made are organic.

Another six elements make up around 0.85 per cent of our bodily mass, but they are necessary for life: potassium, phosphorus, sulphur, sodium, chlorine, magnesium and iron.

The tiny fraction that is left comprises a few trace elements and these, too, are vital. They include fluorine, zinc, copper, lithium and iodine.

When these elements combine, in ways that are dizzyingly myriad and complex, in some extraordinary way they come alive. Life is a chemical system that extracts energy out of its environment to power itself.[12] In their complex, collective, self-sustaining wonder, the elements out of which we are made allow us to move, breathe, digest, sense, reproduce, be aware and think. They form cells and the living tissue of our hearts and livers, skin and bone, muscles and nerves. The elements are also the stuff out of which our brains are made. The human brain is a 1,400-gram tangle of neurons and blood vessels, a jelly-like mass of trillions of individual atoms, atoms that in some gloriously mysterious way become aware of their own existence and able to reflect on that very same self-awareness. They become self-conscious. They see a world around them. And they begin to wonder.

Part VII

One World

18

It Takes All Sorts

This brain of ours, this self-conscious bundle of living matter has not only turned its gaze outwards to try to make sense of the external world, it has also reflected on its own internal make-up and character. Inspired by the success of physics, chemistry, biology and geology, nineteenth-century social researchers felt the need to emulate their scientific methods of enquiry and investigation. Perhaps social scientists should measure, count, statistically analyse, order and classify human behaviour? Maybe social and behavioural observations should be more objective, rigorous and systematic? Perhaps psychologists could experiment on human populations to see whether people respond differently to, say, stress or rules or discrimination?

However, human personality and behaviour are much trickier to fathom than the effect of acids on metals, or the life-cycle of the butterfly, as difficult as those things are. Our self-aware, self-reflective natures mischievously enter the social science equation. As the social sciences conduct much of their research using interviews, conversation and language, the idea of taking an objective stand-point can soon get lost. We are a species immersed in language and it is within language, both verbal and non-verbal, that our psychological selves constantly form and re-form.

Language carries meaning and meaning can be endlessly interpreted. Moreover, it is we, the observer and observed, who are doing the interpreting even as we engage and interact. The interpersonal world is fluid. It is slippery. It is reflexive. 'I think that she thinks that I think that he thinks …' It is a world of beliefs, actions and intentions that shift and change as we engage with others. Things get even more complicated if you attempt to compare and contrast personalities and behaviour between cultures, and across time and place. Not only are languages different, the assumptions, values, norms, mores and traditions are also different.

In his 2019 book review of David Shariatmadari's, *Don't Believe a Word: The Surprising Truth about Language*, Joe Moran, writes:

> Shariatmadari borrows from Iris Murdoch's idea of language as a net cast over the mind, constraining our thoughts according to how its knots and threads land – wrinkled in some places, straight in others. Every language is a different throw of the net. Language sieves and strains reality but never imprisons it. There are holes for the real world to escape … words … aren't a condiment you sprinkle on top of reality; they are the marinade that alters the taste of everything. … When we learn how the world is made through words, we also learn to be sceptical of our current iteration of reality and more tolerant of other perspectives. If life can be lived differently worded, it can be differently lived.[1]

Nevertheless, in spite of the Alice-Through-the-Looking-Glass, hermeneutical, head-spinning confusion of people thinking about people thinking about people, in the spirit of this book we shall take a step back to see what psychologists have managed to say about the types and variety of human behaviour and personality. There is certainly fun to be had in classifying different types of personality. It is the stuff of pop psychology and newspaper quizzes; it is the basis on which some businesses choose who to hire and fire; it lies behind the work of counsellors and psychotherapists; and, at a push, it might help us see whether certain personality types crop up more frequently amongst the ranks of the scientific classifiers and those who look for order in the natural world. Just a note in passing, a surprising number of the leading actors, both scientists and artists in our present story lost one or both parents during their childhoods. Admittedly, early death was a lot more common in past centuries but, even so, the death of a parent when you're a child strikes me as tough and not without psychological consequences.

* * *

One of the earliest beliefs, still going strong today with many credulous people, is that the time of the year you were born and therefore the zodiacal star sign under which you find yourself determines your personality. Astrologers claim that understanding the traits supposedly associated with your zodiac sign can help you understand your basic personality profile, including its strengths and weaknesses.

Let's take a couple of examples.

If you were born between 21 March and 19 April, your star sign is Aries. Astrologers who know about these things suggest that, on the one hand, you tend to be adventurous and energetic, keen and confidant, sharp and quick-witted, friendly but strong-willed. On the other, you are also prone to be impulsive and impatient, competitive and quick-tempered. Or take Librans, those born between 23 September and 22 October, they enjoy relationships but seek balance and harmony. They are diplomatic and easy-going but they are also liable to be indecisive and can be easily influenced and prone to change their minds.

Now admittedly, these are rather crude caricatures of the full astrological picture, but more sophisticated trait profiles have been researched and tested. For example, in a 1985 report in the journal *Nature*, Shawn Carlson described the results of a double-blind test of astrology on a sample of 193 subjects.[2] He found that astrologers scored at a level consistent only with chance when it came to assessing the traits of individuals.

Although not a huge number of scientific studies have been carried out on the accuracy of star signs and their ability to predict personality traits, most of those conducted by research psychologists have found little or no evidence to support their astrological claims. In reality, out there in the cosmos, actual stars evolve according to physical laws. They are born, live and die. The cosmos and night sky have an ever-shifting geometry. Their configuration and appearance from any fixed stand-point, such as planet Earth, constantly changes. The constellations as they appear today will be different to how they look in the future. Nevertheless, astrologers and those who follow the stars continue to believe – and maybe there's no harm in that.

However, there is evidence that the time of the year you were born does have an impact on your chances of sporting, even academic, success and the likelihood of your getting into a top-rated university. This is all to do with the physical, developmental and cognitive differences between children born at the beginning or the end of any one defined year, whether this is a calendar year or a school year. If the school year begins in September, children born in September have an advantage over children born in the August of the following year because they have an extra eleven or twelve months to grow and develop. This is exacerbated in the early stages of puberty when children can shoot up in a single year.

This is called the Relative Age Effect.[3] It is determined by the cut-off date for any age group competition or category. The common practice of placing children into age groups for sport benefits those who are more developed physically, emotionally and cognitively. This favours those who have birthdays at the beginning of the academic year.

For example, in English school football, children are placed into year groups based on whether they are born after the 1 September and before the end of August the following year. A study by Iñigo Mujika and colleagues found that in English football youth academies (for boys aged sixteen to twenty years), 57 per cent of youngsters were born in September, November or December whilst only fourteen per cent celebrated their birthdays in June, July or August.[4] Similar effects are found across many sports, including ice hockey, rugby and Olympic athletics, whatever dates are used for determining the age band in which you are placed.

If the sport uses the calendar year, January to December, for its adolescent age categorisation, then in these cases it is those born within January to March who are more likely to be chosen and succeed than those born between October and December. What's more, success breeds success. You are likely to persist at something new if you enjoy early recognition and triumph. Those who are younger and not picked are more likely to lose confidence, commitment and interest. These differences are statistical. There will always be impressive exceptions. However, the bias is there.

* * *

However, when it comes to life in general and looking at the different ways in which people are perceived, relate to others, set about work, achieve success, spend their leisure time, view the world, then individual traits and personality do come into play. Personality types and differences have long fascinated psychologists, novelists and the public at large.

The interest stretches back at least to Classical times. The ancient Egyptians and Mesopotamians were the first to consider how bodily fluids might affect our temperament, feelings and behaviour. However, it was the Greek physician Hippocrates (*c.* 460-*c.* 370 BCE) who tidied up these ideas and gave us the theory of 'humourism', not a joke but the belief that different bodily fluids, which he called 'humours', could affect our moods and behaviour. Too much or too little of a particular humour could upset as well as determine our feelings and actions.

There are four humours, each associated with a different part of the body. They are blood, yellow bile, black bile and phlegm. A few centuries later, another Greek physician, Galen of Pergamon (129-*c.* 200 CE) developed these categories further, recognising that some humours might combine or be dominant.

A person's temperament might be described as *sanguine*, the blood being warm and moist and in the Classical mind most associated with the liver. These qualities were thought to lead to sociable, jolly, touchy-feely behaviour.

Choleric types were said to be outward-going but inclined to be short-tempered. Yellow bile, or choler is bitter. It is produced by the gall bladder, which in these cases was thought to be over-active. Choleric people were said to combine both warm and dry qualities.

Those who are *melancholic* were seen as inward-looking, thoughtful and reserved. Their bile was black and produced by the spleen. They displayed qualities that were both cold and dry.

Phlegmatic types remain unmoved. They don't get flustered. They are stolid. Phlegm was thought to be associated with the lungs which were said to be cold and moist.

The four humours model of temperament continued to influence medical and personality theories right up until the beginning of the Age of Enlightenment in the seventeenth century. Galen believed that blood was the dominant humour, and therefore an excess of this humour was treated by blood-letting and purging. Blood-sucking leeches were also a favoured treatment for many ailments, particularly those where a fever was involved. Victorian physicians were particularly keen on using leeches until studies showed that they did not effect any cures; indeed, their application would often make a patient's health worse.

In a 2014 review of medicine's historical use of blood-letting, D.P. Thomas, a haematologist, wryly notes that leeches have had something of minor renaissance in recent years.[5] They are sometimes used in micro- and plastic surgery for removal of localised collections of blood, as opposed to any systemic or curative effect. The application of a leech to the affected part can have a beneficial effect by removing congested venous blood. The paper reminds us, however, that they are still not a cure for anything, just a neat and efficient way of tidying up a bloody mess.

The idea of the four humours has also influenced poets and playwrights. For example, Shakespearean scholars have looked at how Elizabethan concepts of the humours influenced his plays and the behaviour of his characters. *Henry IV*'s four main characters have been seen as examples of each temperamental type: King Henry IV is portrayed as melancholic, Prince Hal sanguine, Sir Harry Hotspur choleric, and the knight, Sir John Falstaff as phlegmatic. And, of course, right up to the present day we still talk of people feeling melancholic or being phlegmatic, being sanguine or full of bile.

* * *

By the nineteenth and twentieth centuries, psychologists were determined to be more scientific in their approach to the study of personality and individual differences. To talk of a plethora of personality theories might be a little unfair, but quite a number were developed as psychologists attempted to understand and classify our temperamental styles and personality traits.

First, however, we need to ask what is personality? In its one sentence definition, the American Psychological Association says that personality refers to individual differences in characteristic patterns of thinking, feeling and behaving. Expanding this definition allows us to include moods, attitudes and opinions. Also, the way we interact with other people says a lot about our personality.

Sigmund Freud recognised a number of traits that if strongly present could lead to poor and troubled mental health.[6] He saw patients whom he said were *neurotic*. Some he described as *hysterical*. Others he felt were showing *obsessive* and *compulsive* traits. He also suggested that there were five stages of psychosexual development progressing through oral, anal, phallic, latency and genital. The only one still used colloquially these days is when someone is described as 'anal retentive', a person who tends to be rather obsessive, mean, stubborn and reluctant to give and share. Harsh and early potty training is blamed! Hold on to that idea.

The Swiss psychoanalyst, Carl Jung collaborated and corresponded with Freud, although the two eventually parted company and headed down rather different psychological paths. Jung was one of the first people to categorise people as either *introverts* or *extroverts*. In Jung's 1921 definitions, introverts are prone to reflect, contemplate, daydream, be shy and not want a social life that is too busy and full. In contrast, extroverts do enjoy being sociable.[7] Their behaviour is focussed on the outside world. They are lively and energetic. They can be the life and soul of any party.

Hans Eysenck was born in Berlin in 1916 but moved to London during the 1930s. He spent the rest of his life living and working in Britain. During the 1940s he worked at London's Maudsley psychiatric hospital. His job was to make an initial assessment of each patient to help psychiatrists make their diagnosis. To help sharpen his assessments, Eysenck developed a questionnaire which asked about the patient's behaviour. In a later study he applied this questionnaire to 700 soldiers who had been admitted to the hospital, often as a result of their war experiences. Using statistical techniques, he identified two major, first-order, personality traits. This allowed him to represent behaviour along two intersecting dimensions.

One dimension ran from introversion to extroversion[8]. The other ran from neuroticism to stability.[9] The behaviour associated with introverts and extroverts had much in common with Jung's types.

Eysenck described *extroverts* as very sociable. They enjoy the buzz of social life, seek constant stimulation and are easily bored. Although they are optimists by nature, they can be impulsive and inclined to take risks. In contrast, *introverts* seek the quiet life. They try to keep their emotions under control. They come across as reserved, serious, predictable and perhaps inclined to be rather pessimistic. We all lie on a spectrum somewhere between these two extremes.

People assessed as high in *neuroticism* are emotionally unstable. They are prone to overreact. They don't cope well with stress. They worry and fret. Or they erupt and rage. They don't easily calm down. In contrast, people who are described as emotionally and behaviourally *stable* remain calm under pressure. They weigh things up and remain level-headed. We all lie somewhere between these two extremes.

Testing people to determine where they lie along each of these two dimensions produces four possible combinations, and therefore four general personality types.

For example, people who score high on both extroversion and neuroticism exhibit behaviour that might be described as excitable, restless and impulsive. Those who display both extrovert and stable traits are more likely to be easy-going, sociable, lively, even keen to get into leadership roles. Unstable-introverts are not very sociable. They can be moody, anxious and pessimistic. Finally, stable-introverts are seen as thoughtful, self-controlled, reliable and even-tempered; people who don't court a busy social life, but respond to relationships with respect and courtesy.

There is one final possible spin given to this classification. Those with a Classical eye and a witty outlook have mapped the four humours of Hippocrates onto these four Eysenckian types to give us:

Melancholic: unstable-introverts.
Phlegmatic: stable-introverts.
Sanguine: stable-extroverts.
Choleric: unstable-extroverts.

Eysenck's classifications have an intuitive appeal. We all know people who fit each type, or so we believe. They are the heroes and anti-heroes of novels and plays. They describe the dedicated scientists who quietly explore a single obsession. There are nerds and geeks. There are exhibitionists and show-offs. Our individual differences make social life interesting, more colourful, less bland. They add challenge as we negotiate everyday relationships, at work, at home, at play. They are the stuff of gossip, novels, films and drama.

* * *

Over subsequent years, a number of psychologists, including Ernest Tupes, Raymond Christal, Raymond Cattell, Lewis Goldberg, Paul Costa and Robert Macrae, further analysed and elaborated our behavioural traits. Each research team developed its own particular model to capture the rich variety of people's personality make-up and behavioural style. The teams' various efforts share many similarities and together they are generally known as the 'Big Five' model of personality traits.[10]

The models contain a lot of fascinating detail. Each one of the five traits represents a continuum. An individual can fall anywhere along a trait's defining characteristics, from high presence to low. At the end of a test, a subject will be given a profile of where they lie along each of the five trait continua. Here is a very brief outline of the Big Five personality traits:

Openness to Experience (from High to Low):
Curious, inquisitive, imaginative, willing to try new things that can sometimes stray into risky behaviour, enjoys variety
versus
Incurious, preference for the familiar and routine, safe, practical, pragmatic, consistent, risk-averse.

Conscientiousness (from High to Low):
Focussed, self-disciplined, dutiful, ambitious, punctual, organised, careful
versus
Easy-going, impulsive, negligent, careless, lazy, flexible, relaxed.

Extroversion (from High to Low):
Sociable, outgoing, enthusiastic, exuberant
versus
Reserved, quiet, low-key, introverted, thoughtful.

Agreeableness (High to Low):
Considerate, kind, likes harmony, acquiescent, willing to compromise, trustworthy
versus
Disagreeable, self-interested, uncooperative, suspicious.

Neuroticism (from High to Low):
Negative emotional bias, emotional instability, vulnerable to stress, pessimistic
versus
Confident, emotionally stable, calm, reliable.

These 'Big Five' personality traits give us the acronym OCEAN. It reminds us that sailing the seas of human behaviour and social relationships can be choppy.

Psychologists have been keen to see whether people in different population groups, defined by such things as occupation or political persuasion, show distinctive profiles when their Big Five personality traits are assessed and compared. The types of people who feature throughout this book – scientists and creative artists – have certainly been studied along these lines.

Not surprisingly, in general, scientists are found to be more open-minded, intrinsically motivated, introverted and focussed. Indeed, introverted individuals are more likely to pursue careers in scientifically-based, systematising occupations. However, there are exceptions. A significant minority of scientists score high on extroversion and sociability. These more socially extrovert scientists are more likely to work in academic settings, particularly where there are opportunities to perform, give lectures, lead teams, be media-friendly and enthuse about their discipline to anyone who will listen.

The most creative people, and this includes ground-breaking scientists as well as artists who come up with new ways of seeing and thinking about the world, appear most open to new experiences. They are people who are less conventional, more driven and, perhaps unexpectedly, less conscientious and more impulsive. Original thinkers don't take the world for granted. They see beneath, behind and beyond the surface of things and, when their work is seen, heard, read and done, we view the world differently and thrillingly anew.

* * *

However, there is something which constantly challenges what psycho-social scientists try to say and do. When men and women observe human actions and behaviour, they find themselves trying to find order in a world that is more fluid and flexible, more reflexive and less universal than we find in the physical world. Social science classifications feel less solid, more open to dispute. Their labels are more labile.

Some doubt whether the major traits mean the same thing as you move from one culture to another. Others have found differences across age and gender. For example, the science writer Dana Smith reports on a meta-analysis of one and a half million people which found that women over the age of forty tended to be low in neuroticism and high in openness, agreeableness, extroversion and conscientiousness.[11] In contrast, young men scored more highly on self-centredness and extroversion, medium ratings for neuroticism, along with low openness, agreeableness and conscientiousness. It seems that as we age and gain experience, our personality profiles can and do change. Time can often, but not always, moderate some of our biologically based, psychological dispositions.

In his book, *Personality Isn't Permanent*, the American psychologist, Benjamin Hardy goes further.[12] He says that our personalities are not set in stone. He doubts that we have a true, fixed, core authentic self. Our personality traits can change over time. We can become more self-controlled and perhaps be less adventurous as we get older. New jobs and new friends can shift our self-perception and lead to new behaviour. We can consciously alter our disposition if we try. However, many of us suspect that, at heart, we haven't changed that much over our lifetime. We just learn to recognise when we're about to be unreasonable, unsociable or excessive and, ideally, hold back, take a deep breath and restrain ourselves. Well, that's the hope.

* * *

It is because we can reflect on what we say and do that we can think about our purported character and attributed behaviour, thereby altering them in the reflective process. This means that the psycho-social sciences find themselves operating in a much fuzzier world than the physical sciences, perhaps with the exception of quantum physics. The psychologist Lucy Foulkes writes that we lose something if we attempt to reduce ourselves into types that are too simple, too categorical: 'When you use a label to describe someone, and that includes yourself, you can turn a multi-faceted, endlessly complicated character into a flat stereotype.'[13]

In his book *What it Means to Be Human*, the philosopher Robert Rowland Smith reflects that:

> being human means dealing with our fate. … Whether our fate is lucky or unlucky, we are dealt a hand. We might be born into poverty or affluence, good or bad health, peace or war – but playing that hand is up to us. And so it is that tension between being determined by our circumstances and determining ourselves is an essential part of being human.[14]

Thus, mind is notoriously more difficult to grasp than matter. It seems that movement between social and psychological categories is entirely possible. In psychological schemes, there is none of the eternal elegance that we find in the classification of the elements and the beauty of the Periodic Table. Stellar evolution is entirely predictable, given the laws of physics. The geological timeline is what it is.

Nonetheless, whatever the challenges associated with trying to make sense of human personality and behaviour, it is in our nature to weigh up our fellow men and women. We are a social species. We constantly strive for social understanding. Our very success lies in our ability to cooperate and collaborate and, even though these are easier said than done, they are essential for our survival. They make our world go round.

19

Sense and Sensibility

We shall consider just one more psychological 'typology'. It's particularly germane to what we've been considering throughout these pages. According to the psychologist Simon Baron-Cohen, there are two human talents that help us make sense of the world of things, on the one hand, and the world of people, on the other.[1]

Making sense of the physical world and wondering how things work is helped when we approach matters *systematically*. However, when it comes to understanding people and the social world, a degree of *empathy* is required, that is the ability to see and feel things from other people's point of view and then successfully communicate that understanding.[2]

At a stretch, systematising skills and empathising talents might roughly equate with approaching the world either scientifically or artistically. Most of us are reasonably proficient in both skills. Our *balanced* approach allows us to feel confident when dealing with everyday physical problems, on the one hand, and social relationships, on the other.

The light in the bedside table lamp goes out – it could be that the bulb needs replacing or maybe the fuse in the plug has blown. Kate says she'll check the bulb first and, if that doesn't do the trick, she'll check the fuse. The problem and its analysis are conducted systematically, logically, sequentially. Her father needs the lamp to help him read his newspaper. He gets tetchy and says 'everything is going wrong today. I can't read without that light.' But he's had a bad week. His failing eyesight has also meant that he can't drive anymore. 'I know, Dad, it's been a rotten few days. It must be very frustrating. But we'll soon have the light fixed. And don't forget, they've introduced that new bus service into town. It gets you there in ten minutes. And you can travel free! You've got your bus pass!' The response shows empathy and good humour. Kate's Dad smiles.

However, there are people who tend strongly towards one end or the other of this systematising-empathy continuum. Some people have above average systematising skills, while others seem naturally gifted empathisers.

The scientists we have met in this book have shown great curiosity about the natural world. They look at nature and wonder why things are like they are. In Baron-Cohen's words, they are 'pattern seekers'. They look for order and seek the reason why of things. They observe, measure, count, note, classify and theorise. They love detail and are curious about how things work and appear the way they do. Their gaze is objective; their approach is systematic. Whether it's the stars in the heavens, the clouds in the sky, the birds in the air, the rocks underground, or the elements all around, their wonder turns to curiosity, their curiosity to questions, their questions to observation, and their observations to a search for order, patterns and ultimately explanations. Systematisers and pattern seekers want to make sense of the appearance of things and the reason why of things.

Gifted empathisers also wonder about the world, not just the world of people but the world of nature too – mountains, rivers, oceans, trees, life. However, their response is subjective. It is their *experience of* and *reaction to* things that intrigues; and, whether it's in paint, poetry or prose, the artist seeks to communicate his or her subjective experience. Empathy, then, is both the ability to feel and understand the meaning of things *in themselves*, and then successfully to communicate the meaning of that subjective experience artistically in words, paint or sound.

The concept of empathy has its origins in the philosophy of aesthetics. Late nineteenth-century German philosophers used the word *mitgefühl* and sometimes *einfühlung*, later translated as empathy, when discussing aesthetics. One of the earliest appearances of the word was in 1846. It was used by the German poet and novelist, Friedrich Theodor Vischer to discuss the pleasure we experience when we contemplate a work of art. The word represented an attempt to describe our ability to get 'inside' a work or object of beauty by, for example, projecting ourselves and our feelings 'into' a painting, a sculpture, a piece of music, and even into the beauty and sublimity of nature itself. As we resonate with the work of art or the wonder of nature, the feelings generated are projected into, and then felt to be a quality of that work of art, that experience of nature.

If we can 'feel our way into' a work of art, a landscape, a starlit sky, a restless ocean in an act of empathy, our understanding of the world and our place in it increases, our appreciation deepens. We feel ourselves reacting both viscerally and emotionally. We have an aesthetic experience. The artist, Paul Klee said that 'art does not reproduce the visible; rather, it makes visible'. He encouraged his students to: 'sense the total nature of things [by] entering the conception of the natural object, be this object plant, animal, or human being. … The object grows beyond its appearance through our knowledge of its inner nature.'[3]

Artistically immersing yourself in nature makes the world a richer, more dense, more textured place, and, in turn, this absorption in the very fabric of things helps you feel at one with the world and its beauty, wonder and mystery. The early Romantics reacted against what they saw as the impersonal logic of the newly emerging Enlightenment sciences. Yes, they agreed, you could order, systematise and explain nature, but science and its objectivity has nothing to say about what it feels like to be in the world, what it is like to experience life, to be in the midst of colour, shape and sound, to be a human being. In his book, *The Magus of the North*, the philosopher Isaiah Berlin celebrates the life of the German philosopher Johann Georg Hamann (1730-88). He begins his book with this claim: 'The most passionate, consistent, extreme and implacable enemy of the Enlightenment and, in particular, of all forms of rationalism of his time … was Johann Georg Hamann. His influence, direct and indirect, upon the romantic revolt against universalism and scientific method in any guise was considerable and perhaps crucial.'[4]

Hamann contrasts the imagination, passion, introspection and intuitive insights of the artist with the lifeless approach of the systematisers and dissectors, the theorists and the reasoners. Direct revelation, writes Berlin, not analysis, was at the heart of Hamann's romantic vision.

Romantics saw men and women as part of nature. Consciousness could be enhanced and deepened by immersing oneself sensually and emotionally in the world. For the Romantics, the human experience can only be understood and appreciated if we recognise that we are found in, and formed by, nature. We can't stand apart from it. We are embodied creatures: more than reason; more than thought. In human affairs experience so often outbids explanation. Reflecting on the subjective self is what gives life its meaning. Contemplating nature enriches our being and deepens our sense of self.

In 1798 Wordsworth was on a walking tour along the Welsh Borders with his sister Dorothy. During their wanderings he felt the landscape enter his being. He could 'see into the life of things'. His poem, 'Lines Composed a Few Miles above Tintern Abbey, On Revisiting the Banks of the Wye during a Tour, July 13, 1798', began to form in his mind.[5] The following lines are taken from a section of the third stanza:

For I have learned
To look on nature, not as in the hour
Of thoughtless youth; but hearing oftentimes
The still sad music of humanity,
Nor harsh nor grating, though of ample power
To chasten and subdue. – And I have felt
A presence that disturbs me with the joy
Of elevated thoughts.

While the 'Age of Enlightenment' was celebrating the power of human reason to fathom nature rationally, the 'Age of Sensibility' was valuing our ability to experience nature directly through the senses, unmediated by thought or theory. Science discovered calculated, deduced and reasoned. It sought cause and effect. Art created, made, expressed and realised our inner visions, our subjective consciousness. It spoke to our place in the world. Throughout the eighteenth century, both Science and Sensibility, Reason and Romance, Analysis and Synthesis were gathering pace. It was under their shared banner that Immanuel Kant exhorted us to 'dare to understand'.[6]

For Romantics, it's as we contemplate the outer landscape that our internal landscape of sense and self, thought and feeling change. Deeper notes of understanding become possible. As we understand more deeply and feel more profoundly, so our resonance and oneness with the world increases. This was the way in which Coleridge thought about poetry. Sublime landscapes of wonder can and do influence who we are. There is a reflexive relationship between contemplating nature's beauty and deepening our consciousness of self. Thus, the living of life itself becomes the source of its own meaning. Those with an 'ecological consciousness' understand the interconnectedness of all things and that we separate ourselves from nature at our peril. Wordsworth, of course, felt no such separation.[7]

Here is an extract from his 'The Tables Turned':

> And hark! how blithe the throstle sings!
> He, too, is no mean preacher:
> Come forth into the light of things,
> Let Nature be your teacher.

Nan Shepherd also knew about such feelings. In her book, *The Living Mountain*, she writes about her time on and amongst the Cairngorms of Scotland.[8] For her, walking is 'a journey into Being; for as I penetrate more deeply into the mountain's life, I penetrate also into my own. For an hour I am beyond desire. … I am not out of myself, but in myself: I am.'[9] For Shepherd, 'place and mind … interpenetrate until the nature of both are altered'.[10] Subject and object become caught in an inflationary loop of sensory excitement in which the self feels both lost and infinite. There is no longer any sense of the internal and external. In moment of ecstasy, we find our self, our very being dissolved in nature. We feel at one with the world.

* * *

However, in the minds of many people, the difference between the scientific and artistic gaze is not so great. Both can approach nature in a state of wonder. To understand, first we need to wonder. Wonder engages our imagination and then invites us to explore, scientifically, poetically, artistically, philosophically. Scientists and artists are curious both about the material world and our relationship with that world.

Tristan Gooley sees rainbows in raindrops.[11] He thinks the analytic mind, a knowledge of physics and a poetic sense can stand side by side. In Richard Dawkins' book, *Unweaving the Rainbow*, the evolutionary biologist writes that:

> The feeling of awed wonder that science can give us is one of the highest experiences of which the human psyche is capable. It is a deep aesthetic passion to rank with the finest that music and poetry can deliver. It is truly one of

> the things that makes life worth living and it does so, if anything, more effectively if it convinces us that the time we have for living is finite.[12]

The physicist and Nobel laureate, Richard Feynman, whom we first met in Chapter 1 also felt puzzled when people didn't seem to appreciate that great scientists needed to be every bit as imaginative and creative as great artists. He makes the point in the case of 'a friend who's an artist and has sometimes taken a view which I don't agree with very well. He'll hold up a flower and say "look how beautiful it is".' Feynman agrees, it is beautiful. However, scientists might point out that the flower's beauty and the wonder it induces only increases when it is understood that the light of the sun gives it vibrancy, colour, life and complexity. For Feynman science only adds to the flower's beauty, mystery and awe.[13]

There is one particular genre of writing that wanders happily between the arts and the sciences. At its best, and in the hands of the most gifted, nature writing transcends any distinction between the factual and philosophical, the scientific and aesthetic. Science, wonder, poetry, reflection and description transport us through woods and over mountains, along rivers and by the sea, among the flowers and into the buzz and roar of life itself. The young nature writer, Dara McNulty reflects in sensuous prose of his intense connection and relationship with nature,[14] echoing John Clare's poem, 'All Nature Has a Feeling', in which 'woods, fields, brooks are life eternal', The naturalist Helen Macdonald writes beautifully, poetically even, about nature, in general, and birds, in particular. In her book, *Vesper Flights*, she echoes Feynman's passion for science and understanding: 'there's an immense intellectual pleasure involved in making identifications, and each time you learn to recognise a new species of animal or plant, the natural world becomes a more complicated and remarkable place, pulling intricate variety out of a background blur of nameless grey and green'.[15]

An environmental aesthetics can also lead to an 'ecological consciousness', which, in turn, can promote a political awareness, especially in these days of pollution, climate change and loss of biodiversity. Although science gives us the facts, it is the humanities that help us understand the world, how we look at it and how we feel about it.

The human capacity to wonder makes the stories we've been following just one single story, uniting art and science, subject and object, synthesis and analysis, and the heavens above and the earth below. At the deepest levels, the world is a seamless place. It is a dense fabric of woven threads. Follow one thread and you follow all threads – elements, stars, planets, rocks, oceans, clouds, life, humanity, consciousness, self-consciousness, wonder, curiosity, art, science, creativity, understanding, the appearance of order and the emergence of meaning in a meaningless universe. It's all one, beautiful whole.

20

The Art of Science

We began this journey in Great Langdale, deep in the heart of the English Lake District. This is a place of beauty and grandeur, where earth and sky create feelings of wonder.

We met a number of men and women who saw order and felt poetry as they walked by lakes and climbed mountains. Both their intellects and imaginations were aroused. Theirs was an age of romantic science as well as romantic art. They were storytellers as well as pattern-seekers and surprisingly often their lives and works crossed and connected.

The Keswick clock repairer, Jonathan Otley, became a lifelong friend of his fellow Cumbrian, John Dalton. They shared a love of the weather. Dalton's curiosity about the very small helped him to understand the character of atoms and the chemistry of compounds. Humphry Davy was a chemist interested in the elements and their chemical behaviour. He was the first to discover and isolate many of them himself. Although he was not always complimentary about Dalton's rigour as an experimentalist, he recognised the older man's theoretical brilliance. In spite of their own failures to crack the order and logic that underpinned the elements, Dalton's and Davy's work paved the way for others to look for and find those patterns, work that would eventually lead to Mendeleev and his Periodic Table of the chemical elements.

Luke Howard brought order to the skies with his cloud classification. Howard had been familiar with John Dalton's book, *Meteorological Observations and Essays*, published in 1793.[1] These overlapping interests resulted in the two men enjoying a lifelong correspondence.

In 1837, Howard dedicated his *Seven Lectures on Meteorology* to John Dalton in recognition of their forty years of friendship.[2]

The German writer and poet, Goethe was a fan of Howard and his classification of clouds. He believed that a romantic sensibility could inspire and inform both art and science. In contrast, Wordsworth remained wary of science's 'dissection' of nature. Coleridge was less hostile. He was friendly with the chemist Humphry Davy and attended many of his lectures. Also, of course, there was that remarkable climb up Helvellyn in 1805 that brought together Davy and poets, William Wordsworth, Robert Southey and Walter Scott.

In spite of his romantic worries about science's attitude to nature, Wordsworth did collaborate with scientists on at least three occasions. In 1800 he asked Davy if he would proof-read the second edition of *Lyrical Ballads*, to which the young scientist agreed. As well as his poems, Wordsworth had also written a *Guide to the Lakes.*[3] Recognising that nineteenth-century tourists liked a few scientific facts to inform their guides, Wordsworth invited a couple of science experts to contribute. The 'blind philosopher' of Kendal, Thomas Gough had been John Dalton's mentor when the young man was teaching in the town with his brother. He agreed to write a section 'promoting' the botany of the lakes. Wordsworth also asked Adam Sedgwick, professor of geology at the University of Cambridge, to write a few brief 'letters' on the geology of the area which would be added to later editions of his *Guide to the Lakes*. The guides sold well, even better than Wordsworth's poetry.

Wordsworth and Sedgwick got to know one another. When he was in the Lake District, Sedgwick would sometimes stay with the poet Robert Southey and, if time and circumstance allowed, he would catch up with Wordsworth. There had also been some friendly correspondence between them in which Sedgwick chided Wordsworth for being rude about rock-smashing geologists in his 1814 poem, 'The Excursion – Book Third – Despondency':

> He, who with pocket hammer smites the edge
> Of every luckless rock or stone that stands.

After reading the poem, Sedgwick wrote 'that one of your greatest works seems to contain a poetic ban against "my brethren of the hammer"'. However, in friendly reply Wordsworth said that Sedgwick shouldn't take his words too literally.

Sedgwick, it might be remembered, was also in regular contact with Dalton's friend, Jonathan Otley, who, even though he was an amateur, knew as much about Lakeland's geology as anyone. Sedgwick even went for a walk up Helvellyn with Otley and Dalton in the summer of 1824. Although Sedgwick was 20 years younger than the Keswick clock repairer, the two of them would meet, stroll and try to make sense of the rocks, minerals and stratigraphy of Lakeland's hills and dales. Helped by his chats with Otley, between 1831 and 1855 the Cambridge professor published a series of papers on the rocks and structure of the Cumbrian mountains.

Otley had got the local geological sequence right but it was Sedgwick who glimpsed the bigger picture, the deeper order, and the outline of a grander geological timescale. In recognition of his work in Wales, it was Sedgwick who named the period in which the rocks occurred the *Cambrian*. With his colleague and occasional combatant, the man from the Scottish Highlands, Roderick Murchison, he also named the slightly younger rocks found in Devon the *Devonian*.

Murchison was a wealthy man. After time in the army he took to a life of leisure. Then Humphry Davy entered his life. Davy urged Murchison to turn his undoubted talents to science instead of wasting his days riding horses and hunting. It was the science of geology that excited the Scotsman and it was Murchison who named another major geological period – the *Silurian*, after the ancient tribe, the Silures, who lived along the English-Welsh borders.

During their later lifetimes, Sedgwick and Murchison disputed where the Cambrian period ended and the younger Silurian period began. They couldn't agree. The dispute wasn't resolved until after their deaths. A solution was offered by Charles Lapworth, professor of geology at the newly established University of Birmingham. He suggested that the disputed rocks should form an entirely new period which would separate the other two. He called it the *Ordovician*, younger than the Cambrian but older than the Silurian. Ironically, the rocks of the central Lake District, which Sedgwick mapped so assiduously, are now allocated to the Ordovician period and not Sedgwick's beloved Cambrian.

While he was at Cambridge, Charles Darwin attended some of Sedgwick's geology lectures. In 1831 he accompanied the professor on a geological field trip to Wales before taking up the offer of joining Robert FitzRoy on the *Beagle* expedition. Darwin and Sedgwick began a correspondence that lasted many years. However, in 1859, their friendship was severely tested when Darwin sent Sedgwick a first-edition copy of *On the Origin of Species by Means of Natural Selection*. Sedgwick was a religious man. He was the son of an Anglican vicar and he himself was ordained as a priest in 1818. The Reverend Professor Adam Sedgwick never accepted the case for evolution, replying to Darwin that he read his book 'with more pain than pleasure'.

The irony was that it was Sedgwick's own work on ancient rocks and fossils that in part provided Darwin with the vast passages of time that his theory of evolution needed to make it work. Darwin had also read Charles Lyell's three-volume book, *Principles of Geology*, while he had been sailing around the world on HMS *Beagle*.[4] In Darwin's mind, an appreciation of geological time and the changing fossil record added further support to his own revolutionary ideas.

One more influence on Darwin's thinking might be worth mentioning as we trace the interlaced lives of these pioneering pattern-seekers. John Herschel was the son of the astronomer, William Herschel. As well as following in his father's footsteps as an astronomer, he also made significant contributions to mathematics, botany and chemistry. He was knighted in 1831. Darwin had read and was impressed by John Herschel's book, *A Preliminary Discourse on the Study of Natural Philosophy*, published in 1830, the year before Darwin graduated.[5] In 1836 the *Beagle* with Darwin aboard arrived in Cape Town, South Africa where Herschel had helped set up an astronomical observatory. The two men met.[6]

In the months before Darwin's arrival, John Herschel had been thinking about evolution, in general – of the stars, plants and animals and plants. John's father, William Herschel had explored the idea that stars might evolve, from gaseous nebulae to newborn stars. The young Herschel continued to work on his father's ideas. Herschel extended his thoughts on stellar evolution to plants and animals. He felt that the living world was dynamic. Herschel talked about his ideas with Darwin and the conversation lodged in the naturalist's mind. Twenty years later in the opening paragraph of *On the Origin of Species* Darwin wrote:

> When on board HMS 'Beagle', as naturalist, I was much struck with certain facts on the distribution of organic beings inhabiting South America. These facts seemed to throw some light on the origin of species – that mystery

> of mysteries, as it has been called by one of our greatest philosophers.[7]

He was referring to John Herschel when he wrote of 'one of our greatest philosophers'. He sent Herschel an advance copy of the book with a note saying how much he admired and had been influenced by Sir John's own work. Herschel wasn't entirely convinced by Darwin's arguments. He had doubts about the mechanisms that Darwin said drove evolution. However, the two men were reconciled in death. Charles Darwin and John Herschel are buried in adjacent graves in the north-east corner of the nave in Westminster Abbey, not too far from the memorial dedicated to John's father, William Herschel. Darwin's tombstone is a bright white marble and literally abutting it is the dark grey tombstone of Sir John Herschel. Only a little further along the nave are the tombstones of some of the other scientists mentioned throughout these pages, including Isaac Newton, Charles Lyell, Ernest Rutherford and Lord Kelvin. The poets have their own corner – poet's corner – in the south transept. Even in death, the living world insists on keeping the arts and sciences apart even though a sense of shared wonder brought them together in life.

* * *

This quick reprise is to remind us that the criss-crossed lives of so many scientists who saw order in the natural world reflect the underlying interrelatedness of all things.

For its third meeting, the newly established British Association for the Advancement of Science met in June 1833 at the University of Cambridge. It brought together many of the great scientists of the day. Amongst those attending were the physicist, Michael Faraday, the chemist and meteorologist, John Dalton, the astronomer and chemist, John Herschel, the geologist, Adam Sedgwick, the mathematician, and the first to conceive the idea of a programmable digital computer, Charles Babbage, the economist, Thomas Malthus and the ailing, but still indefatigably curious, 60-year-old Samuel Taylor Coleridge. Charles Darwin was on his *Beagle* expedition, 'botanising' in South America.

This was also the meeting at which discussions took place about what to call the men and women of science. 'Natural philosophers' as a name had served well for many years but there was a feeling that, as the polymath and Master of Trinity College, Cambridge,

William Whewell put it, 'There was no general term by which these gentleman could describe themselves with reference to their pursuits.' In his report of the British Association's 1833 gathering published in the *Quarterly Review* of 1834, he wrote: '"Philosophers" was felt to be too wide and lofty a term, and was very properly forbidden by Mr Coleridge. … "Savans" was rather assuming and beside too French; but some ingenious gentleman proposed that by analogy with "artist", they might form "scientist".'

The 'ingenious gentleman' turned out to be Whewell himself. The word 'scientist' quickly became popular and by 1840 it had been recognised by the Oxford English Dictionary. The scientists of the late eighteenth and early nineteenth centuries quite happily wondered over all of nature. John Dalton studied the wind and the rain as well as chemical compounds and atomic weights. Humphry Davy gave lectures on geology, physics and chemistry as well as writing poetry. Charles Darwin read widely about plants and animals, geological time and stellar evolution.

It was only as scientific knowledge of particular subjects increased and became ever-more detailed and sophisticated that the specificity and rigour of individual disciplines began to define the men and women of science as either chemists or biologists, physicists or geologists, astronomers or mathematicians. Polymaths were becoming a rare breed.

* * *

However, there is a current demand that once again we should think holistically about nature, across and beyond the usual disciplinary boundaries. Our success in applying science to the exploitation of nature has not been without consequences. Enlightenment science had encouraged us to look at nature objectively. We did not see ourselves as part of the planetary equation. We sought to understand nature so that we might tame her, order her, exploit her. We mined the earth, we farmed the animals, we grew the crops, and we reworked the world's rocky treasures into an excess of material stuff from metals to plastics, concrete to glass, steam-driven engines to electrically powered devices.[8]

We learned to move faster, go further, keep warmer, stay cooler, eat more exotically, live more comfortably, spend more extravagantly. In the course of all this hubris and profligacy, we have ended up degrading the land, polluting the earth, heating the atmosphere, melting the ice, changing the climate, diminishing biodiversity and risking a sixth mass extinction. In spite of Coleridge's warnings in his poem, 'The Rime of the Ancient Mariner', the crimes against nature that the Romantic poets feared have now been committed. We have killed the albatross and are paying the price, spiritually, materially and environmentally.

None of the traditional sciences on their own seemed capable of handling the range and interconnectedness of these environmental concerns. If we were to understand nature in all her dynamic complexity, more integrated scientific approaches were called for, and perhaps more maverick minds to champion them. James Lovelock was one such mind.[9]

* * *

Lovelock's early career experiences included photography, chemistry, medical research and cryogenics. In 1961 he began working for the National Aeronautics and Space Administration, NASA. By the late 1970s he was involved in the development of instruments that could measure and analyse the gases that the Viking landers might find when they touched down on Mars.

An earlier invention of Lovelock's – the electron capture detector – helped in the discovery of CFCs (chlorofluorocarbons) high in the stratosphere. The gas was used in refrigerators, aerosols spray cans and solvents. Later research by Frank Sherwood Rowland and Mario Molina established that the CFCs that escaped into the atmosphere were implicated in the destruction of the ozone layer, the layer that helps shield the earth from the sun's harmful ultraviolet rays. Ozone loss is a major environmental worry. The gas is a molecule of three oxygen atoms (O_3). Its loss increases the amount of ultraviolet (UV) radiation that reaches the Earth's surface, especially in the polar regions. UV light increases the risk of skin cancer, eye cataracts, and genetic and immune system damage. The work of Rowland and Molina helped politicians agree the Montreal Protocol, ratified in 1987. The protocol was the first of several international enactments designed to halt the production and use of ozone-depleting chemicals.

For many decades Lovelock worked as an independent scientist and inventor based in south-west England. In his book, *Homage to Gaia: The Life of an Independent Scientist*, he said that he was 'a general practitioner' in a world of specialists.[10] He felt that the increasingly finer divisions that characterised much of academic life made it more difficult for people to come up with original ideas, especially ideas that spanned more than one discipline. Being independent, he felt he could enjoy more freedom of thought and for him one such thought was the Gaia hypothesis.

It was during the 1960s that James Lovelock came up with the idea that the Earth could be seen as a self-regulating, living system. His neighbour and friend, the novelist William Golding, suggested the scientist name his hypothesis Gaia after the Greek goddess of the Earth. Lovelock outlined his hypothesis in a number of journal articles, work which culminated in his 1979 book, *Gaia: A New Look at life on Earth.*[11]

At first, his ideas didn't attract much attention but gradually the scientific community began to take an interest. The Gaia hypothesis proposed that all organisms and their inorganic surroundings on Earth are closely integrated to form a single and self-regulating complex system conducive to the maintenance of life. The idea suggested that there are any number of complex, *non-linear* feedback loops operating on a planetary scale that affect the atmosphere, the climate, life on the land, and life in the sea.

Feedback loops between life, land, air and water ensure that oxygen, temperature and light radiation levels stay within limits suitable for plants and animals. When one of nature's elements or cycles starts to get out of kilter, disturbing the planet's homeostatic equilibrium, other natural elements and cycles work to bring it back again. In this way, conditions for life on Earth are continually optimised. It was a revolutionary idea that saw links between biology, geology, physics and the Earth's chemistry.

Unsurprisingly, as well as attracting scientific attention, the idea also caught the imagination of those who had a more mystical take on the planet's health and wellbeing. Naming the hypothesis after a Greek goddess of the Earth only fed into their spiritual interpretation of how they viewed the 'living' planet. However, from the outset, Lovelock and others were clear that there were no conscious processes going on, no personification of the planet intended, no spiritual meaning to what was happening. It was just the natural sciences in action, without meaning, without intent, without feeling. The American biologist, Lynn Margulis was an early supporter of the Gaia hypothesis. In her 1998 book, *Symbiotic Planet*, she rebuked any notion that the planet should be understood as a single living organism.[12] There is just one huge ecosystem operating across the earth's surface.

In collaboration with the Manchester Science Festival, on 13 February 2021, the London Science Museum hosted an online event to discuss the Gaia hypothesis. It was titled 'Climate Talks: Earth, But Not As We Know It: Lovelock's Legacy and Our Future'. Aged 101, James Lovelock was interviewed and his thoughts were used to structure the day. This is what he had to say about Gaia:

> Gaia is not an entity that … decides. … It's just cybernetic feedback, there's no kind of thought involved in it. I mean, if you find too many clouds up in the sky by air pollution or something, it'll do all sorts of things, and one of them that's obvious, it'll reflect sunlight back to space, so it could have a cooling effect. On the other hand, it may reflect infrared radiation back to the earth and have a warming effect. So, it's physics rather than emotion that's involved in the choices by the system.

Gaia theory, as it is referred to nowadays, has been extensively researched. There is broad backing for the idea that biological and physical systems interact in highly complex ways, but any notion that the whole Earth might be seen as a living, self-sustaining organism receives less support. There are feedback loops and knock-on effects, but there is no inherent, purposeful drive to maintain life or keep temperatures ambient. These things may or may not happen depending on how the systems interact and play out. If conditions do remain conducive to life, these are seen as undirected emergent properties of the system.

All of this defines a trans-disciplinary field we now call 'earth system sciences', testimony to Lovelock's belief that to understand the planet we need to consider how all the physical and social sciences relate and interact, particularly the dynamic interplay between the geosphere and biosphere, and between human behaviour and the natural world. This is particularly true if we are to understand and do something about human-induced climate change, pollution and land degradation. As a species, we have become a dominant, even dangerous force on the planet.

* * *

The interrelationship of the multiple systems that have led to global heating and climate change are now familiar. Here is just one example of the cybernetic web of system complexity that might, after taking a deep breath, go something like this:

> The ingenuity of men and women taught us how to turn some rocks into pure metals. Fire and heat were involved which meant chopping down trees and burning wood. Later technologies realised that higher temperatures and more energy could be achieved by burning oil, coal and other fossil fuels. This involved digging up the ground, drilling for oil and pumping out gas. It took millions of years and complex geological processes for these fossil fuels to form. They represent 'trapped' sunlight, the ancient energy captured by photosynthesising trees and plants that died, were buried deep and compacted to form layers of coal, reservoirs of oil, and pockets of underground gas. Burning fossil fuels, whether to heat homes, cook food or make iron and steel, produces carbon dioxide. What had taken nature millions of years to sequester was being released back into the atmosphere in a blip of geological time. The invention of the steam engine at the beginning of the Industrial Revolution also relied on the burning of fossil fuels on a huge scale. Burning fossil fuels to heat water to make steam to drive engines led to more and more carbon dioxide being released; and, when engineers worked out how to use steam to drive turbines to make electricity, the production and consumption of fossil fuels rose exponentially, even before the invention of the internal combustion engine fuelled by petrol. In 1750 the level of carbon dioxide in the atmosphere was around 280 parts per million. In 2022, levels were running around 420 parts per million. Carbon dioxide is a 'greenhouse' gas, which is to say that it absorbs and therefore traps reflected infrared heat radiation from the sun resulting in a gradual warming up of the atmosphere, known as global heating. The global annual temperature has increased at an average rate of 0.07 °C per decade since 1880 and over twice that rate (+0.18 °C) since 1981. The seven warmest years between 1880 and 2023 have all occurred over the last decade, while nine of the ten warmest years have occurred since 2005, with 2020 average global temperatures around 1.2 °C higher than

> 1850 values and rising. Higher temperatures mean more energy in the atmosphere which leads to more turbulent and extreme weather patterns. Some places experience more storms, heavier rainfall and floods. Other places suffer drought, desertification and crop failure. Increased famines lead to large-scale population migrations which create political tensions and conflict. People die. Many plants and animals lose their habitats. Species become extinct. Biodiversity decreases. A sixth mass extinction looms. More carbon dioxide in the atmosphere means that more is absorbed by the warming oceans. Carbon dioxide in water produces a weak solution of carbonic acid which dissolves calcium carbonate out of which shells, many algae and corals are made. Warming oceans and heating atmosphere also melt more of the world's ice which raises global sea levels, disrupts ocean currents, changes weather pattern, and upsets and destroys marine life, floods low-lying land, displaces populations. Less ice exposes more 'dark' sea water and land-based rock which absorb more heat, adding further to rises in global temperatures.

Well, you get the idea. Because the mechanisms are non-linear, it is possible to 'enter' these chains at any point and tell similar stories. We could begin with oil and its use in the manufacture of plastics and how plastics are polluting both land and sea and killing wildlife on a global scale. We could look at the way people in crowded cities sell live animals for food, allowing the transmission of novel viruses from animals to humans causing global pandemics, increasing death rates and disrupting economies.

Or we could trace the history of agriculture. In 2019 Hannah Ritchie and Max Roser wrote that for much of human history, the world was mainly a wilderness of forests, grasslands and shrubs.[13] A thousand years ago they estimate that only four million square kilometres, or four per cent of the world's ice-free and non-barren land area was used for farming. Today, 71 per cent of the world's land is regarded as habitable, half of which is now used for agriculture. To achieve this, forests have been felled, woods cleared, rivers diverted, marshes drained and lakes pumped dry. Cattle and sheep, cereals and grain crops have replaced the rich biodiversity supported by natural habitats. Many fear that the combined effect of changing agricultural patterns and global heating is leading to a sixth mass extinction.

The *Living Planet Report 2022* of the World Wild Fund for Nature and the Zoological Society of London found that from 1970 to 2018, there was an average 69 per cent decline in the relative population abundance of monitored mammals, birds, reptiles, amphibians and fish.[14] We are in the midst of a biodiversity and climate crisis which is taking us rapidly along the road towards the collapse of the Earth's systems.

'The 2023 State of the Climate Report: Entering Uncharted Territory', written by William J. Ripple and colleagues, identifies 35 'vital signs' which track the planet's health.[15] They observe that 20 of these are in a critical state. 'Life on planet Earth', they say, 'is under siege.' The emission of greenhouse gases, global temperatures, wildfires and sea levels continue to rise. The European Union's Copernicus Climate Change Service reported that 2024 has been the hottest year for at least the last 125,000 years with average temperatures 1.5 °C above pre-industrial levels. Glaciers and ice sheets are melting at alarming rates. More areas of the world are becoming uninhabitable.

Each story of knock-ons, feedback loops and tipping points involves a knowledge of chemistry, physics, biology, meteorology, geology, the social sciences and all those elements that make up the earth system sciences whose beginnings we saw forming in the minds of late eighteenth- and early nineteenth-century classifiers, systematisers and pattern-seekers.

* * *

The classifications and patterns that we construct help us to make sense of, and navigate our way in the world. We are an order-searching, storytelling, meaning-making, curiosity-driven species. However, nature itself is seamless. It is we who feel wonder and awe as we parse the universe and create our stories.

From quantum fluctuations, big bangs, energy, matter, elements, stars, planets, earth, air and water to life, *homo sapiens*, consciousness, self-awareness and the search for meaning, we revel in a universe that is extraordinary and sublimely beautiful. In his book, *First You Write a Sentence*, Joe Moran says that 'Eastern mysticism and modern science agree: reality is an unbroken flow. Nouns divide that flow into things. They press the pause button of language and freeze-frame the real. Verbs set it in motion again.'[16] It is language that helps shape *our* reality.

The earth system sciences remind us, warn us even, that we are part of nature. We are active players on the planetary stage. We cannot stand apart. Our actions have consequences. Let's hope our understanding of what we have done, and continue to do, to the Earth has not come too late for us to do something about global heating, climate change, pollution and the threat of a sixth mass extinction, in which we, as a species, might be a casualty. If we can wonder, we might also learn to respect. If we are as clever as we think we are, there is still hope.

I am looking forward to climbing my next hill where I shall see the heavens above and the earth below, watch a thundercloud tower, gaze at a star-studded sky, catch the schillerising flash of a sunlit, feldspar-rich granite, listen to a beck babble and burble down a hillside, look up as a buzzard soars higher and higher, watch a red admiral settle momentarily on a buddleia, marvel at the tiny perfection of a forget-me-not, and remember the fourteenth-century anchoress, Julian of Norwich and recall her words of optimism as she meditated on life's wonders: 'All shall be well, and all shall be well, and all manner of things shall be well.'[17]

I do hope she's right.

Endnotes

1. Wondering High and Low

1. Helen Macdonald, *Vesper Flights* (London: Jonathan Cape, 2020), p. 248.
2. In August 1802 the poet Samuel Taylor Coleridge climbed Scafell Pike in the Lake District. He recounts the eventful experience in a letter to Sara Hutchinson, sister of Wordsworth's wife, Mary, dated 6 August 1802.
3. Robert Macfarlane, *The Wild Places* (London: Granta Books, 2007), p. 157.
4. Thomas Fletcher Smith, *John Dalton: A Cumbrian Philosopher* (Carlisle: Bookcase, 2015).
5. Thomas Fletcher Smith, *Jonathan Otley: Man of Lakeland* (Carlisle: Bookcase, 2007).
6. Richard Holmes, *Coleridge* (Oxford: Oxford University Press, 1982).
7. Juliet Barker, *Wordsworth: A Life* (London: Viking, 2000).
8. Simon Bainbridge, *Mountaineering and British Romanticism: The Literary Cultures of Climbing, 1770-1836* (Oxford: Oxford University Press, 2020).
9. 'Great things are done when men and mountains meet; / This is not done by jostling in the street.' One of Wordsworth's 'Gnomic Verses'. William Michael Rossetti, *The Poetical Works of William Blake* (London: Forgotten Books, 2018).
10. Theodore Roszak, *The Making of a Counter Culture* (Berkeley: University of California Press, 1995).
11. This question is asked and answered in Julian Baggini's 2005 book, *What's It All About?: Philosophy and the Meaning of Life* (London: Granta Books).
12. Julian of Norwich, *Revelations of Divine Love* (Oxford: Oxford University Press, 2015), p.16.

13. Richard Holmes, *The Age of Wonder* (London: Harper Press, 2008).
14. Samuel Taylor Coleridge (2015). *The Complete Works of Samuel Taylor Coleridge: Poetry, Plays, Literary Essays, Lectures, Autobiography and Letters (Classic Illustrated Edition)*, p.369.
15. E. Aronson, T.D. Wilson and R.M. Akert, *Social Psychology*, 5th edn (Upper Saddle River, NJ: Pearson, 2005).

2. Order and Meaning

1. Penelope Lively, *Ammonites and Leaping Fish: A Life in Time* (London: Fig Tree, 2013).
2. For example, see Carl Gustav Carus, *Nine Letters on Landscape Painting: Written in the Years 1815-1824; with a Letter from Goethe by Way of Introduction* (1831; Los Angeles: Getty Research Institute, 2006).
3. Part of Charles Darwin's famous last sentence in his 1859 book, *On the Origin of Species by Means of Natural Selection, or the Preservation of Favoured Races in the Struggle for Life*, 1st edn (London: John Murray).
4. Richard Feynman, *Feynman Lectures on Physics* (New York, NY: Basic Books, 2010), p 4.
5. Don Cupitt, *The Sea of Faith* (London: BBC Publications, 1984).
6. Bryan Magee, *Ultimate Questions* (Princeton NJ: Princeton University Press, 2017), p 116.
7. Jorge Luis Borges, 'The Analytical Language of John Wilkins', was first printed in *La Nación* on 8 February 1942. A translation of Borges' essay by Lilia Graciela Vázquez is available online at: https://ccrma.stanford.edu/courses/155/assignment/ex1/Borges.pdf (accessed 18 April 2024).
8. Katie Mack, *The End of Everything (Astrophysically Speaking)* (London: Penguin, 2021).
9. Jerome Bruner, 'The Narrative Construction of Reality', *Critical Inquiry* 18, no. 1 (Autumn 1991), pp. 1-21.
10. Richard Holloway, *Stories We Tell Ourselves: Making Meaning in a Meaningless Universe* (Edinburgh: Canongate, 2020), p 30.
11. Iris Murdoch in conversation with Bryan Magee (1977) on the *Men of Ideas* television series: 'Philosophy and Literature with Iris Murdoch', BBC Television [1977]. Available online at: https://www.youtube.com/watch?v=g7fY3GsFzkY (accessed 18 April 2024).
12. Bruner, 'The Narrative Construction of Reality'.
13. F. Heider and M. Simmel, 'An Experimental Study of Apparent Behavior', *American Journal of Psychology* 57, no. 2 (1944), pp. 243-59.

3. Star Struck

1. Bob Dylan, song, *Mr Tambourine Man* (1965).
2. Gerard Manley Hopkins, 'The Starlight Night' (1877), in *The Poems of Gerard Manley Hopkins*, edited with notes by Robert Bridges (2018), (Oxford: Oxford University Press).
3. William T. Vollmann, *Uncentering the Earth: Copernicus and the Revolution of the Heavenly Spheres* (New York, NY: W.W. Norton, 2006).
4. Albert van Helden, Sven Dupré, Rob van Gent and Huib Zuidervaart (eds), *The Origins of the Telescope* (Amsterdam: Amsterdam University Press, 2010).
5. John L. Heilbron, *Galileo* (Oxford: Oxford University Press, 2012).
6. Massimo Bucciantini, Michele Camerota and Franco Giudice, *Galileo's Telescope: A European Story*, trans. Catherine Bolton (Cambridge, MA: Harvard University Press, 2015).
7. Audrey T. Carpenter, *John Theophilus Desaguliers: A Natural Philosopher, Engineer and Freemason in Newtonian England* (London: Continuum, 2011).
8. Wolfgang Steinicke, *William Herschel: Discoverer of the Deep Sky* (Watford: Books on Demand, 2021).
9. Holmes, *The Age of Wonder*, p. 205.
10. Louise Glück, 'The Telescope', in Louise Glück, *Averno* (London: Penguin, 2021).
11. John Keats, 'On First Looking into Chapman's Homer' (1816), in *John Keats: Selected Poems*, ed. John Barnard (London: Penguin, 2007), p. 12.
12. Holmes, *The Age of Wonder*.
13. Erasmus Darwin, 'The Botanic Garden' (1792), Part 1 Canto IV, lines 375-76, quoted by Adam Komisaruk and Allison Dushane (eds), *The Botanic Garden by Erasmus Darwin* (London: Routledge, 2017).
14. Cited in Holmes, *The Age of Wonder*, p. 210.
    14 Cited in Holmes, *The Age of Wonder*, p 73.

4. Let Me Play among the Stars

1. Charles Coulston Gillispie, *Pierre-Simon Laplace, 1749-1827: A Life in Exact Science* (Princeton, NJ: Princeton University Press, 2000).
2. Myles W. Jackson, *Spectrum of Belief: Joseph von Fraunhofer and the Craft of Precision Optics* (Cambridge, MA: MIT Press, 2000).
3. Dava Sobel, *The Glass Universe: How the Ladies of the Harvard Observatory Took the Measure of the Stars* (London: Penguin, 2016).

4. Donovan Moore, *What Stars Are Made Of: The Life of Cecilia Payne-Gaposchkin* (Cambridge, MA: Harvard University Press, 2020).
5. Ian Ridpath, *A Dictionary of Astronomy*, 2nd edn (Oxford: Oxford University Press, 2012).
6. Geoff McNamara, *Clocks in the Sky: The Story of Pulsars* (New York, NY: Springer Praxis Books, 2008).
7. Alexander S. Sharov and Igor D. Novikov, *Edwin Hubble: The Discoverer of the Big Bang Universe* (Cambridge: Cambridge University Press, 2008).
8. Thomas Hardy, *Two on a Tower: A Romance* (1882; London: Penguin, 1999).
9. Tremain, Rose (1985), The Swimming Pool Season, London: Sceptre edition, pp 237-8.
10. Sharov and Novikov, *Edwin Hubble.*
11. Mack, *The End of Everything (Astrophysically Speaking)*, p 32.
12. Brian Greene, *Until the End of Time: Mind, Matter, and Our Search for Meaning in an Evolving Universe* (London: Penguin, 2021), p. 5.
13. Sarah Williams, 'The Old Astronomer', in Sarah Williams, *Twilight Hours: A Legacy of Verse* (London: Strahan & Co., 1868).
14. W.H. Auden, 'The More Loving One', in W.H. Auden, *Homage to Clio* (New York, NY: Random House, 1960).

5. Head in the Clouds

1. John Ruskin, *The Works of John Ruskin*, ed. Alexander Wedderburn and Edward Tyas Cook (Cambridge: Cambridge University Press, 1903-12), vol. 3, section 3, 'Of Truth of Skies'.
2. Virginia Woolf, 'On Being Ill', first published in *The New Criterion* 4, no. 1 (January 1926) (London: Renard Press, 2023).
3. Alice Oswald and Paul Keegan (eds), *Gigantic Cinema: A Weather Anthology* (London: Jonathan Cape, 2020).
4. Shelley's poem, 'The Cloud', was originally published in 1820 by Charles and James Ollier in a collection titled *Prometheus Unbound, A Lyrical Drama, in Four Acts, with Other Poems.*
5. After he left his school teaching post in Kendal in 1793 John Dalton moved to New College, Manchester, where he established himself as Professor of Mathematics and Natural Philosophy. The college was one of the 'dissenting academies' set up to provide higher education for non-conformists, that is, those who did not belong to the Church of England and who were barred from entering the universities. He also joined the Manchester Literary and Philosophical Society. His daily life was regular, structured and predictable. He never married, claiming 'I never had the time.'

6. Smith, *John Dalton.*
7. Howard Oliver and Sylvia Oliver, 'Meteorologist's Profile: John Dalton', *Weather* 58, no. 6 (2003), pp. 206-11.
8. Luke Howard, On the Modifications of Clouds (London: John Churchill & Sons, 1803).
9. Rhodri Lewis, 'Shakespeare's Clouds and the Image Made by Chance', *Essays in Criticism* 62, no. 1 (January 2012), pp. 1-24.
10. Richard Hamblyn, *The Invention of Clouds: How an Amateur Meteorologist Forged the Language of the Skies* (London: Picador, 2011). In 1823 Luke Howard moved with his family to live in Ackworth, a couple of miles south of Pontefract, Yorkshire. He continued to commute to London to visit his factory for the next nineteen years. In 1852, Mariabella, his wife, died, and he returned to the capital to live with his eldest son, Robert, at 7 Bruce Grove, Tottenham. At the grand age of 91, on 21 March 1864, Luke Howard died.
11. Luke Howard, *On the Modifications of Clouds* (London: John Churchill & Sons, 1803).
12. Luke Howard, *Seven Lectures on Meteorology* (1837; Cambridge: Cambridge University Press, 2011).
13. Jean-Baptiste Lamarck, 'Nouvelle définition des termes que j'emploie pour exprimer certaines formes des nuages qu'il importe de distinguer dans l'annotation de l'état du ciel', *Annuaire météorologique pour l'an XIII de la République Française*, no. 3 (1805), pp. 112-33.
14. Quoted in Stanley David Gedzelman, 'Cloud Classification before Luke Howard', *Bulletin of the American Meteorological Society* 70, no. 4 (1989), p. 381.
15. Hamblyn, *The Invention of Clouds.*
16. See https://www.tottenhamclouds.org.uk/goethe-discovers-luke-howard.html (accessed 19 April 2024).
17. Quoted in Alison Meier, 'How the Naming of Clouds Changed the Skies of Art', *Hyperallergic* (a forum for discussing art headquartered in Brooklyn, New York City), 7 January 2016. Available online at: https://hyperallergic.com/261023/how-the-naming-of-clouds-changed-the-skies-of-art/ (accessed 20 April 2024).
18. John E. Thornes, *John Constable's Skies: A Fusion of Art and Science* (Birmingham: Birmingham University Press, 1999).
19. John Ruskin, *Modern Painters*, Volume 3 (1856). Available online via Project Gutenberg, updated 25 January 2021.
20. Mark Evans, *Constable's Skies: Paintings and Sketches by John Constable* (London: Thames & Hudson, 2018).
21. Thomas Forster, *Researches about Atmospheric Phaenomena*, 2nd edn (London: Baldwin, Cradock & Joy, 1815), p. 3.
22. Quoted in Thornes, *John Constable's Skies.*

6. Weather Forecasts and Cloudy Thinking

1. John Gribbin and Mary Gribbin, *FitzRoy: The Remarkable Story of Darwin's Captain and the Invention of the Weather Forecast* (Scotts Valley, CA: CreateSpace Independent Publishing Platform, 2016); UK Met Office, 'Robert FitzRoy and the Early Met Office': https://www.metoffice.gov.uk/research/library-and-archive/archive-hidden-treasures/robert-fitzroy (accessed 21 April 2024).
2. UK Met Office, ibid.
3. Biography in Britannica, The Editors of Encyclopaedia, 'Lewis Fry Richardson', *Encyclopaedia Britannica*, 4 April 2024, https://www.britannica.com/biography/Lewis-Fry-Richardson (accessed 21 April 2024).
4. World Meteorological Association, *International Cloud Atlas*: https://cloudatlas.wmo.int/en/cloud-classification-summary.html (accessed 21 April 2024).
5. Rebecca J. Rosen, 'Clouds: The Most Useful Metaphor of All Time?', *The Atlantic*, 30 September 2011.
6. William Wordsworth, 'I Wandered Lonely as a Cloud', in William Wordsworth, *Poems in Two Volumes* (London: Longman, Hurst, Rees, Orme & Brown, 1807).
7. David Mitchell, *Cloud Atlas* (London: Sceptre Books, 2014).

7. Down to Earth

1. William Whiston, *A New Theory of the Earth: from Its Original, to the Consummation of All Things* (1696; Madrid: Hard Press Publishing, 2019).
2. Ray Perman, *James Hutton: The Genius of Time* (Edinburgh: Birlinn Books, 2022); Dennis R. Dean, *James Hutton and the History of Geology* (Ithaca, NY: Cornell University Press, 1992).
3. John Playfair, *Illustrations of the Huttonian Theory of the Earth* (Edinburgh: Cadell & Davies, 1802).
4. Sir Charles Lyell was a nineteenth-century Scottish geologist and the author of *Principles of Geology*, first published in 1830-33 by John Murray, London.
5. Horace Bénédict de Saussure (1740-99) was born in a town not far from Geneva, Switzerland. He explored the Alps and their glaciers and in the process established himself as a pioneering meteorologist, geologist, botanist, physicist and mountaineer.
6. Jules Verne, *Journey to the Centre of the Earth* (1864; Oxford: Oxford University Press, 2008).

8. Mary Anning and 'Strata' Smith

1. Charlotte Smith, 'From Beachy Head', in Charlotte Smith, *Beachy Head with Other Poems* (London: J. Johnson, 1707).
2. Kurt Badt, *John Constable's Clouds* (London: Routledge & Kegan Paul, 1950).
3. The portrait hangs in the Ashmolean Museum, Oxford.
4. Although John Ruskin invited John Everett Millais to paint his portrait, he hadn't planned to lose his wife, Effie, to the artist. After six years, Effie, left her unconsummated marriage to marry Millais. Their marriage was consummated. The couple went on to have eight children.
5. Shelley Emling, *The Fossil Hunter: Dinosaurs, Evolution, and the Woman Whose Discoveries Changed the World* (London: Palgrave Macmillan, 2011); Marie-Claire Eylott, 'Mary Anning: The Unsung Hero of Fossil Discovery'; see Natural History Museum: https://www.nhm.ac.uk/discover/mary-anning-unsung-hero.html (accessed 22 April 2024).
6. Tracy Chevalier, *Remarkable Creatures* (London: The Borough Press, 2014).
7. Simon Winchester, *The Map that Changed the World: The Tale of William Smith and the Birth of a Science* (London: Viking, 2001); John L. Morton, *Strata: The Remarkable Life Story of William Smith, the Father of English Geology* (Horsham: Brocken Spectre Publishing, 2004).
8. Maura Dooley, 'Treasure Island', in Michael McKimm (ed.), *Map: Poems After William Smith's Geological Map of 1815* (Chadwell Heath: Worple Press, 2015).
9. For some years after the publication of his map, William Smith found himself in financial difficulties. To pay off some of his debts he sold his fossil collection and books to the British Museum in London. Still unable to pay his debts, in 1819 he spent ten weeks in the King's Bench Prison for debtors in London.
10. Smith, *Jonathan Otley*.
11. In 1881 Charles Lapworth became the first professor of geology at Mason Science College, later to become the University of Birmingham.

9. Geological Time and the Restless Planet

1. Joe D.D. Burchfield, *Lord Kelvin and the Age of the Earth* (Chicago: University of Chicago Press, 1990).

2. Kelvin is perhaps best known for being the first person to work out the value of absolute zero, the temperature at which, put simply, atoms no longer transmit any thermal energy and, save for the weird effects of quantum mechanics, all internal motion ceases. It is not possible for temperatures to get any lower than this absolute point. The value of absolute zero calculated by Kelvin, which has been revised only slightly over the years, was –273.15 °C. In honour of his work, all temperatures which work from absolute zero as their base are talked about in terms of degrees Kelvin (°K). The freezing point of water on this scale, therefore, is approximately +273 °K.
3. Claude J. Allègre, *Isotope Geology*, trans. Christopher Sutcliffe (Cambridge: Cambridge University Press, 2008).
4. Wolfgang Frisch, Martin Meschede and Ronald C. Blakey, *Plate Tectonics: Continental Drift and Mountain Building* (Berlin: Springer, 2022).
5. T. Mott Greene, *Alfred Wegener: Science, Exploration, and the Theory of Continental Drift* (Princeton, NJ: Princeton University Press, 2018).
6. Cherry Lewis, *The Dating Game* (Cambridge: Cambridge University Press, 2012); Arthur Holmes, *Principles of Physical Geology* (London: Thomas Nelson & Sons, 1965).
7. Frisch, Meschede and Blakey, *Plate Tectonics.*
8. Verne, *Journey to the Centre of the Earth*, p. 76.
9. Neil Hodgson, "Time Tide, Blanket Cover, Zone Fossil" Geological Society Geopoetry Day, Edinburgh, 1 October 2020 < https://www.youtube.com/watch?v=Xzs5YMhJiAk > [1 May 2024].
10. Richard Fortey, *The Earth: An Intimate History* (London: Harper Perennial, 2005); Nigel Woodcock and Rob Strachan, *Geological History of Britain and Ireland* (Oxford: Blackwell, 2012).

10. Plants and Animals

1. Paul Nurse, *What Is Life?* (Oxford: David Fickling Books, 2021).
2. Sophia M. Connell (ed.), *The Cambridge Companion to Aristotle's Biology* (Cambridge: Cambridge University Press, 2021); Armand Marie Leroi, *The Lagoon: How Aristotle Invented Science* (London: Bloomsbury, 2014).
3. Gunnar Broberg, *The Man Who Organized Nature: The Life of Linnaeus* (Princeton, NJ: Princeton University Press, 2023).
4. P.D. James, *Time to Be in Earnest: A Fragment of Autobiography* (London: Faber & Faber, 2000), p. 22.
5. John Gray, *Feline Philosophy: Cats and the Meaning of Life* (London: Allen Lane, 2020).

6. During his late twenties and early thirties, Linnaeus travelled and worked around Europe before returning to Sweden in June 1738. He became engaged to Sara Elisabeth Moræa. Three months later, he moved to Stockholm to work as a doctor where he also became involved in founding the Royal Swedish Academy of Science. In 1739 he married Sara. They went on to have six children together.

11. *On the Origin of Species*

1. The Lunar Society met when there was a full moon to discuss matters of shared interest, particularly around the subject of natural philosophy. Self-mockingly, they called themselves 'the lunatiks'. Charles Darwin's maternal grandfather, Josiah Wedgwood, was a pottery manufacturer and leading figure in the industrial revolution. He was also an original member of the Lunar Society.
2. See Chapter 6 for more on the life and work of Robert FitzRoy.
3. Josiah Wedgwood II was the son of the industrialist and potter, Josiah Wedgwood. He continued his father's work and also was Member of Parliament for Stoke-upon-Trent from 1832 to 1835. He was a keen supporter of the abolition of slavery. In 1798 Josiah and his brother Thomas offered the poet Samuel Taylor Coleridge a life annuity of £150 so that he could pursue his literary and philosophical interests without worrying too much about money.
4. Janet Browne, *Charles Darwin: Voyaging: Volume 1* (London: Pimlico, 1996); Janet Browne, *Charles Darwin: The Power of Place: Volume 2* (London: Pimlico, 2003).
5. David Lack, *Darwin's Finches* (Cambridge: Cambridge University Press, 1983).
6. Holmes, *The Age of Wonder.*
7. Alfred Russel Wallace was born in 1823. He was a biologist, anthropologist and explorer.
8. Darwin Correspondence Project, University of Cambridge, 'Letter no. 2299': https://www.darwinproject.ac.uk/letter/?docId=letters/DCP-LETT-2299.xml (accessed 23 April 2024).
9. C.R. Darwin, *On the Origin of Species by Means of Natural Selection, or the Preservation of Favoured Races in the Struggle for Life*, 1st edn (London: John Murray, 1859).
10. John Abraham Heraud, *The Descent into Hell, with an Analysis and Notes: To Which Are Added, Uriel, a Fragment, and Three Odes* (1835; Whitefish, MT: Kessinger Publishing, 2009).
11. Richard Dawkins, *Unweaving the Rainbow: Science, Delusion and the Appetite for Wonder* (London: Allen Lane/Penguin Press, 1998).

12. Daniel Dennett, *Darwin's Dangerous Idea: Evolution and the Meanings of Life* (New York: Simon & Schuster, 1995).
13. Charles Darwin, *The Variations of Animals and Plants under Domestication*, 2nd edn (London: John Murray, 1882).
14. Charles Darwin, *The Descent of Man* (London: John Murray, 1871).
15. Charles Darwin, *The Expression of the Emotions in Man and Animals* (London: John Murray, 1872).
16. Charles Darwin, *The Formation of Vegetable Mould Through the Action of Worms* (London: John Murray, 1882).
17. Ruth Padel, *Darwin: A Life in Poems* (London: Vintage, 2010).
18. Richard Holmes, 'Giving to a Blind Man Eyes', *The Guardian*, 14 March 2009.

12. Genetics

1. Vitezslav Orel, *Gregor Mendel: The First Geneticist*, trans. Stephen Finn (Oxford: Oxford University Press, 1996).
2. Nurse, *What Is Life?*
3. Sean B. Carroll, *Endless Forms Most Beautiful: The New Science of Evo Devo and the Making of the Animal Kingdom* (London: Weidenfeld & Nicolson, 2006).
4. Ibid., p. 3.
5. Ibid., p. 10.
6. Thomas Hardy, *The Complete Poetical Works of Thomas Hardy: Volume II: Satires of Circumstance, Moments of Vision, Late Lyrics and Earlier*, ed. Samuel Hynes (Oxford: Oxford University Press, 1983).
7. Richard C. Francis, *Epigenetics: How Environment Shapes Our Genes* (New York, NY: W.W. Norton, 2012).
8. C. McEwen and B. McEwen, 'Social Structure, Adversity, Toxic Stress, and Intergenerational Poverty: An Early Childhood Model', *Annual Review of Sociology* 43, no. 1 (2017), pp. 445-72.
9. R.F. Anda, J.B. Croft, V.J. Felitti *et al.*, 'Adverse Childhood Experiences and Smoking during Adolescence and Adulthood', *Journal of the American Medical Association*, 282, no. 17 (1999), pp. 1652-58.
10. H.G. Wells, *The Time Machine* (London: Heinemann, 1895); H.G. Wells, *The War of the Worlds* (London: Heinemann, 1898); Joseph Conrad, *Heart of Darkness* (1902; London: Penguin Classics, 2024); R.L. Stevenson, *The Strange Case of Dr Jekyll and Mr Hyde* (1886; Oxford: Oxford University Press, 2008); Margaret Atwood, *The Handmaid's Tale* (London: Vintage, 1996); Margaret Atwood, *MaddAddam Trilogy* (Toronto: McClelland & Stewart, 2013);

A.S. Byatt, *A Whistling Woman* (London: Vintage, 2003); Paul Hamann-Rose, *Genetics and the Novel: Reimagining Life Through Fiction* (London: Palgrave Macmillan, 2024).

11. Patrick Barkham, *The Butterfly Isles: A Summer Search of Our Emperors and Admirals* (London: Granta, 2010).

13. The Philosopher's Stone

1. John Milton, *Paradise Lost: Books V-VI* (1667; Cambridge: Cambridge University Press, 1975), V, l. 439.
2. Paul Strathern, *Mendeleyev's Dream: The Quest for the Elements* (London: Hamish Hamilton, 2000), p. 58.
3. Jorge Luis Borges' poem, 'Browning Decides to Be a Poet', in Lowell Dunham and Ivar Ivask (eds), *The Cardinal Points of Borges* (Norman: University of Oklahoma Press, 1971).

14. The Rise of the Chemist

1. Robert Boyle was born in Ireland in 1627, the fourteenth child of the first Earl of Cork. He was schooled in England and by his late twenties was living and working in Oxford, before finally moving to London in 1668. He was interested in physics and chemistry, both practically and theoretically and was one of the leading figures who founded the Royal Society of London in 1663. In his later years, Boyle suffered from poor health. He died, aged 64, on the very last day of 1691 and was buried in the churchyard of St Martin-in-the-Fields, London.
2. Robert Boyle, *The Sceptical Chymist: Or Chymico-Physical Doubts and Paradoxes* (London: F. Crooke, 1661); available online at Project Gutenberg: https://www.gutenberg.org/ebooks/22914 (accessed 24 April 2024).

15. In Their Element

1. Humphry Davy, 'The Sons of Genius', quoted in Holmes, *The Age of Wonder*, p. 244.
2. Wordsworth's letter to Davy, quoted in Barker, *Wordsworth*; Wordsworth to Davy, 29 July 1800, pp. 289-90. Based on Coleridge's word, in 1800 Wordsworth invited Davy to correct and proof-read the second edition of their anthology, *Lyrical Ballads*. This book of poems marks the beginning of the Romantic Movement in England

and contains Coleridge's 'Rime of the Ancient Mariner' and Wordsworth's 'Lines Composed a Few Miles above Tintern Abbey'. Wordsworth's letter to Davy, written in August 1800, should hearten all schoolchildren struggling with spelling and punctuation: "Dear Sir, So I venture to address you though I have not had the happiness of being personally known to you. You would greatly oblige me by looking over the enclosed poems and correcting any thing you find amiss in the punctuation a business at which I am ashamed to say I am no adept. … I write to request that you would have the goodness to look over the proof-sheets of the 2nd volume before they are finally struck off. … Yours sincerely, W. Wordsworth".

3. Robert Southey quoted in Holmes, *The Age of Wonder*, p. 264.
4. In 1812 Humphry Davy married the rich socialite and widow, Jane Kerr. She attended many of Davy's lectures and had long held a great interest in the emerging sciences. The couple had no children and Davy left most of his scientific papers to his brother, John, who had enjoyed a career as a chemist (discovering the gas phosgene) and medical doctor. In 1844 John Davy moved with his wife to Ambleside in the Lake District where he became the family doctor to the Wordsworths, who were living at Rydal Mount, a mile up the road.
5. D.S.L. Cardwell (ed.), *John Dalton and the Progress of Science* (Manchester: Manchester University Press, 1968); Smith, *John Dalton: A Cumbrian Philosopher.*
6. Strathern, *Mendeleyev's Dream*, p. 58.
7. Ibid., p. 258.
8. Ibid., p. 259.

16. The Periodic Table

1. Michael D. Gordin, *A Well-Ordered Thing: Dmitrii Mendeleev and the Shadow of the Periodic Table* (Princeton, NJ: Princeton Univeristy Press, 2018); Strathern, *Mendeleyev's Dream.*
2. Dmitri Mendeleev was the youngest of seventeen children. As a boy, Mendeleev was taught Latin and Ancient Greek, neither of which he liked or excelled at. However, he did receive some private tutoring in the sciences from the husband of one of his elder sisters and this he did enjoy.
3. Dmitry Ivanovich Mendeleyev, *The Principles of Chemistry* (1868; St Albans: Wentworth Press, 2016).
4. Julius Lothar Meyer (1830-95) was a German chemist.
5. Paul-Émile Lecoq de Boisbaudran discovered a number of elements including dysprosium, gallium and some of the rare earths. He was a pioneer in the field of spectroscopy.

6. In 1886 Clemens Alexander Winkler (1838-1904) discovered the element germanium, which he isolated from argyrodite, a silver germanium sulphide mineral.
7. Eric R. Scerri, 'Happy 150th Birthday to the Periodic Table', *Chemistry European Journal* 25, no. 31 (2019), pp. 7410-15.
8. Primo Levi, *The Periodic Table* (London: Abacus, 1986).
9. Ibid., pp. 27-28.
10. Ibid., pp. 232-33.

17. Sentient Stardust

1. John Joseph Thomson was born in Manchester in 1856. While at the University of Cambridge he discovered the electron. In 1906 was awarded the Nobel Prize for physics for his work on the conduction of electricity in gases.
2. Ernest Rutherford (1871-1937) was born in New Zealand. In 1895 he moved to the University of Cambridge where he carried out research with J.J. Thomson on the atom at its structure. He also conducted research into radioactivity.
3. Niels Henrik David Bohr (1885-1962) was a Danish physicist known for his work on the structure of the atom and quantic theory. He received the Nobel Prize in Physics in 1922.
4. Abraham Pais, *Niels Bohr's Times: In Physics, Philosophy and Polity* (Oxford: Clarendon Press, 1993).
5. Werner Heisenberg quotes Bohr in his book, *Physics and Beyond* (New York, NY: Harper & Row, 1971), p. 206.
6. Barbara Ryden, *Introduction to Cosmology* (Cambridge: Cambridge University Press, 2016).
7. Fred Hoyle, 'The Synthesis of the Elements from Hydrogen', *Monthly Notices of the Royal Astronomical Society* 106 (1946), pp. 343-83.
8. Carl Sagan, *Cosmos: A Personal Voyage*, TV series, PBS America (1980).
9. Picking up the allusion, in her song, 'Woodstock', Joni Mitchell sings: 'We are stardust. We are golden', as she asks might we get back to an age of innocence.
10. Nikita Gill's poem '93 Percent Stardust' in her book of poems, *Your Soul Is a River* (Williamsburg, Brooklyn: Thought Catalog Books, 2018).
11. William Wordsworth, 'The Stars Are Mansions Built by Nature's Hand' (1820).
12. Gaia Vince, *Transcendence: How Humans Evolved through Fire, Language, Beauty and Time* (London: Allen Lane, 2020).

18. It Takes All Sorts

1. Joe Moran, 'Don't Believe a Word by David Shariatmadari Review – The Truth about Language', *The Guardian*, 10 August 2019.
2. Shawn Carlson, 'A Double-Blind Test of Astrology', *Nature* 318 (1985), pp. 419-25.
3. A. Kelly, J. Côté, M. Jeffreys and J. Turnnidge, *Birth Advantages and Relative Age Effects in Sport: Exploring Organizational Structures and Creating Appropriate Settings* (London: Routledge, 2021).
4. I. Mujika, R. Vaeyens, S.P. Matthys *et al.*, 'The Relative Age Effect in a Professional Football Club Setting', *Journal of Sports Science* 27, no. 11 (2009), pp. 1153-58.
5. D.P. Thomas, 'The Demise of Blood-letting', *Journal of the Royal College of Physicians* 44, no. 1 (2014), pp. 72-77.
6. Sigmund Freud, *The Psychopathology of Everyday Life* (1904; Cambridge: Cambridge University Press, 2010).
7. Carl Jung, *Psychological Types* (1921; London: Routledge, 2016).
8. *Extravert* and *extraversion* were Eysenck's original spellings and these are still used today in many psychology textbooks. However, today the more common spellings, particularly outside psychology, are *extrovert* and *extroversion*. Although the spellings are different the meanings are the same.
9. Hans J. Eysenck and Sybil Eysenck, *Personality Structure and Measurement* (1969; London: Routledge, 2014).
10. Gerald Matthews, *Personality Traits* (Cambridge: Cambridge University Press, 2009).
11. Dana G. Smith, 'Big Data Gives the "Big 5" Personality Traits a Makeover', *Scientific American*, 18 September 2018.
12. Benjamin Hardy, *Personality Isn't Permanent: Break Free from Self-Limiting Beliefs and Rewrite Your Story* (New York, NY: Portfolio, 2020).
13. Lucy Foulkes, 'The Big Idea: Is It Your Personality, or a Disorder?', *The Guardian*, 16 October 2021, p. 77.
14. Robert Rowland Smith, *What It Means to Be Human: A Philosophical Memoir* (London: Fourth Estate, 2019), p. 3.

19. Sense and Sensibility

1. Simon Baron-Cohen, *Zero Degrees of Empathy* (London: Penguin, 2012); Simon Baron-Cohen, *The Pattern Seekers: A New Theory of Human Invention* (London: Penguin, 2022).
2. David Howe, *Empathy: What It Is and Why It Matters* (London: Palgrave Macmillan, 2012).

3. Paul Klee, 'The Play of Forces at the Bauhaus' (1921), quoted in L. Wix, 'Aesthetic Empathy in Teaching Art to Children: The Work of Friedl Dicker-Brandeis in Terezin', *Art Therapy* 26, no. 4 (2009), pp. 152-58; p. 153.
4. Isaiah Berlin, *The Magus of the North: J.G. Hamann and the Origins of Modern Irrationalism* (London: Fontana Press, 1993), p. 1.
5. William Wordsworth, 'Lines Composed a Few Miles above Tintern Abbey, on Revisiting the Banks of the Wye during a Tour, July 13, 1798', in William Wordsworth and Samuel Taylor Coleridge, *Lyrical Ballads 1798 and 1802*, ed. Fiona Stafford (Oxford: Oxford University Press, 2013).
6. 'Sapere Aude!' – in the opening paragraph of 'An Answer to the Question: What Is Enlightenment?' by Immanuel Kant (1784). The translation of Kant's essay by Ted Humphrey (Hackett Publishing, 1992) is available online via the New York Public Library website: https://www.nypl.org/sites/default/files/kant_whatisenlightenment.pdf (accessed 26 April 2024).
7. William Wordsworth, 'The Tables Turned' (1798), in Wordsworth and Coleridge, *Lyrical Ballads 1798 and 1802*.
8. Nan Shepherd, *The Living Mountain: A Celebration of the Cairngorms Mountains of Scotland* (Edinburgh: Canongate Books, 2011).
9. Ibid., p. 108.
10. Ibid.
11. Tristan Gooley, *How to Read Water: Clues, Signs & Patterns from Puddles to the Sea* (London: Sceptre, 2016).
12. Dawkins, *Unweaving the Rainbow*, p. x.
13. Richard P. Feynman, *The Pleasure of Finding Things Out: The Best Short Works of Richard P. Feynman* (Cambridge, MA: Perseus Books, 1999), p. 2.
14. Dara McAnulty, *Diary of a Young Naturalist* (London: Ebury Press, 2021).
15. Macdonald, *Vesper Flights*, p. 21.

20: The Art of Science

1. John Dalton, *Meteorological Observations and Essays* (1793; Cambridge: Cambridge University Press, 2011).
2. Howard, *Seven Lectures on Meteorology*.
3. William Wordsworth, *Guide to the Lakes* (1835; Oxford: Oxford University Press, 2022).
4. Charles Lyell, *Principles of Geology* (1830-33; London: Penguin, 1997).
5. John F.W. Herschel, *A Preliminary Discourse on the Study of Natural Philosophy* (1830; Chicago: Chicago University Press, 1987).

6. B. Warner, 'Charles Darwin and John Herschel', *South African Journal of Science* 105, no. 11/12 (2009), pp. 432-39.
7. Darwin, *On the Origin of Species*, opening two sentences of the book.
8. David Howe, *Extraction to Extinction: Rethinking Our Relationship with Earth's Natural Resources* (Salford: Saraband, 2021).
9. James Lovelock was born on 26 July 1919 in Letchworth, England, and died on his 103rd birthday on 26 July 2022.
10. James Lovelock, *Homage to Gaia: The Life of an Independent Scientist* (London: Souvenir Press, 2019).
11. James Lovelock, *Gaia: A New Look at Life on Earth* (Oxford: Oxford University Press, 2016).
12. Lynn Margulis, *Symbiotic Planet: A New Look at Evolution* (New York, NY: Basic Books, 1998).
13. Hannah Ritchie and Max Roser, *Land Use*, September 2019, published online at Our World in Data. Available online at: https://ourworldindata.org/land-use (accessed 26 April 2024).
14. World Wild Fund for Nature in collaboration with Zoological Society of London, *Living Planet Report 2022: Building a Nature-Positive Society* (Gland, Switzerland: WWF, 2022).
15. William J. Ripple, Christopher Wolf, Jillian W. Gregg *et al.*, 'The 2023 State of the Climate Report: Entering Uncharted Territory', *BioScience* 73, no. 12 (2023), pp. 841-50.
16. Joe Moran, *First You Write a Sentence* (London: Penguin, 2018), p. 16.
17. Julian of Norwich, *Revelations of Divine Love*.

Bibliography

Allègre, Claude J., *Isotope Geology*, trans. Christopher Sutcliffe (Cambridge: Cambridge University Press, 2008)

Anda, R.F., J.B. Croft, V.J. Felitti, D. Nordenberg, W.H. Giles, D.F. Williamson and G.A. Giovino, 'Adverse Childhood Experiences and Smoking during Adolescence and Adulthood', *Journal of the American Medical Association* 282, no. 17 (1999), pp. 1652-58

Aronson, E., T.D. Wilson and R.M. Akert, *Social Psychology*, 5th edn (Upper Saddle River, NJ: Pearson, 2005)

Auden, W.H., *Homage to Clio* (New York, NY: Random House, 1960)

Badt, Kurt, *John Constable's Clouds* (London: Routledge & Kegan Paul, 1950)

Baggini, Julian, *What's It All About?: Philosophy and the Meaning of Life* (London: Granta Books, 2005)

Bainbridge, Simon, *Mountaineering and British Romanticism: The Literary Cultures of Climbing, 1770-1836* (Oxford: Oxford University Press, 2020)

Barker, Juliet, *Wordsworth: A Life* (London: Viking, 2000)

Barkham, Patrick, *The Butterfly Isles: A Summer Search of Our Emperors and Admirals* (London: Granta, 2010)

Baron-Cohen, Simon, *The Pattern Seekers: A New Theory of Human Invention* (London: Penguin, 2022)

———, *Zero Degrees of Empathy* (London: Penguin, 2012)

Bate, Jonathan, *The Song of the Earth* (Cambridge, MA: Harvard University Press, 2000)

Berlin, Isaiah, *The Magus of the North: J.G. Hamann and the Origins of Modern Irrationalism* (London: Fontana Press, 1993)

Borges, Jorge Luis, 'The Analytical Language of John Wilkins', was first printed in *La Nación* on 8 February 1942; a translation of Borges' essay by Lilia Graciela Vázquez is available online at: https://ccrma.stanford.edu/courses/155/assignment/ex1/Borges.pdf (accessed 18 April 2024)

Boyle, Robert, *The Sceptical Chymist: Or Chymico-Physical Doubts and Paradoxes* (London: F. Crooke, 1661); available online at Project

Gutenberg: https://www.gutenberg.org/ebooks/22914 (accessed 24 April 2024)

Britannica, The Editors of Encyclopaedia, 'Lewis Fry Richardson', *Encyclopaedia Britannica*, 4 April 2024: https://www.britannica.com/biography/Lewis-Fry-Richardson (accessed 21 April 2024)

Broberg, Gunnar, *The Man Who Organized Nature: The Life of Linnaeus* (Princeton, NJ: Princeton University Press, 2023)

Browne, Janet, *Charles Darwin: Voyaging: Volume 1* (London: Pimlico, 1996); and *Charles Darwin: The Power of Place: Volume 2* (London: Pimlico, 2003)

Bruner, Jerome, 'The Narrative Construction of Reality', *Critical Inquiry* 18, no. 1 (Autumn 1991), pp. 1-21

Bucciantini, Massimo, Michele Camerota and Franco Giudice, *Galileo's Telescope: A European Story*, trans. Catherine Bolton (Cambridge, MA: Harvard University Press, 2015)

Burchfield, Joe D.D., *Lord Kelvin and the Age of the Earth* (Chicago: University of Chicago Press, 1990)

Cardwell, D.S.L., (ed.), *John Dalton and the Progress of Science* (Manchester: Manchester University Press, 1968)

Calaprice, A., (ed.), *The Ultimate Quotable Einstein* (Princeton, NJ: Princeton University Press, 2011)

Carlson, S., 'A Double-blind Test of Astrology', Nature 318, no. 6045 (1985), pp. 419-25

Carpenter, Audrey T., *John Theophilus Desaguliers: A Natural Philosopher, Engineer and Freemason in Newtonian England* (London: Continuum, 2011)

Carroll, Sean B., *Endless Forms Most Beautiful: The New Science of Evo Devo and the Making of the Animal Kingdom* (London: Weidenfeld & Nicolson, 2006)

Carus, Carl Gustav, *Nine Letters on Landscape Painting: Written in the Years 1815-1824; with a Letter from Goethe by Way of Introduction* (1831; Los Angeles: Getty Research Institute, 2006)

Chevalier, Tracy, *Remarkable Creatures* (London: The Borough Press, 2014)

Connell, Sophia M., (ed.), *The Cambridge Companion to Aristotle's Biology* (Cambridge: Cambridge University Press, 2021)

Cupitt, Don, *The Sea of Faith: Christianity in Change* (London: BBC Publications, 1984)

Cuvier, George, *The Animal Kingdom* (1817; Cambridge: Cambridge University Press, 2012)

Dalton, John, *Meteorological Observations and Essays* (1793; Cambridge: Cambridge University Press, 2011)

Darwin, Charles, *On the Origin of Species by Means of Natural Selection* (London: John Murray, 1859)

Darwin Correspondence Project, University of Cambridge, 'Letter no. 2299', J.D. Hooker and Charles Lyell to the Linnean Society, 30 June 1858: https://www.darwinproject.ac.uk/letter/?docId=letters/DCP-LETT-2299.xml (accessed 23 April 2024)

———, 'Letter no. 2548', Adam Sedgwick to C.R. Darwin, 24 November 1859: https://www.darwinproject.ac.uk/letter/?docId=letters/DCP-LETT-2548.xml (accessed 23 April 2024)

Dawkins, Richard, *Unweaving the Rainbow: Science, Delusion and the Appetite for Wonder* (London: Allen Lane/Penguin Press, 1998)

Dean, Dennis R., *James Hutton and the History of Geology* (Ithaca, NY: Cornell University Press, 1992)

Dennett, Daniel, Darwin's Dangerous Idea: Evolution and the Meanings of Life (New York, NY: Simon & Schuster, 1995)

Desaguliers, J.T., The Newtonian System of the World: The Best Model of Government: An Allegorical Poem (Westminster: J. Roberts, 1728); available online at: https://archive.org/details/b30415615/page/n3/mode/2up (accessed 26 April 2024)

Descartes, René, *Discourse on the Method of Rightly Conducting the Reason and Seeking the Truth in the Sciences*, edited by Charles W. Eliot (1635; New York, NY: P.F. Collier & Son, 1909)

Dunham, Lowell, and Ivar Ivask (eds), *The Cardinal Points of Borges* (Norman: University of Oklahoma Press, 1971)

Emling, Shelley, *The Fossil Hunter: Dinosaurs, Evolution, and the Woman Whose Discoveries Changed the World* (London: Palgrave Macmillan, 2011)

Evans, Mark, *Constable's Skies: Paintings and Sketches by John Constable* (London: Thames & Hudson, 2018)

Eylott, Marie-Claire, 'Mary Anning: The Unsung Hero of Fossil Discovery', Natural History Museum; available online at: https://www.nhm.ac.uk/discover/mary-anning-unsung-hero.html (accessed 22 April 2024)

Eysenck, Hans, *Dimensions of Personality* (New Brunswick, NJ: Transaction Publishers, 1997)

———, and Sybil Eysenck, *Personality Structure and Measurement* (1969; London: Routledge, 2014)

Feynman, Richard P., *Feynman Lectures on Physics* (New York, NY: Basic Books, 2010)

———, 'How Did It Get that Way? The Relation of Physics to Other Sciences', in *Feynman Lectures on Physics*, Vol. 1, ch. 3, sections 3-7

———, *The Pleasure of Finding Things Out: The Best Short Works of Richard P. Feynman* (Cambridge, MA: Perseus Books, 1999)

Forster, Thomas, *Researches about Atmospheric Phaenomena*, 2nd edn (London: Baldwin, Cradock & Joy, 1815)

Fortey, Richard, *The Earth: An Intimate History* (London: Harper Perennial, 2005)

Foulkes, Lucy, 'The Big Idea: Is It Your Personality, or a Disorder?', *The Guardian*, 16 October 2021, p. 77

Francis, Richard C., *Epigenetics: How Environment Shapes Our Genes* (New York, NY: W.W. Norton, 2012)

Freud, Sigmund, *The Psychopathology of Everyday Life* (1904; Cambridge: Cambridge University Press, 2010)

Frisch, Wolfgang, Martin Meschede and Ronald C. Blakey, *Plate Tectonics: Continental Drift and Mountain Building* (Berlin: Springer, 2022)

Gedzelman, Stanley David, 'Cloud Classification before Luke Howard', *Bulletin of the American Meteorological Society* 70, no. 4 (1989), pp. 381-95

Gill, Nikita, *Your Soul Is a River* (Williamsburg, Brooklyn: Thought Catalog Books, 2018)

Gillispie, Charles Coulston, *Pierre-Simon Laplace, 1749-1827: A Life in Exact Science* (Princeton, NJ: Princeton University Press, 2000)

Glück, Louise, *Averno* (London: Penguin, 2021)

Gooley, Tristan, *How to Read Water: Clues, Signs & Patterns from Puddles to the Sea* (London: Sceptre, 2016)

Gordin, Michael D., *A Well-Ordered Thing: Dmitrii Mendeleev and the Shadow of the Periodic Table* (Princeton, NJ: Princeton Univeristy Press, 2018)

Gray, John, *Feline Philosophy: Cats and the Meaning of Life* (London: Allen Lane, 2020)

———, *Straw Dogs: Thoughts on Humans and Other Animals* (London: Granta Books, 2003)

Greene, Brian, *Until the End of Time: Mind, Matter, and Our Search for Meaning in an Evolving Universe* (London: Penguin, 2021)

Greene, Mott T., *Alfred Wegener: Science, Exploration, and the Theory of Continental Drift* (Princeton, NJ: Princeton University Press, 2018)

Gribbin, John, and Mary Gribbin, *FitzRoy: The Remarkable Story of Darwin's Captain and the Invention of the Weather Forecast* (Scotts Valley, CA: CreateSpace Independent Publishing Platform, 2016)

Hamann-Rose, Paul, *Genetics and the Novel: Reimagining Life Through Fiction* (London: Palgrave Macmillan, 2024)

Hamblyn, Richard, *The Invention of Clouds: How an Amateur Meteorologist Forged the Language of the Skies* (London: Picador, 2011)

Hardy, Benjamin, *Personality Isn't Permanent: Break Free from Self-Limiting Beliefs and Rewrite Your Story* (New York, NY: Portfolio, 2020)

Hardy, Thomas, *The Complete Poetical Works of Thomas Hardy: Volume II: Satires of Circumstance, Moments of Vision, Late Lyrics and Earlier*, ed. Samuel Hynes (Oxford: Oxford University Press, 1983)

———, *Two on a Tower: A Romance* (1882; London: Penguin, 1999)

Heider, F., and M. Simmel, 'An Experimental Study of Apparent Behavior', *American Journal of Psychology* 57, no. 2 (1944), pp. 243-59
Heilbron, John L., *Galileo* (Oxford: Oxford University Press, 2012)
Heisenberg, Werner, *Physics and Beyond* (New York, NY: Harper & Row, 1971)
Helden, Albert van, Sven Dupré, Rob van Gent and Huib Zuidervaart (eds), *The Origins of the Telescope* (Amsterdam: Amsterdam University Press, 2010)
Heraud, John Abraham, *The Descent into Hell, with an Analysis and Notes: To Which Are Added, Uriel, a Fragment, and Three Odes* (1835; Whitefish, MT: Kessinger Publishing, 2009)
Herschel, John F.W., *A Preliminary Discourse on the Study of Natural Philosophy* (1830; Chicago: Chicago University Press, 1987)
Hill, Andrew, *Ruskinland: How John Ruskin Shapes Our World* (London: Pallas Athene, 2019)
Holden, Edward S., *Sir William Herschel: His Life and Works* (New York, NY: Charles Scribner's Sons, 1881)
Holloway, Richard, *Stories We Tell Ourselves: Making Meaning in a Meaningless Universe* (Edinburgh: Canongate, 2020)
Holmes, Arthur, *Principles of Physical Geology* (London: Thomas Nelson & Sons, 1965)
Holmes, Richard, *The Age of Wonder* (London: Harper Press, 2008)
———, *Coleridge* (Oxford: Oxford University Press, 1982)
———, 'Giving to a Blind Man Eyes', *The Guardian*, 14 March 2009
Hopkins, Gerard Manley, *The Poems of Gerard Manley Hopkins*, edited with notes by Robert Bridges (Oxford: Oxford University Press), 1956, Third edition
Howard, Luke, *On the Modifications of Clouds* (London: John Churchill & Sons, 1803)
———, *Seven Lectures on Meteorology* (1837; Cambridge: Cambridge University Press, 2011)
Howe, David, *Empathy: What It Is and Why It Matters* (London: Palgrave Macmillan, 2012)
———, *Extraction to Extinction: Rethinking Our Relationship with Earth's Natural Resources* (Salford: Saraband, 2021)
Hoyle, Fred, 'The Synthesis of the Elements from Hydrogen', *Monthly Notices of the Royal Astronomical Society* 106 (1946)
International Geosphere-Biosphere Programme, 'Challenges of a Changing Earth: Global Change Open Science Conference', Amsterdam, The Netherlands, 13 July 2001
Jackson, Myles W., *Spectrum of Belief: Joseph von Fraunhofer and the Craft of Precision Optics* (Cambridge, MA: MIT Press, 2000)
James, P.D., *Time to Be in Earnest: A Fragment of Autobiography* (London: Faber & Faber, 2000)

Jamie, Kathleen, (ed.), *Antlers of Water: Writing on the Nature and Environment of Scotland* (Edinburgh: Canongate Books, 2015)
Julian of Norwich, *Revelations of Divine Love* (Oxford: Oxford University Press, 2015)
Jung, Carl, *Psychological Types* (1921; London: Routledge, 2016)
Kant, Immanuel, 'An Answer to the Question: What Is Enlightenment?' (1784), trans. Ted Humphrey (Hackett Publishing, 1992); available online via the New York Public Library website: https://www.nypl.org/sites/default/files/kant_whatisenlightenment.pdf (accessed 26 April 2024)
Keats, John, *John Keats: Selected Poems*, ed. John Barnard (London: Penguin, 2007)
Kelly, A., J. Côté, M. Jeffreys and J. Turnnidge, *Birth Advantages and Relative Age Effects in Sport: Exploring Organizational Structures and Creating Appropriate Settings* (London: Routledge, 2021)
Klee, Paul, 'The Play of Forces at the Bauhaus' (1921)
Komisaruk, Adam, and Allison Dushane (eds), *The Botanic Garden by Erasmus Darwin* (London: Routledge, 2017)
Lack, David, *Darwin's Finches* (Cambridge: Cambridge University Press, 1983)
Lamarck, Jean-Baptiste, 'Nouvelle définition des termes que j'emploie pour exprimer certaines formes des nuages qu'il importe de distinguer dans l'annotation de l'état du ciel', *Annuaire météorologique pour l'an XIII de la République Française*, no. 3 (1805), pp. 112-33
Leroi, Armand Marie, *The Lagoon: How Aristotle Invented Science* (London: Bloomsbury Circus, 2014)
Levi, Primo, *The Periodic Table* (London: Abacus, 1986)
Lewis, Cherry, *The Dating Game* (Cambridge: Cambridge University Press, 2012)
Lewis, Rhodri, 'Shakespeare's Clouds and the Image Made by Chance', *Essays in Criticism* 62, no. 1 (2012), pp. 1-24
Lively, Penelope, *Ammonites and Leaping Fish: A Life in Time* (London: Fig Tree, 2013)
Lounsbury, John Baldwin, Nancy Foster, Hamali Patel, Patrick Carmody, Lucy W. Gibson and Deborah R. Stairs, 'An Investigation of the Personality Traits of Scientists Versus Nonscientists and Their Relationship with Career Satisfaction', *R&D Management* 42, no. 1 (2012)
Lovelock, James, *Gaia: A New Look at Life on Earth* (Oxford: Oxford University Press, 1979)
———, *Homage to Gaia: The Life of an Independent Scientist* (Oxford: Oxford University Press, 2014)
Lyell, Charles, *Principles of Geology* (1830-33; London: Penguin, 1997)
Macdonald, Helen, *H is for Hawk* (London: Vintage, 2015)
———, *Vesper Flights* (London: Jonathan Cape, 2020)

Macfarlane, Robert, *The Wild Places* (London: Granta Books, 2007)
———, and Jackie Morris, *The Lost Spells* (London: Hamish Hamilton, 2020)
Mack, Katie, *The End of Everything (Astrophysically Speaking)* (London: Penguin, 2021)
Magee, Bryan, *Ultimate Questions* (Princeton, NJ: Princeton University Press, 2017)
Margulis, Lynn, *Symbiotic Planet: A New Look at Evolution* (New York, NY: Basic Books, 1998)
Matthews, Gerald, *Personality Traits* (Cambridge: Cambridge University Press, 2009)
McAnulty, Dara, *Diary of a Young Naturalist* (London: Ebury Press, 2021)
McCrae, Robert R., and Paul Costa Jr, *Personality in Adulthood: A Five-Factor Theory Perspective* (New York, NY: Guilford Press, 2005)
McEwen, C., and B. McEwen, 'Social Structure, Adversity, Toxic Stress, and Intergenerational Poverty: An Early Childhood Model', *Annual Review of Sociology* 43, no. 1 (2017), pp. 445-72
McKimm, Michael, (ed.), *Map: Poems After William Smith's Geological Map of 1815* (Chadwell Heath: Worple Press, 2015)
McNamara, Geoff, *Clocks in the Sky: The Story of Pulsars* (New York, NY: Springer Praxis Books, 2008)
McNee, Alan, *The New Mountaineer in Late Victorian Britain: Materiality, Modernity, and the Haptic Sublime* (London: Palgrave Macmillan, 2017)
Mendeleyev, Dmitry Ivanovich, *The Principles of Chemistry* (1868; St Albans: Wentworth Press, 2016)
Milton, John, *Paradise Lost: Books V-VI* (1667; Cambridge: Cambridge University Press, 1975)
Mitchell, David, *Cloud Atlas* (London: Sceptre Books, 2014)
Moore, Donovan, *What Stars Are Made Of: The Life of Cecilia Payne-Gaposchkin* (Cambridge, MA: Harvard University Press, 2020)
Moran, Joe, 'Don't Believe a Word by David Shariatmadari Review – The Truth about Language', *The Guardian*, 10 August 2019
———, *First You Write a Sentence* (London: Penguin, 2018)
Morton, John L., *Strata: The Remarkable Life Story of William Smith, the Father of English Geology* (Horsham: Brocken Spectre Publishing, 2004)
Mujika, I., R. Vaeyens, S.P. Matthys, J. Santisteban, J. Goiriena and R. Philippaerts, 'The Relative Age Effect in a Professional Football Club Setting', *Journal of Sports Science* 27, no. 11 (2009), pp. 1153-58
Murdoch, Iris, 'Philosophy and Literature with Iris Murdoch', *Men of Ideas* [TV series], BBC Television [1977]; available online at: https://www.youtube.com/watch?v=g7fY3GsFzkY (accessed 18 April 2024)
Nin, Anaïs, *Seduction of the Minotaur* (Denver, CO: Swallow Press, 1961)
Nurse, Paul, *What Is Life?* (Oxford: David Fickling Books, 2020)
Oldroyd, David, *Thinking about the Earth: A History of Ideas in Geology* (London: Athlone, 1996)

Oliver, Howard, and Sylvia Oliver, 'Meteorologist's Profile: John Dalton', *Weather* 58, no. 6 (2003), pp. 206-11
Orel, Vitezslav, *Gregor Mendel: The First Geneticist*, trans. Stephen Finn (Oxford: Oxford University Press, 1996)
Oswald, Alice, and Paul Keegan (eds), *Gigantic Cinema: A Weather Anthology* (London: Jonathan Cape 2020)
Padel, Ruth, *Darwin: A Life in Poems* (London: Vintage, 2010)
Pais, Abraham, *Niels Bohr's Times: In Physics, Philosophy and Polity* (Oxford: Clarendon Press, 1993)
Patel, R., A.M. Nevill, R. Cloak, T. Smith and M. Wyon, 'Relative Age, Maturation, Anthropometry and Physical Performance Characteristics of Players within an Elite Youth Football Academy', *International Journal of Sports Science and Coaching* 14, no. 3 (2019), pp. 714-25
Pedgley, D.E., 'Luke Howard and His Clouds', *Weather* 58, no. 2 (2003), pp. 51-55
Perman, Ray, *James Hutton: The Genius of Time* (Edinburgh: Birlinn Books, 2022)
Playfair, John, *Illustrations of the Huttonian Theory of the Earth* (Edinburgh: Cadell & Davies, 1802)
Pullman, Philip, '25 Years of *His Dark Materials*: Philip Pullman on the Journey of a Lifetime', *The Guardian*, 10 October 2020, p. 8
Repcheck, J., *The Man Who Found Time: James Hutton and the Discovery of the Earth's Antiquity* (London: Pocket Books, 2004)
Ridpath, Ian, *A Dictionary of Astronomy*, 2nd edn (Oxford: Oxford University Press, 2012)
Ripple, William J., Christopher Wolf, Jillian W. Gregg, Johan Rockström, Thomas M. Newsome, Beverly E. Law, Luiz Marques, Timothy M. Lenton, Chi Xu, Saleemul Huq, Leon Simons and Sir David Anthony King, 'The 2023 State of the Climate Report: Entering Uncharted Territory', *BioScience* 73, no. 12 (2023), pp. 841-50
Ritchie, Hannah, and Max Roser, *Land Use*, September 2019, published online at Our World in Data; available online at: https://ourworldindata.org/land-use (accessed 26 April 2024)
Roberts, Alice, *The Incredible Unlikeliness of Being: Evolution and the Making of You* (London: Heron Books, 2014)
Rosen, Rebecca J., 'Clouds: The Most Useful Metaphor of All Time?', *The Atlantic*, 30 September 2011
Ross, Marlon B., 'Romantic Quest and Conquest: Troping Masculine Power in the Crisis of Poetic Identity', in Anne K. Mellor (ed.), *Romanticism and Feminism* (Bloomington: Indiana University Press, 1988), pp. 26-51
Rossetti, William Michael, *The Poetical Works of William Blake* (London: Forgotten Books, 2018)
Roszak, Theodore, *The Making of a Counter Culture* (Berkeley: University of California Press, 1995)

Ruskin, John, *Modern Painters*, Volume 3 (1856); available online via Project Gutenberg, updated 25 January 2021

——, *Selections from the Works of John Ruskin*, ed. Chauncey Tinker (Cambridge, MA: Riverside Press, 1908) ; available online via Project Gutenberg

——, *The Works of John Ruskin*, ed. Alexander Wedderburn and Edward Tyas Cook (Cambridge: Cambridge University Press, 1903-12), vol. 3, section 3, 'Of Truth of Skies'

Ryden, Barbara, *Introduction to Cosmology* (Cambridge: Cambridge University Press, 2016)

Sacks, Oliver, *The Man Who Mistook His Wife for a Hat* (London: Picador, 1985)

Sagan, Carl, *Cosmos: A Personal Voyage*, TV series, PBS America (1980)

Salinero, J.J., B.P. González, P. Burillo and M.L. Lesma, 'Relative Age Effect in European Professional Football: Analysis by Position', *Journal of Human Sport and Exercise* 8, no. 4 (2013), pp. 966-73

Saussure, Horace de, *Voyages dans Les Alpes* (Neuchâtel: Chez Samuel Fauche, 1796)

Scerri, Eric R., 'Happy 150th Birthday to the Periodic Table', *Chemistry European Journal* 25, no. 31 (2019), pp. 7410-15

Sharov, Alexander S., and Igor D. Novikov, *Edwin Hubble: The Discoverer of the Big Bang Universe* (Cambridge: Cambridge University Press, 2008)

Shelley, Percy Bysshe, *Prometheus Unbound, A Lyrical Drama, in Four Acts, with Other Poems* (London: C. & J. Ollier, 1820)

Shepherd, Nan, *The Living Mountain: A Celebration of the Cairngorms Mountains of Scotland* (Edinburgh: Canongate Books, 2011)

Smith, Charlotte, *Beachy Head with Other Poems* (London: J. Johnson, 1707)

Smith, Dana G., 'Big Data Gives the "Big 5" Personality Traits a Makeover', *Scientific American*, 18 September 2018

Smith, Robert Rowland, *What It Means to Be Human: A Philosophical Memoir* (London: Fourth Estate, 2019)

Smith, Thomas Fletcher, *John Dalton: A Cumbrian Philosopher* (Carlisle: Bookcase, 2015)

——, *Jonathan Otley: Man of Lakeland* (Carlisle: Bookcase, 2007)

Sobel, Dava, *The Glass Universe: How the Ladies of the Harvard Observatory Took the Measure of the Stars* (London: Penguin, 2016)

Solms, Mark, *The Hidden Spring: A Journey to the Source of Consciousness* (London: Profile, 2021)

Spector, Tami I., 'The Art of the Periodic Table', *Leonardo Music Journal* 52, no. 3 (2019), pp. 292-99

Steinicke, Wolfgang, *William Herschel: Discoverer of the Deep Sky* (Watford: Books on Demand, 2021)

Strathern, Paul, *Mendeleyev's Dream: The Quest for the Elements* (London: Hamish Hamilton, 2000)

Thomas, D.P., 'The Demise of Blood-letting', *Journal of the Royal College of Physicians, Edinburgh* 44, no. 1 (2014), pp. 72-77
Thornes, John E., *John Constable's Skies: A Fusion of Art and Science* (Birmingham: Birmingham University Press, 1999)
Trout, J.D., *Wondrous Truths: The Improbable Triumph of Modern Science* (Oxford: Oxford University Press, 2016)
UK Met Office, 'Robert FitzRoy and the Early Met Office': https://www.metoffice.gov.uk/research/library-and-archive/archive-hidden-treasures/robert-fitzroy (accessed 21 April 2024)
Verne, Jules, *Journey to the Centre of the Earth* (1864; Oxford: Oxford University Press, 2008)
Vince, Gaia, *Transcendence: How Humans Evolved through Fire, Language, Beauty and Time* (London: Allen Lane, 2020)
Vollmann, William T., *Uncentering the Earth: Copernicus and the Revolution of the Heavenly Spheres* (New York, NY: W.W. Norton, 2006)
Warner, B., 'Charles Darwin and John Herschel', *South African Journal of Science* 105, no. 11/12 (2009), pp. 432-39
Whiston, William, *A New Theory of the Earth: from Its Original, to the Consummation of All Things* (1696; Madrid: Hard Press Publishing, 2019)
Williams, Sarah, *Twilight Hours: A Legacy of Verse* (London: Strahan & Co., 1868)
Winchester, Simon, *The Map that Changed the World: The Tale of William Smith and the Birth of a Science* (London: Viking, 2001)
Wix, L., 'Aesthetic Empathy in Teaching Art to Children: The Work of Friedl Dicker-Brandeis in Terezin', *Art Therapy* 26, no. 4 (2009), pp. 152-58
Woodcock, Nigel, and Rob Strachan, *Geological History of Britain and Ireland* (Oxford: Blackwell, 2012)
Woolf, Virginia, 'On Being Ill', first published in *The New Criterion* 4, no. 1 (January 1926) (London: Renard Press, 2023)
Wordsworth, William, *Guide to the Lakes* (1835; Oxford: Oxford University Press, 2022)
———, *Poems in Two Volumes* (London: Longman, Hurst, Rees, Orme & Brown, 1807)
———, and Samuel Taylor Coleridge, *Lyrical Ballads 1798 and 1802*, ed. Fiona Stafford (Oxford: Oxford University Press, 2013)
World Meteorological Association, *International Cloud Atlas*: https://cloudatlas.wmo.int/en/cloud-classification-summary.html (accessed 21 April 2024)
World Wild Fund for Nature in collaboration with Zoological Society of London, *Living Planet Report 2022: Building a Nature-Positive Society* (Gland, Switzerland: WWF, 2022)

Index

You may also be interested in:

Where All the Ladders Start

A Study of Poems, Poets and the People who Inspired Them

by Julian Lovelock

Who were Shakespeare's 'Friend' and the 'Dark Lady'? Why did Donne risk his life and ruin his career for a seventeen-year-old girl? Why did Wordsworth's sister retire to her bed on his wedding day? Writing never takes place in a vacuum and much of the finest poetry in the English language has been inspired by particular people – patrons, spouses, lovers, friends, or just casual acquaintances. Whether relegated to an obscurity they do not deserve or thrust into prominence they did not seek, their importance to the creative process is inescapable.

In *Where All the Ladders Start*, Julian Lovelock discusses with characteristic incisiveness and enthusiasm nine major British poets and the real lives behind some of their most personal and significant works. Along the way he shows how poetry has developed over the past four hundred years and provides suggestions for further reading, while for convenience all of the relevant poems and extracts are reproduced in full. Written for both the seasoned reader and the student encountering these poems for the first time, Lovelock's analysis will inspire and entertain in equal measure.

Julian Lovelock has spent his life in education, as a teacher, headmaster and university lecturer. He is now a Senior Research Fellow in the Department of English at the University of Buckingham, where he was previously Dean of Arts and Languages and Pro Vice-Chancellor.

His most recent publications with The Lutterworth Press are *From Morality to Mayhem: The Fall and Rise of the English School Story* (2018) and *The Business of Reading: A Hundred Years of the English Novel* (2022).

Published 2023

Paperback ISBN: 978 0 7188 9724 6
PDF ISBN: 978 0 7188 9725 3
ePub ISBN: 978 0 7188 9726 0

You may also be interested in:

The Shadow of the Telescope

A Biography of John Herschel

by Gunther Buttman

Gunther Buttman's *The Shadow of the Telescope* was the first full-length biography of the nineteenth-century astronomer, Sir John Herschel. First published in German, this intriguing text chronicles the life and works of the third of the Herschel astronomers, the son of William and the nephew of Caroline. John was extremely intelligent, graduating as Senior Wrangler in the notoriously difficult Mathematical Tripos at Cambridge University. While less famous than his father and aunt, he nevertheless went on to make important discoveries in the field of astronomy. He named seven moons of Saturn and four moons of Uranus, the planet his father had only recently discovered.

Making admirable use of John's unpublished correspondence, diaries, and notebooks, Buttman covers his extensive astronomical observations at Cape Town in South Africa, his pioneering work in photography and in physical optics in Britain, his unhappy experiences as Master of the Mint, and much more.

Gunther Buttmann's other biographical subjects include William Herschel, Caroline Herschel and Friedrich Ratzel. His studies of them have been hailed as definitive works in astronomers' biography.

Published 2022

Paperback ISBN: 978 0 7188 9527 3
PDF ISBN: 978 0 7188 4744 9
ePub ISBN: 978 0 7188 4745 6

You may also be interested in:

Blasted with Antiquity

Old Age and the Consolations of Literature

by David Ellis

Given the increasing number of old people, the proliferation of books about old age is hardly surprising. Most of these come from cultural historians or social scientists and, when those with a literary background have tackled the subject, they have largely done so through what are known as period studies. In *Blasted with Antiquity*, David Ellis provides an alternative. Skipping nimbly from Cicero to Shakespeare, and from Wordsworth to Dickens and beyond, he discusses various aspects of old age with the help of writers across European history who have usually been regarded as worth listening to.

Eschewing extended literary analyses, Ellis addresses retirement, physical decay, sex in old age, the importance of family, legacy, wills and nostalgia, as well of course as dying itself. While remaining alert to current trends, his approach is consciously that of the old way of teaching English rather than the new. Whether 'blasted with antiquity' like Falstaff in *Henry IV Part Two*, or with the 'shining morning face' of an unwilling student, his accessible and witty style will appeal to young and old alike.

David Ellis is Emeritus Professor of English Literature at the University of Kent and has published around twenty books on Shakespeare, leading figures of the Romantic era, and D.H. Lawrence. In 2012 he received the Harry T. Moore Award for distinguished services to D.H. Lawrence studies.

Published 2023

Paperback ISBN: 978 0 7188 9718 5
PDF ISBN: 978 0 7188 9717 8
ePub ISBN: 978 0 7188 9716 1

You may also be interested in:

The Language of Science

From the Vernacular to the Technical

by Maurice Crosland

Where do scientific terms come from? Why are they so similar in so many languages? How was the new nomenclature spread across the world? *The Language of Science* analyses the development of scientific vocabulary from its basic origins in everyday agricultural work, through to the need for a measurement system when it came to trading, to the scientific innovations of the seventeenth century and a subsequent period of consolidation in the eighteenth century.

This is a period of great relevance in history of science and a strong focus of Crosland's work. The time between 1750 and 1800 saw many movements trying to organise and revolutionise scientific names and units – the significance of which is often overlooked. Crosland talks here about the development of language in botany, chemistry and the metric system, drawing a connection between the three fields and the development of the sciences in general. The final chapter pays close attention to how the international conferences helped in the adoption and standardisation of the new language.

Crosland's approach to the subject matter is very clear and concise. *The Language of Science* will be of interest to anyone who wants to know more about history of language, social history and of course science. The author popularises an often intimidating and complex segment of the English language. Scientists and non-scientists alike will find this book stimulating and thought-provoking.

Maurice Pierre Crosland is an eminent academic. Having lectured at Leeds and been a Professor at Berkeley Cornell, Pensylvania, he is Emeritus Professor of History of Science at the University of Kent. He has published several works of great value, including *The Science of Matter* and *Science under Control*. He has a lifelong interest in the language and the history of science, and is Honorary Editor of the British Journal of Science, as well as President of the British Society for the History of Science.

Published 2006

Paperback ISBN: 978 0 7188 3060 1

You may also be interested in:

The Business of Reading

A Hundred Years of the English Novel

by Julian Lovelock

In *The Business of Reading*, Julian Lovelock charts the development of the English novel over the past hundred years. Smuggling in titles from Scotland, Ireland and the Caribbean, he focuses on twenty texts written since the end of the First World War, some well-known but others less so, placing them in their historical context. Novelists represented range from D.H. Lawrence, E.M. Forster and Virginia Woolf, through Graham Greene, Kingsley Amis and Iris Murdoch, to such contemporary writers as Ian McEwan, Maggie O'Farrell and Graham Swift.

Written in a lucid style that reflects his expertise and enthusiasm, Lovelock's innovative selection, perceptive analysis and lightness of touch will appeal to the general reader, the book club member and the student. He argues that our response as readers is an important part of the creative process, and while he mainly avoids the critical '-isms' that have characterised recent academic debate, he introduces such concepts as intertextuality, metafiction and the role of the often unreliable narrator, showing how an appreciation of the way the language of fiction works can only add to our understanding and enjoyment.

Julian Lovelock has spent his life in education, as a teacher, headmaster and university lecturer. He is now a Senior Research Fellow in the Department of English at the University of Buckingham, where he was previously Dean of Arts and Languages and Pro Vice-Chancellor.

His many publications include *Swallows, Amazons and Coots: A Reading of Arthur Ransome* (2016) and *From Morality to Mayhem: The Fall and Rise of the English School Story* (2018), both published by the Lutterworth Press.

Published 2022

Paperback ISBN: 978 0 7188 9595 2
PDF ISBN: 978 0 7188 9596 9
ePub ISBN: 978 0 7188 9597 6

Printed and bound by CPI Group (UK) Ltd, Croydon, CR0 4YY

16/07/2026

02169150-0001